CB048043

iDentities

PAUL SELIGSON and LUIZ OTÁVIO BARROS

1

STUDENT'S BOOK

To the student

High-intermediate and advanced students often face a challenge when they study English: continuing to make steady progress in their skills and fluency. In *Identities*, we've tried to address that challenge in ways we hope you'll enjoy.

Identities offers you rich content in each of the four skills – reading, writing, listening and speaking – as well as grammar, pronunciation and vocabulary. Here are just some of the ways we try to make all of these areas useful for you.

Natural, authentic, and entertaining material continues to develop your listening comprehension. To help you, *Identities* is unique in offering "Listen to check" activities throughout the unit. Good pronunciation improves your understanding, too, and you'll find new pronunciation points, fully integrated with speaking activities. Pink syllables show you how to stress new words.

Of course, you want to keep improving your speaking skills, too. In each unit you will find relevant and realistic...

- *Make it personal* activities, where you can express your ideas and talk about yourself – with speech balloons that show you how to begin.
- *How to say it* activities to introduce you to more advanced conversational strategies and expressions.
- A *Keep talking* section in the last lesson to consolidate and use the language you've learned.

What's more, every lesson offers a song line linked to the content to help you remember the lesson.

Identities fully develops your reading skills through high-interest articles, blog posts, and interviews on many new topics, which help you to understand main ideas quickly, focus on reference words, make inferences, and more.

Every unit also offers contextualized writing practice that follows directly from the topics you will discuss in *Keep talking*. The activities give you a chance to practice the kinds of tasks you may need to do in real life.

Finally, *Identities* recognizes your need to keep improving your grammar and expanding your vocabulary.

- Grammar points in every unit focus on usage and form, as well as introducing you to aspects of more formal written English.
- *Grammar Expansion* section allows you to work on even more challenging structures.
- Grammar boxes give you a chance to discover rules by yourself so they stay with you.
- New structures are *always* presented in context so you can see exactly how they are used in natural conversation.

Vocabulary-development activities introduce you to high-frequency words, expressions, and phrasal verbs, which are always in context. You will also find frequent *Common mistake* boxes, covering grammar points and vocabulary, as well as purple language boxes with helpful information on more aspects of English.

As you work through *Identities*, you will notice that it's both serious and fun. We hope you will notice increased fluency and accuracy after every unit. And, above all, we hope attending English class will be your favorite weekly activity!

Language Map

	Speaking / Topic	Grammar	Vocabulary / Strategies	Writing
1	1.1 What's the story behind your name?		Family: compound words and phrasal verbs	
	1.2 Do / Did you get along with your parents?	Using *-ing* forms: subjects, verbs, and expressions	Common uses of *get*	
	1.3 How many pets have you lived with?		Suffixes for nouns and adjectives	
	1.4 What difficult people do you know?	Using the infinitive with adjectives: active and passive sentences		
	1.5 Do you still make voice calls?		Developing an argument (1)	An effective paragraph: topic sentences; using connectors
2	2.1 What's most on your mind right now?		Noun modifiers: nouns and adjectives; expressing surprise	
	2.2 Do you worry about your diet?	Using noun, verb, and sentence complements	Expressions for food habits	
	2.3 Who's the smartest person you know?		Describing ability; reference words	
	2.4 Do you enjoy science fiction?	Degrees of certainty: *may, might, must, can,* and *could*		
	2.5 What was the last test you took?		Expressing advantages and disadvantages; agreeing and disagreeing	A for-and-against essay: listing pros and cons, contrasting, and reaching a conclusion
	Review 1 *p.26*			
3	3.1 Do you get embarrassed easily?	Narrative style	Physical actions; creating suspense	
	3.2 How often do you take selfies?	Past narration: simple, continuous, and perfect tenses; spoken grammar	Longer numbers	
	3.3 What invention can't you live without?		Words to describe inventions; binomials: repeated words, opposites, and related words	
	3.4 What was your favorite activity as a child?	Describing past habits and states: simple past, *used to*, and *would*		
	3.5 What makes you really happy?			Telling a story (1): linking words to sequence events
4	4.1 Are you ever deceived by ads?		False advertising: phrasal verbs; developing an argument (2)	
	4.2 Are teachers important in the digital age?	Conjunctions to compare and contrast ideas: *although, (even) though, despite, in spite of, unlike, while,* and *whereas*		
	4.3 What was the last rumor you heard?		Time expressions; similes	
	4.4 How would you describe yourself?	Reflexive pronouns with *-self / -selves*; reciprocal actions with *each other / one another*	Avoiding repetition	
	4.5 How many pairs of glasses do you own?		Figurative expressions	A product review: making generalizations
	Review 2 *p.48*			

Language Map

	Speaking / Topic	Grammar	Vocabulary / Strategies	Writing
5 5.1	What's your biggest life decision so far?		Collocations with verbs to discuss adversity; building a narrative	
5.2	What would you love to be able to do?	Imaginary situations (1): *wish* and *if only*	Expressing encouragement	
5.3	How important is a college degree?		Expressing negative ideas; prefixes: *over-*, *under-*, and *inter-*	
5.4	Did you make any mistakes today?	Imaginary situations (2): mixed conditionals		
5.5	How lucky are you?			Telling a story (2): using a good range of adjectives
6 6.1	Have you ever Googled yourself?		Verbs and expressions for online privacy	
6.2	Do you worry about privacy?	Using passive structures: *be*, modal verbs, and *have*	Responding to an argument	
6.3	What makes you suspicious?		More privacy words and expressions	
6.4	Are you into social media?	Question words with *-ever*: *who*, *what*, *which*, *when*, and *where*		
6.5	Who do you share your secrets with?			A *how to ...* guide: giving specific directions
Review 3 *p.70*				
7 7.1	How important is music to you?		Success expressions; talking about changing tastes	
7.2	What was your most recent disappointment?	Conjunctions to express purpose and reason: *(in order) to*, *so (that)*, *as*, *since*, *because (of)*, and *due to*	Uses of *so*	
7.3	What's the best movie you've seen?		Failure expressions; words that are nouns, verbs, or both	
7.4	When was the last time you went to a museum?	Modifying nouns: *another*, *some other* and *the others*		
7.5	Which musician do you listen to the most?			Writing a review: using adverbs effectively
8 8.1	Has fear ever held you back?		Expressing fears; physical symptoms of fear	
8.2	Are you good at improvising?	Describing past ability: *could* and *was / were able to*		
8.3	How much attention do you pay to the news?		Common verb + noun collocations	
8.4	What prevents you from traveling more?	Expressing obligation, permission, and advice: *must / have (got) to*, *had better*, *be allowed to*, *be supposed to*, and *should / ought to*		
8.5	Who do you usually turn to for advice?			A message of advice: using friendly comments for naturalness
Review 4 *p.92*				

Language Map

	Speaking / Topic	Grammar	Vocabulary / Strategies	Writing
9 9.1	How much time do you spend on your own?	Word order for objects and phrasal verbs	Verbs and expressions for interacting with people	
9.2	What behavior is rude in your culture?	Uses of *which* in non-restrictive clauses		
9.3	What does your age group worry about the most?		Describing attitudes	
9.4	Would you be a good detective?	Reduced relative clauses: active and passive		
9.5	What do you spend the most money on?		Developing an argument (3)	A problem-solution essay: conjunctions to express purpose, to compare, to concede, and to express reason
10 10.1	How do you like to get around town?		Phrasal verbs; talking about unexpected events	
10.2	What's your idea of a perfect vacation?	Negative questions; indirect questions: *Wh-* and *yes-no*	Forming nouns from phrasal verbs	
10.3	Which foreign country would you most like to live in?		Words with literal and figurative meanings	
10.4	Has your daily routine changed over time?	Talking about acquired habits: *be* and *get used to*		
10.5	Which are your two favorite cities and why?			A travel report: using synonyms and figurative expressions in descriptions
Review 5 *p.114*				
11 11.1	What recent news has caught your eye?		Words and expressions for talking about the news	
11.2	Have you ever laughed at the wrong moment?	Reporting what people say (1): reported statements and questions		
11.3	What was the last video you shared?		Expressions for emotional reactions	
11.4	What's your definition of gossip?	Reporting what people say (2): reporting patterns with the infinitive and base form	Expressions for gossiping	
11.5	Would you enjoy being world famous?			A letter of complaint: writing a formal email
12 12.1	How optimistic are you?		Expressing optimism and pessimism	
12.2	Will the world be better in 100 years?	Talking about the future (1): predictions with *going to*, *will*, future perfect and future continuous	Uses of *by*; other ways to make predictions	
12.3	What's the coldest place you've been to?		Expressions for discussing innovation	
12.4	What was the last excuse you made?	Talking about the future (2): expressing plans and intentions, decisions, and scheduled events; time clauses		
12.5	What will your life be like 10 years from now?		Expressions for degrees of certainty	An email to your future self: using adverbs for emphasis
Review 6 *p.136*				

1 What's the story behind your name?

1 Listening

A Answer the title question. Do any of the photos remind you of your own family?

> My mother named me George after George Clooney. She's always been a fan. It means "farmer" in Greek.

Common mistake

The second photo ~~remembers~~ reminds me of my family.

B 1.1 Listen to the start of a documentary about families. Choose the correct title.

- [ ] *All you need is love* – why family still matters in the U.S. today.
- [ ] *Everybody's changing* – a look at 21st century American families.

C Read *Family members*. Do you have all of these relatives in your family?

Family members

You can use the bold words and prefixes to form different family words:

- I love my husband, but I find his mother really difficult. Is she a typical mother-**in-law**, I wonder.
- I grew up an **only** child, but Dad and his new wife had twins! Now I have not just one **half** brother, but two! My **step**mother was as surprised as I was!
- I was raised by a **single** mom. My dad died before I was born.

D 1.2 Listen to the second part and order the photos 1–3. There's one extra family.

E 1.2 Listen again. T (true), F (false), or NI (no information)? Who do you think had the most difficult childhood?

1 Marco lived in a spacious apartment in Manhattan.
2 Marco and his stepfather have always been friendly with each other.
3 Karin's family used to make a lot of money.
4 Karin sometimes wishes she'd had a different adolescence.
5 Josh was very close to his grandma and his aunt.
6 Josh probably never met his great-grandmother.

> The one whose childhood sounded the most difficult to me was ...

F **Make it personal** Do you agree with 1–4? Give examples.

1 "Family doesn't necessarily mean mother and father."
2 "Love is love. I know they say 'Blood is thicker than water,' but genetics makes no difference at all."
3 "Parents shouldn't prioritize their careers over their kids."
4 "In my experience, older parents have just as much energy as younger parents."

I agree with the second one. Blood relationships are not the most important thing.

Yeah, absolutely. I have an adopted sister and we adore each other.

2 Vocabulary: Family

A ▶ 1.3 Match the bold expressions in each group to their definitions. Listen to check.

1 Jeff and I didn't **get along** at all.
2 We always **made up** a few minutes later.

a ☐ become friends again after an argument
b ☐ have a good relationship

---

3 I **looked after** her while Mom and Dad were at work.
4 I think she really **looks up to** me.

c ☐ take care of somebody / something
d ☐ respect or admire

---

5 I was **brought up** by my grandmother.
6 I guess it **runs in the family**.

e ☐ care for a child and help him / her grow up
f ☐ be a common family characteristic

B In pairs, using only the photos and bold words, remember all you can about each family. What can you guess about the extra family?

I think the boy is older than the girl.

C Complete questions 1–6 with the bold words in A, changing the verb tense and form as necessary.

What do your families have in common?

1 As a child, were you *brought up* with lots of strict rules?
2 Today, who do you really ________ in your family? Why do you admire him / her?
3 Are there any family members you don't ________ with?
4 Have you ever had an argument with a relative? How long did it take you to ________ ?
5 Do / Did you ever have to ________ younger / aging relatives? Do / Did you enjoy it?
6 Can you think of one physical characteristic that ________ ?

D **Make it personal** Read *Phrasal verbs*. Then in pairs, ask and answer the questions in C. Ask follow-up questions, too. How many things in common?

Phrasal verbs

Remember phrasal verbs are either separable (***bring up*** *a child* = ***bring*** *a child* ***up***) or inseparable (***look back on*** *my childhood*). Most two-particle phrasal verbs are inseparable:

I really **look up to** my father / him.

Try saying the sentence out loud. If it sounds wrong, the verb might be inseparable:

Could you ~~look my kids after~~ ***look after*** *my kids* while I'm away?

As a child, were you brought up with lots of strict rules?

Well, my parents were really strict with me, but they let my little brother do anything he wanted.

3 Language in use

A Which uses of *get* below are you familiar with? Which sentences are true for you?

Common uses of *get*

1 *receive* or *have*: I never **got** an allowance.
2 *become*: I **get** bored during family meals.
3 *be able to*: When I was younger, I never **got** to drive Mom's car.
4 *arrive*: My parents insist I **get** home by 10 p.m.
5 *understand*: No one in my family **gets** me.

B When did you last hear / say the quotes in 1–4? Remember any similar ones?

Here's one: "I'll take away your (phone) unless you do as you're told."

C 1.4 Read Carol's review and match quotes 1–4 in B with her son's advice a–d. Listen to check.

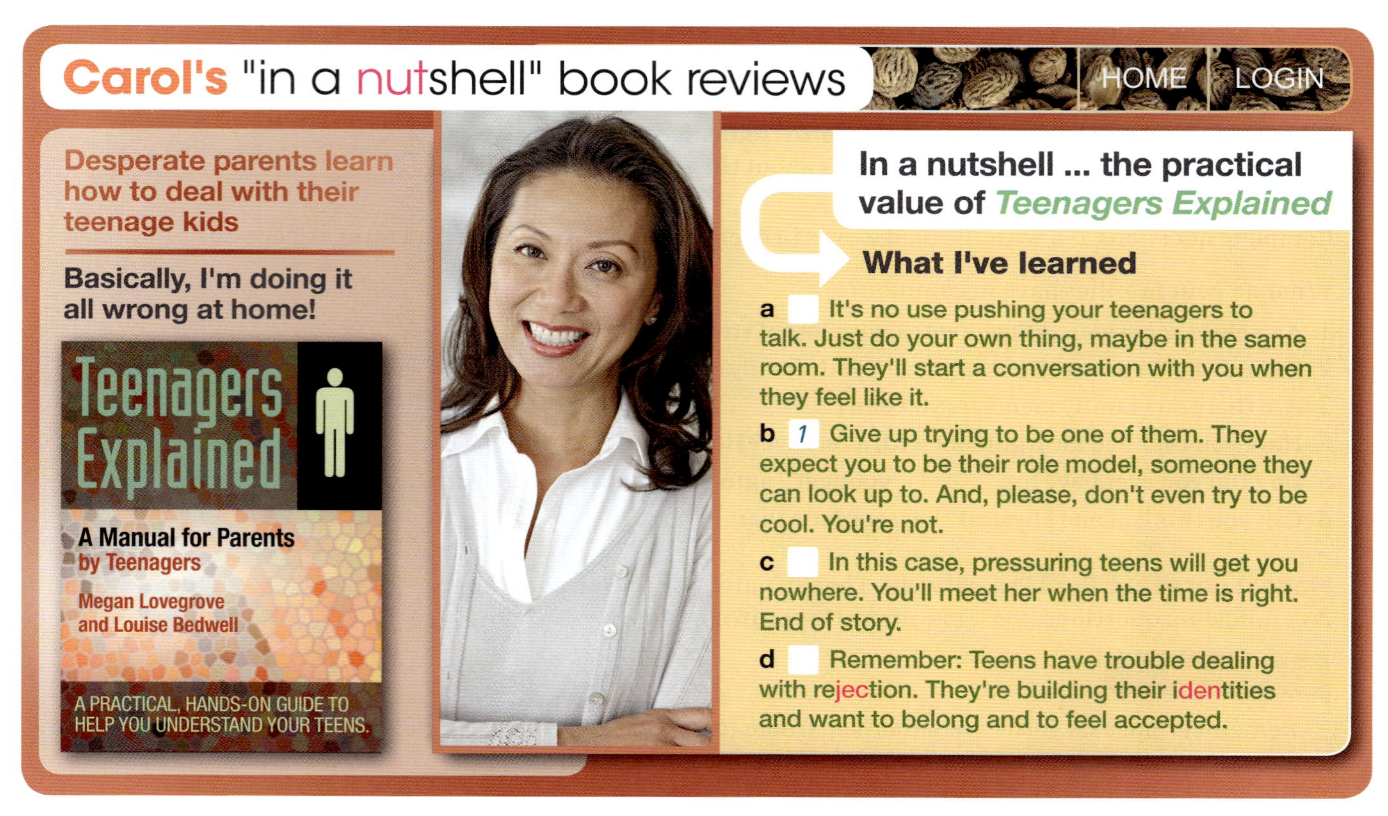

D Make it personal In pairs, answer 1–4. Do you generally agree with the advice in C?

1 What's your favorite piece of advice?
2 Would you like to read the book?
3 Who in your family "gets" / "got" you as a teen?
4 Summarize your family "in a nutshell."

I really like "It's no use pushing your teenagers to talk." I think they need to pick the right time.

4 Grammar: Using *-ing* forms

A Read and match 1–4 to examples a–d in Carol's review.

Common mistake

I have a hard time ~~to deal~~ *dealing* with my son.

Using *-ing forms:* subjects, verbs, and expressions	
1 as subject of a sentence *c*	**Raising teenagers** is a challenge. **Not listening to them** is the worst thing you can do.
2 after a phrasal verb ☐	If she doesn't want to talk, **carry on doing** what you're doing.
3 in a negative point of view ☐	**It's no good / It's not worth / There's no point arguing** with teenagers.
4 in some expressions of difficulty ☐	Parents **have difficulty / a hard time talking** to children. **I can't help saying** yes, no matter how hard I try to say no.

» Grammar expansion p.138

B 1.5 Rephrase Carol's advice to her son 1–6 (before the book!) using an *-ing* verb as subject. Choose from these verbs, adding a preposition if necessary. Listen to check.

do	eat	hang out	listen	read	risk (v)	spend

1 "Fruit every morning is good for you."
2 "Too much time in front of that computer will hurt your eyes."
3 "Good literature will help you write better."
4 "Loud music can damage your ears."
5 "Too much exercise isn't good for you."
6 "Those guys will get you into trouble."

"Eating fruit every morning is good for you."

Hmm ... I hear this one almost every day.

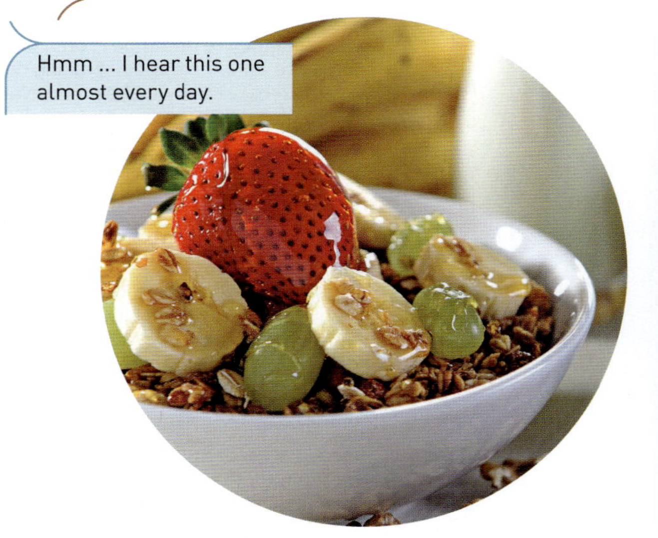

C 1.6 Rewrite 1–5 using the expressions in bold. Listen to check. Do you think Carol became a better parent after the book?

1 Don't try to convince me. [**no use**] *It's no use trying to convince me.*
2 Continue to do what you were doing. [**carry on**]
3 It's hard not to wonder why you've been so quiet lately. [**can't help**]
4 Are you finding it hard to sleep? [**having trouble**]
5 It's not a good idea to live in the past. [**not worth**]

D **Make it personal** Choose a situation and role play a parent / teen conversation. Use expressions from the grammar box and **C**.

1 Teen: You want to go abroad on your own.
2 Parent: Your son / daughter never helps around the house.
3 Teen: You don't want your mom / dad to remarry.
4 Parent: The last phone bill was way too high.
5 Teen: You want to drop out of school and get a job instead.
6 Parent: You don't like the people your son / daughter has been hanging out with.

Mom, there's something I've been meaning to tell you. You see, I ...

... And that's my final answer. There's no point even mentioning it again!

5 Reading

My cousin has a birthday party for her dog every year. It's no use trying to stop her!

A In pairs, do you know people who have pets like this? Why do so many people treat their pets as equal members of the family?

B 1.7 Read and complete the discussion forum with 1–4. Listen to check. In pairs, remember the pronunciation of the highlighted words.

1 owning a pet is good for your health
2 pets can help children develop emotionally
3 pets can teach us how to be responsible
4 owning a pet helps you meet new people

Pet Support

Home | Request | Solutions | Forum | Login

Just got a Labrador. Cutest thing ever! But why do you think people grow so attached to their pets?

(Don6) When I adopted Mindy, I did it mostly for companionship. But I soon realized her value went beyond that. You see, because they're dependent on us for exercise, food, and health care, [a] ________________. They provide structure. In the process of taking care of your pet, you create a routine together. For example, I don't need to set the alarm clock – Mindy wakes me up at 7:00 every morning! So here's my advice: If you're considering parenthood, get a dog first. At times your house will look as if it's been hit by a tornado, I know, but you won't regret it.

(Ann) I know this may sound odd, but I think [b] ________________. I adopted a homeless dog a while back, and I take her for a long walk every day. On the way, I always run into lots of people I stop and talk to. I've even learned some of my neighbors' names – people I've "known" for a hundred years. My life is never filled with boredom. Coco makes my life interesting every day! Here's what I truly love about Coco, though: she somehow knows when I'm having a bad day, and she always tries to make me feel better.

(BarryM) My 10-year-old used to have trouble getting along with the other kids. He was the class bully and didn't have a single friend. Last year we got him a cat, and now he's a different child, a million times more caring and affectionate. I think Michael learned that if he wanted to be liked and trusted by the cat, he would need to treat her carefully and kindly. I think he's learning to put himself in the pet's position, trying to feel the way she does. Clearly, [c] ________________. What a wonderful experience this has been. Now I understand why cats are three times more popular than dogs.

(Cindy52) Here's something nobody's mentioned: [d] ________________. On those (many…) days when I might be tempted to skip a workout to catch my favorite TV show, all I need to do is look at Fred standing by the door, anxiously waiting to go for his daily walk. That usually gives me the push I need to get off the couch. To my doctor's amazement, my cholesterol levels are down, and so is my blood pressure. I feel like a 20-year-old! It turns out my daily walks with Fred have proved more effective than any prescription drug.

C Re-read the discussion forum. Write the people's names.

1 *Ann* is feeling more connected to her community.
2 ________ is not naturally inclined to an active lifestyle.
3 ________ thinks pets can prepare you to raise children.
4 ________ thinks having a pet can help you develop empathy.
5 ________ thinks pets are intuitive.

D Exaggeration is often used for emphasis. Find one example in each paragraph.

*At times your house will look as if it's **been hit by a tornado.***

E **Make it personal** Do you know anyone who has experienced any of the four benefits of pet ownership in B? Can you think of any others?

Me! Number 4! I met my wife while I was buying tropical fish in a pet shop.

6 Vocabulary: Suffixes

A 1.8 Read *If you know suffixes*. Then scan 5B and put the highlighted words in the chart according to their stress. Listen to check. How did you identify the part of speech?

If you know suffixes, you can ...

1. recognize parts of speech (noun, verb, adjective, etc.).
2. infer meaning (e.g., *less* = without / *careless* = without care).
3. expand your vocabulary by "anglicizing" similar words from other languages (Spanish *–miento* = English *–ment: movimiento = movement*).

Nouns		Adjectives	
O o 1 *boredom*	O o o 3 ______	O o 5 *homeless*	O o o 7 ______
o O o 2 ______	o O o o 4 ______	o O o 6 ______	o O o o 8 ______

Nouns
achievement
annoyance
existence
failure
friendship
happiness
neighborhood
security
stardom

Adjectives
affectionate
careless
comparative
courageous
effective
helpful
preventable

B 1.8 Listen again. Circle the correct rules.

1. Suffixes are [**always** / **never**] stressed.
2. Suffixes are [**often** / **rarely**] pronounced with a schwa /ə/.

C 1.9 Complete the text with the correct suffixes. Listen to check. Do you agree with these research results?

I'm a dog person, but I'm not very talkative.

Are you a cat person or a dog person?

A recent study found significant personality differ*ences* between those who self-identified as either dog people or cat people. Dog owners tend to be more extroverted, talk____, and approach____ than cat owners. They also have greater self-discipline and tend to score higher on assertive____. Dog people like to stick to plans and are not particularly adventur____.

Cat owner____ is usually associated with open____ to new ideas and different beliefs. Cat people are less predict____, and more imagin____, and they value their personal free____ more than dog people. Because cats require less mainten____ than dogs, cat people are more likely to be busy individuals who work a lot and have less time for close relation____.

D 1.10 **Make it personal** Listen to two friends playing a guessing game.

1. Who are they comparing? Check (✔) the correct answer after the beep.
   - ☐ day people vs. night people
   - ☐ motorcyclists vs. drivers
   - ☐ couch potatoes vs. workout enthusiasts
   - ☐ small town people vs. big city people
   - ☐ women vs. men
2. In pairs, play the game:
   A Compare two groups. Include suffixes from **C**.
   B Guess who **A** is comparing.

They tend to be really courageous, and they usually value their freedom.

I think you're talking about ...

7 Listening

A In pairs, what characteristics do difficult people have in common?

> Difficult people don't listen. They just talk.

B 1.11 Listen to / Watch (0.00–2.46) Mary Bolster discuss difficult people and choose the correct answers.

1 Mary Bolster is ...
- [ ] a psychologist.
- [ ] the editor of a health magazine.
- [ ] a doctor.

2 She talks about all of these difficult people except ...
- [ ] salespeople.
- [ ] parents.
- [ ] bosses.
- [ ] coworkers.

Stacey Tisdale

Mary Bolster

C 1.11 Listen / Watch again. True (T) or False (F)? Which of the speaker's reasons do you remember?

The best way to deal with difficult people is to ...

1 try to change how you react to them.
2 just state the facts as neutrally as possible.
3 act hurt so they feel guilty.
4 make sure they know you're angry.

D **Make it personal** Have you ever followed the advice in the video? Did it work?

> Well, I once had a teacher who was very unreasonable, and I felt totally stressed out. I decided to ...

8 Language in use

A 1.12 Read and complete the webpage with 1–4. Listen to check. Did you learn any new ways of dealing with difficult people?

1 It's important for you to put yourself in other people's positions
2 It's useful to give yourself time to think
3 These guidelines will make it easier for you to be understood
4 It feels good to be heard

THIS WEEK'S SURVIVAL TIPS

Topic of the week: Dealing with difficult people

Coming up soon:
- Meeting your in-laws for the first time
- New Year's Eve with the whole family
- Your first day at school / work
- Your first job interview
- Passing your driver's test
- An oral test in English
- Saying "no" to people you love

Five easy ways to help you talk to difficult people:

a Pause and take a deep breath. Count to ten, if necessary. ________________ and assess the situation. The less you react, the better.

b Think like them. ________________ so you can see the situation from another perspective. Listen carefully. If you were in their situation, what would it feel like?

c Concede a little. Even if you agree with only one percent of what they are saying, let them know. Remember: ________________ and have your opinion valued.

d Watch your body language. Look the other person in the eye, smile if you can, and don't cross your arms. ________________ . Remember: Successful communication is less than ten percent verbal.

e Above all, be patient.

B Make it personal Which tip in A is best in your opinion? Can you suggest any others?

> I like the first one because I tend to lose my temper very easily – especially with my little brother.

9 Grammar: Using the infinitive with adjectives

A Read and check (✔) the correct rules in the grammar box.

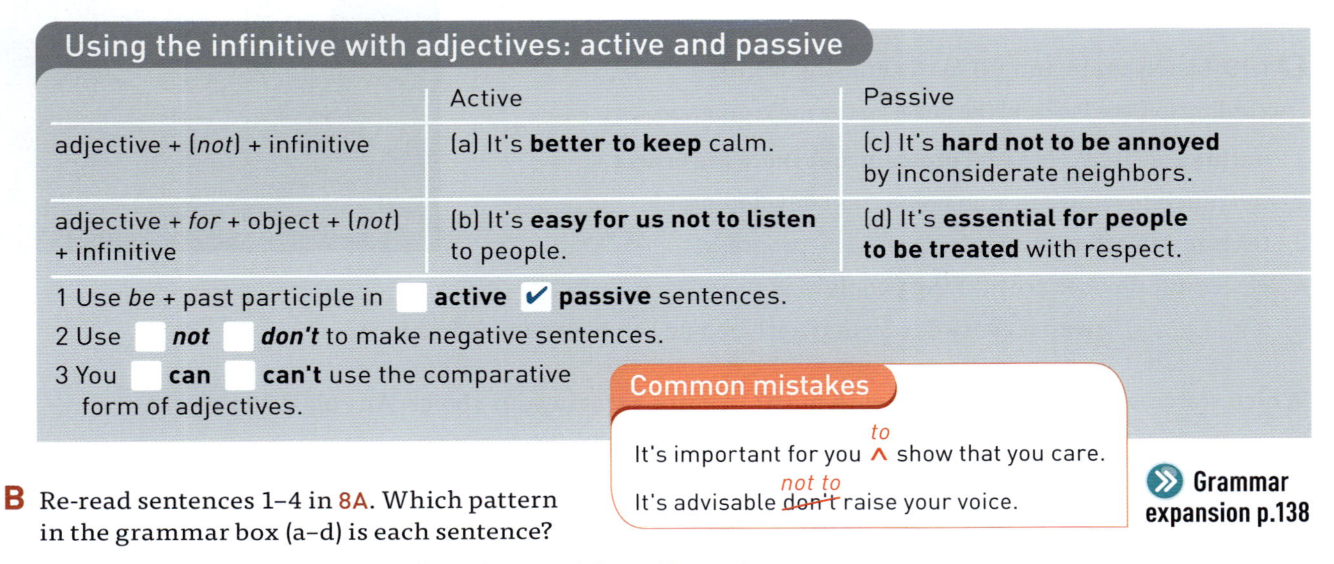

Using the infinitive with adjectives: active and passive

	Active	Passive
adjective + (*not*) + infinitive	(a) It's **better to keep** calm.	(c) It's **hard not to be annoyed** by inconsiderate neighbors.
adjective + *for* + object + (*not*) + infinitive	(b) It's **easy for us not to listen** to people.	(d) It's **essential for people to be treated** with respect.

1 Use *be* + past participle in ☐ **active** ✔ **passive** sentences.
2 Use ☐ ***not*** ☐ ***don't*** to make negative sentences.
3 You ☐ **can** ☐ **can't** use the comparative form of adjectives.

Common mistakes

It's important for you ~~^~~ *to* show that you care.
It's advisable ~~don't~~ *not to* raise your voice.

» Grammar expansion p.138

B Re-read sentences 1–4 in 8A. Which pattern in the grammar box (a–d) is each sentence?

It's important for you to put yourself in other people's positions – b

C ▶ 1.13 Read the end of the webpage in 8A and correct four mistakes. Then listen to four students checking their answers in class.

> I hope these tips will make it easier ^ *for* you to handle some of the toxic people around you at home, school, or work. But keep in mind that it's important choose your battles wisely. There will be times when you will be successful and times when it will be very difficult for the other person to persuade. In those cases, it's no use trying. Remember: It's impossible you change someone. Change comes from within.

D Complete survival tips 1–6, making them negative or passive, if necessary.

How to survive your first job interview!

1 OK / you / be nervous *It's OK for you to be nervous.*
2 natural / they / be curious / you
3 important / arrive late
4 advisable / you / dress smartly
5 essential / keep checking / phone
6 important / intimidate / by the questions

E Make it personal Choose another situation from the website in 8A. In groups, create five survival tips and add more details. Share them with the class. What's the most popular tip?

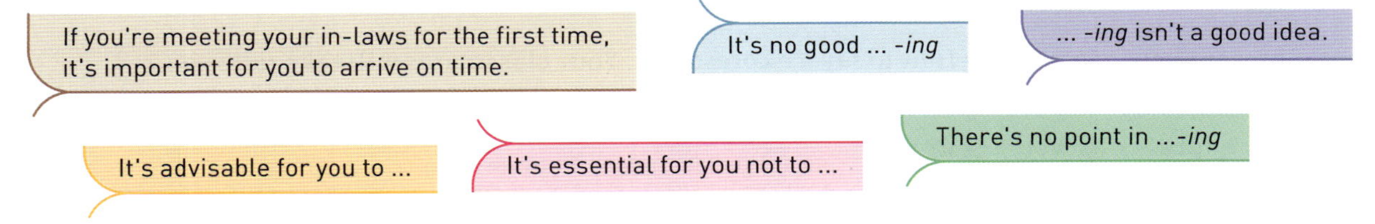

10 Listening

A 1.14 What do you think Steve Jobs' opinion on technology was? Listen to the beginning of a radio program to check.

- [ ] We should limit how much technology our kids use at home.
- [ ] We should encourage our kids to be as digitally connected as possible.

B 1.15 In pairs, list three possible arguments for Jobs' opinion. Listen to the rest of the interview. Were any of your ideas mentioned?

C 1.15 Listen again and fill in the missing words.

According to Dave Jackson, the guest on the radio program, ...

1. online *bullying* is a real problem, but there are others.
2. too much texting can stop teens from developing ________ .
3. texting can affect students' ________ progress.
4. electronic devices are making people ________ .
5. it's ________ to chat every day by text with people you haven't met face to face.

Steve Jobs, co-founder, chairman and CEO of Apple Inc. (1955–2011)

D Which statement in **C** do you agree with most? In pairs, explain your choice. Any big differences?

> I believe online bullying is a terrible problem, but I agree, too much texting is, too.

11 Keep talking

A 1.16 **How to say it** Complete sentences 1–4. Listen to check. Then repeat, sounding as convincing as you can.

Developing an argument (1)

1. For one *thing* , I believe digital technology is making people crueler.
2. What's ________ , texting is making teens lazy.
3. Not to ________ the fact that we're unlearning how to communicate in the real world.
4. On ________ of that, our digital relationships are becoming too superficial.

B Read Dave Jackson's survey results and choose a statement you strongly agree with. List three arguments to support it.

Summary of results of survey on parenting skills

Statement	Agree	Disagree
It's important for children to receive a weekly allowance.	agree 53%	disagree 47%
Children should grow up as slowly as possible.	agree 82%	disagree 18%
It is also the parents' job – not only the school's – to educate children.	agree 37%	disagree 63%
It's no use choosing your children's careers for them.	agree 64%	disagree 36%
It's essential for parents to be strict with their children.	agree 51%	disagree 49%

C In groups, present your ideas using *How to say it* expressions. Your classmates will take notes on 1–3.

1. Were there any long pauses?
2. How many expressions were used?
3. Were there any important mistakes?

> It's important for children to get a weekly allowance to begin to appreciate money. For one thing ...

12 Writing: An effective paragraph

A Read this paragraph from a student exam. Answer 1–3.

1 How many arguments does the writer use?
2 Which ones do you agree with?
3 Which words / expressions does the writer use to introduce each argument?

Name: ....

Date: ....

IT'S ESSENTIAL FOR SCHOOLS TO HAVE PHONE RULES

If you've ever had to look up a word online, need a quick calculator, or need to check the weather or a fact quickly, you know your phone can be a useful learning resource. However, I believe technology should be restricted in class for three reasons. First, playing games, posting Facebook® updates, and watching videos while the teacher and other students are talking is rude and disrespectful. If cell phones have to be turned off in movie theaters, libraries, during exams, at border controls, and on planes, why are classrooms any different? In addition, texting back and forth in class might generate unnecessary gossip and make everybody uncomfortable. People don't want to think they're being talked about behind their backs. Finally, it's important for students to get used to not going online whenever they want to. Self-discipline and the ability to focus are critically important in today's hyper-connected world. For all of these reasons, I strongly believe that schools should implement stricter phone rules.

B Read *Write it right!* Then underline the topic sentence in **A**.

Write it right!

A topic sentence is the most important sentence in any paragraph because it summarizes the rest of the paragraph for the reader. The topic sentence is sometimes, but not always, the first sentence.

When building your argument, use connectors to add each new idea:

First,
To begin with,
↓
In addition,
Besides that,
Moreover, (more formal)
↓
Finally,
Lastly,

C Read the Common mistakes. Then punctuate the beginning of the paragraph below.

Common mistakes

Hyper-connected kids get bored ~~easily,~~ *easily.*
~~in addition they~~ *In addition, they* find it hard to focus.

There are several advantages to texting over voice calls~~,~~ ~~to~~ *. To* begin with it allows shy people to say things they wouldn't otherwise besides that when you text someone you can think carefully about the message before hitting send.

D **Your turn!** Write a 100-word paragraph arguing in favor of the statement you chose in **11B**.

Before
Order your arguments clearly and logically. Write a topic sentence expressing the main idea of your paragraph.

While
Use a variety of connectors to link your ideas.

After
Proofread your paragraph carefully and check punctuation. Email it to a classmate before sending it to your teacher.

2 What's most on your mind right now?

1 Vocabulary: Noun modifiers

A 2.1 Listen and match people 1–6 to topics a–g. Pause and answer when you hear *Beep!* There is one extra topic.

Different people, different concerns

We asked people what was most on their minds.

a romantic relationships
b family dynamics
c material possessions
d financial problems
e physical appearance
f leisure activities
g peer pressure

B 2.1 Listen again. In pairs, who do you relate to most?

I felt sorry for the guy who had an argument with his father. I'm going through that, too.

C Read *Types of noun modifiers*. Then label the modifiers a–g from A as either A (adjective) or N (noun). Can you add three other combinations of these words?

Types of noun modifiers

We can use both nouns and adjectives to create new expressions:
a **family dinner** (noun + noun) = a dinner for the family
social issues (adjective + noun) = issues in society

romantic relationships – A

How about "family pressure"?

That's a good one. There's a lot of pressure in my family!

D **Make it personal** What's most on your mind these days? Share your thoughts in groups. Ask for and give more details. Any surprises?

I can't stop thinking about my dog. She's been sick for a week now.

Sorry to hear that. Have you taken her to a vet?

Common mistakes

I'm considering / thinking about ~~to go~~ *going* back to school.

Romantic ~~relations~~ *relationships* take up a lot of energy!

I'm thinking about ~~family's~~ / ~~families~~ *family* problems a lot.

I'm considering ...

I keep worrying about ...

I think about ... night and day.

I can't seem to focus on anything but ...

2 Listening

A What's each person's problem in pictures 1–4? What do you think happened?

> This guy was driving with his feet out the window!

B 2.2 Listen to a conversation between April and her dad. Number the opinions 1–4 in the order you hear them.

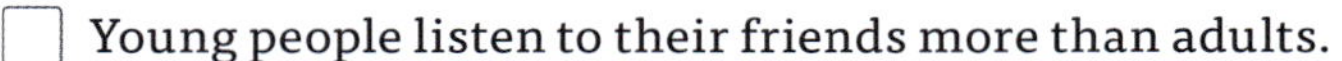

- [ ] Young people listen to their friends more than adults.
- [ ] It's hard for young people to plan and organize so they can reach their goals.
- [1] Young people don't think about the consequences of their actions.
- [ ] Natural body rhythms in young people are different from adults.

C 2.2 Listen again. Who believes 1–6, Dad (D), April (A), or both (B)?

1 Young people's brains are immature until the age of 25.
2 April's last haircut was bad.
3 Teenagers are often tired during the day.
4 April is easily influenced by her friends.
5 Children under 25 should live with their parents.
6 Young people are adults at 18.

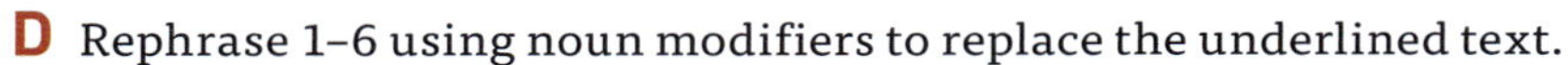

D Rephrase 1–6 using noun modifiers to replace the underlined text.

1 I'm worried about the work you're doing for school.
I'm worried about your schoolwork.
2 I was just reading an article about the brain of the adolescent.
3 You can't argue with facts that are scientific.
4 They make decisions in an instant they often regret.
5 Our patterns of sleep, clocks regulating our bodies, are different.
6 Lots of crashes involving cars are caused by young drivers.

E In pairs, how many noun modifiers can you use to describe the pictures in A? Which reasons in B explain the situations? Similar opinions?

> She sure has an awful haircut! She clearly didn't think about ...

F **Make it personal** Discuss young people's responsibilities.

1 2.3 **How to say it** Complete these expressions from the conversation in B. Then listen to check.

Expressing surprise	
What they said	What they meant
1 I had no idea at *all* (that) ...	I had absolutely no idea (that) ...
2 It never ________ to me (that) ...	I never thought (that) ...
3 You've got to be ________ !	This is a joke, right?
4 It ________ me (that) ...	It really surprises me (that) ...

2 In groups, decide at what age young people should be able to do these things and why. Use *How to say it* expressions.

babysit   drive a car   get a tattoo   get married   join the army   travel abroad alone   vote

> It amazes me that some people say you should be 25 or over to drive a car. I'm 19 and I'm a really careful driver.

> Well, maybe you're the exception and not the rule.

3 Language in use

A 2.4 Listen and fill in the missing words. As you listen, notice the silent /t/ at the end of some words.

the best thing the biggest problem the hardest thing

Sign in | Join

Online Quick Survey

Do you have a sweet tooth?

We asked our readers what sweet **treats** they can't resist. Here's what they told us!

I usually have an [1] ____________ every afternoon. The best thing about it is that it wakes me up for my afternoon classes.

Carmen, 17

[2] ____________ !! The biggest problem is **weight gain** if I have one every day.

Greg, 24

I love a big [3] ____________ for dessert in restaurants. The hardest thing is sharing it with other people!

Marcella, 16

I have two or three [4] ____________ a day. The good thing is the [5] ____________ , which gives me energy. It **keeps me going**, and I really need it because I play a lot of sports.

Dieter, 19

[6] ____________ is my favorite! Going to our local [7] ____________ is a **big deal** for my family. The best part is all the different [8] ____________ , so it never gets boring!

Nancy, 18

There's definitely an advantage to [9] ____________ ! I eat a lot of them to pick me up. However, the **disadvantage** is that they make you feel even more tired later, when the effect **has worn off**.

Ben, 20

In my family, we don't have [10] ____________ like ice cream and cookies, only fruit. My mom says fruit has [11] ____________ .

Jackie, 21

B Complete the definitions with the **highlighted** words from **A**. Change the form if neccesary.

1 To *keep* someone *going* (v) means to give someone strength to continue.
2 A ________ (n) is the opposite of an advantage.
3 It's a ________ (n) means it's important.
4 A ________ (n) is something that gives pleasure or enjoyment.
5 To ________ (v) means to diminish in effect.
6 ________ (n) is the process of becoming heavier.

C **Make it personal** Who in the survey do you identify with most / least? What foods can't you resist? Survey the class to find your top five.

Do you have a sweet tooth?

Not really, but I really can't resist pizza! It's such a great comfort food.

4 Grammar: Using noun, verb, and sentence complements

A Study the sentences 1–3 in the grammar box. Find five similar ones in the survey, and write N (noun), V (verb) or S (sentence) next to each. Then check (✔) the correct rules.

Noun, verb, and sentence complements to describe advantages and disadvantages

1 The problem with cafés **is noise**. (N)
2 The good thing about going to one **is being able to sit down**. (V)
3 The best thing **is (that) they serve nice food**. (S)

After *is*, the form of the verb is an ☐ **infinitive** ☐ ***ing* form**.
When a sentence follows *is*, the word *that* ☐ **is** ☐ **isn't** optional.

Be careful with subject-verb agreement, and make sure sentences have a subject!

One of the best things about restaurants **is** good food.
One disadvantage of **restaurants** is that **they are** often crowded.

Common mistakes

The best thing about ~~fruits~~ *fruit* (NC) is that ~~they have~~ *it has* ~~less~~ *fewer* calories (C) than chocolate.

Remember that count (C) and non-count (NC) nouns are different!

Grammar expansion p.140

B Match the sentence halves. Do you agree with the statements?

1 The best thing about energy drinks is ...
2 The problem with fruit is ...
3 The biggest advantage of vegetables is ...
4 The most difficult thing about eating well is ...
5 The worst thing about junk food is ...

a ☐ that it's expensive, especially if it's organic.
b ☐ knowing what's good for you and what isn't.
c ☐ that they help you stay alert.
d ☐ that it's irresistible!
e ☐ they have less sugar, plus vitamins and minerals.

I definitely agree with the first one. And another good thing about them is ...

C Complete 1–4 with your ideas. In groups, whose were the most original?

1 The best thing about paying taxes is ... , but the worst thing is ...
2 The most difficult thing about studying English is ... , but the most rewarding thing is ...
3 The easiest part of meeting someone new is ... , but the hardest part is ...
4 The biggest advantage of my neighborhood is ... , but the biggest disadvantage is ...

The best thing about paying taxes is that it feels good to be honest, but ...

D Make it personal Choices and more choices!

1 Note down the pluses and minuses of each choice (a–d). Then make a decision.

a On your birthday, would you rather go out to eat or throw a party at home?
b If you want to see a movie with your family, would you rather go to a theater or watch it on TV?
c If you want a new phone, would you rather buy it unlocked or sign up for a plan?
d On vacation, would you rather lie on the beach, hike in the mountains, or go sightseeing in your city?

2 Find a partner who thinks the opposite. Share your arguments. Use expressions from A and B. Can you change people's minds?

Well, the good thing about having a party is that you can invite more people.

Yes, but it's a lot of work.

3 Finally, take a class vote. Which choices win?

5 Vocabulary: Describing ability

A 2.5 Listen to a lecture on six types of intelligence. Number the pictures 1–6.

B 2.5 Guess the missing words in the notes (1–6) on the right. Be careful with verb forms. Listen again to check.

C Write the **highlighted** expressions from the notes in **B** in the chart. Then test your memory in pairs:

A Use the pictures and chart to describe the six types of intelligence.

B Prompt **A** and offer help when needed. Then switch roles.

	☺	☹
at	1 *be good at* 2 ______ 3 ______	be bad / hopeless at (music / singing)
for	4 ______	have no talent for (sports / playing ...)
of	5 ______	be incapable of (learning ...)
to	6 ______	be unable to (learn ...)

Someone who has logical-mathematical intelligence is really good at ...

Common mistake

I find it easy to speak / I'm good at speaking
~~I have facility to speak / speaking~~ in public.

NOTES

Intelligence types / people's abilities:

1 Logical-mathematical: They're good at analyzing and *solving* problems.

2 Verbal-linguistic: They find it easy to tell stories and ______ new concepts.

3 Musical: They're capable of remembering whole songs and ______ notes and tones.

4 Bodily-kinesthetic: They often have a gift for drawing and ______ .

5 Spatial: They're adept at interpreting graphs and ______ maps.

6 Interpersonal: They're skilled at interacting with other people and ______ their emotions and intentions.

D Make it personal In pairs, answer 1–3.

1 Which are your two strongest types of intelligence? How do you know?

2 Which one(s) do you think you should work on? Have you tried?

3 Do you think it makes sense to divide intelligence into different types? Why (not)?

I think my spatial intelligence is good. I find it easy to give directions, and I never get lost.

I'm just the opposite. I can barely understand my GPS!

6 Reading

A 2.6 Read the introduction. Guess the author's answer to the question there. Then listen to or read the article to check.

FISH AND TREES: GARDNER'S MULTIPLE INTELLIGENCES REVISITED

Howard Gardner's theory of multiple intelligences was published in 1983. It is still relevant today and accepted by many as true. But is it a valid way of looking at learning?

Of all the memes I see on my Facebook® wall day after day, there's one that looks particularly clever. It claims that "Everybody's a genius, but if you judge a fish by its ability to climb a tree, you will think it's stupid." In other words, we're all gifted at different things, so we should concentrate on our strengths, not on our weaknesses. People with a high degree of musical intelligence, for example, will excel at playing instruments, but may be hopeless at expressing themselves in writing, or doing math problems in their heads. Fair enough. Who can argue against the notion that each and every one of us is different?

Maybe this explains why Gardner's theory is still popular. In a way, we all like to think of ourselves as unappreciated geniuses whose brilliance remains undiscovered. We're fish, and our teachers and bosses are making us climb trees. But are we really that special? Stephen Hawking is a genius. Mozart was a genius. The fact that my three-year-old can draw a four-legged horse on a rooftop doesn't make her a genius. It simply means she's skilled at drawing pictures of animals, which may or may not help her make a decent living in the future.

Worse still, the theory seems to reinforce the idea that some people have no talent for certain things and that little can be done about it. This, to me, denies the whole point of education, which is to enable people to master new skills and deal with challenges. In my view, you don't need highly developed linguistic intelligence to be able to write a clear essay, or a good degree of bodily intelligence to become a dancer or an athlete.

Any theory that overlooks the importance of motivation, passion, and hard work should not be taken seriously, I believe.

B Re-read. Infer which statements the author would agree with and write Y (yes) or N (no). Underline the evidence in the article.

1 We should only focus on what we're naturally good at.
2 People tend to underestimate their own intelligence.
3 Parents tend to overestimate children's talents.
4 Children with special talents generally become rich later in life.
5 Schools should focus on what students can already do well.
6 You can learn most things if you put your mind to it.

C Read *Reference words*. Then explain what the eight highlighted words in the text refer to.

Reference words

Reference words often refer back to a specific, stated word, but they can refer to a concept, too.

You can't judge a **fish** by **its** ability to climb a tree. **This** idea makes perfect sense to me.
(*Its* = the fish's ability; *This* = the fact that we can't judge a fish.)

D Make it personal Answer 1–3 in groups. Any surprises?

1 Choose a statement in B you agree / disagree with. Explain why.
2 How does / did your school deal with students' different abilities and learning styles?
3 Which skills do these jobs require? Which is the most important intelligence type for each?

actor athlete chef manager nurse parent politician taxi driver teacher

I think it's really important for a teacher to be good at explaining things.

I don't know. A teacher needs to be intuitive – you know, have a gift for reading people's expressions.

7 Listening

A 2.7 Listen to three friends discussing a news report. Who's most convinced that intelligent alien life exists, Theo or Ruby?

B 2.7 Listen again and check (✔) the name(s). In pairs, share your opinion on these statements.

Who believes ...	Theo	Judd	Ruby
1 most UFO stories have a lot in common?		✔	✔
2 it's likely that there's some extraterrestrial life?			
3 maybe aliens talk to each other mentally?			
4 the pyramids were built by aliens?			
5 there's a lot of reliable evidence that aliens do exist?			
6 it's likely that if aliens exist, they are physically similar to us?			

C 2.8 Read the conversations and guess Theo's story. Then listen and number the speech balloons (1–6). How close were you to guessing Theo's story?

Let's see. It was late at night, and he thought somebody was following him. So he was walking outside, right?

Yeah, but what about the vacuum cleaner? What does it have to do with the rest of the story?

8 Grammar: Degrees of certainty with modal verbs

A Study the grammar box and check (✔) the correct rules. Then identify the passive sentence in 7C.

Degrees of certainty: *may, might, must, can,* and *could*

	Present	Past
Maybe it's true.	They **might / may (not) look** like us.	It **might / may (not) have disappeared**.
I'm pretty sure it's true.	It **must (not) be** a UFO.	You **must (not) have felt** scared.
I **really doubt** it's true.	You **can't / couldn't be** serious!	It **can't / couldn't have been** a UFO.

1 Use a modal verb + *be / have been* + past participle to form ☐ **active** ☐ **passive** sentences:
Other planets **might be inhabited** by humans. The scene **could have been captured** on video.

2 Could means *may* or *might* in the ☐ **affirmative** ☐ **negative only**:
It **could have been** a UFO. The scene **could have been captured** on video.

More about ***can*** **and** ***could***

Can is not used in the affirmative to express possibility:
It **could** / **may** / **might be** an alien.

Grammar expansion p.140

B Rephrase 1–6 beginning with the underlined words.

1 I doubt we are alone in the universe.
We can't (couldn't) be alone in the universe.
2 Maybe there is life on other planets.
3 Maybe they use a different form of communication.
4 I doubt the pyramids were built by aliens.
5 (If there are aliens out there), I'm pretty sure they look a lot like us.
6 I'm pretty sure we have been visited by extraterrestrials.

C Make it personal In pairs, rephrase the sentences you disagree with, using a different modal. Are you more like Theo, Ruby, or Judd?

First one ... I think we might be alone in the universe. I mean, who knows.

Common mistakes

That legend must have ~~invented~~ *been invented* by our ancestors.
I think The Loch Ness Monster might ~~had~~ *have* actually existed.

9 Pronunciation: Modal verbs in informal speech

A 2.9 Read and listen to the rules. Then listen to and repeat examples 1–3.

In rapid, informal conversation, it's important to understand these common reductions:
must have = *musta* might have = *mighta* could have = *coulda*
In less informal speech, say *must've*, *might've*, and *could've*.

1 He must have been confused. 2 It might have been a joke. 3 It could have been a UFO.

B Make it personal Think of something hard to explain that happened to you or someone else. Share your stories in groups. Whose explanation is the most logical?

And then when I opened the door, there was nobody there.

Wow! That must have been scary. Were you alone at home?

2.5 What was the last test you took?

10 Listening

A 2.10 Answer 1–4 in the IQ quiz as fast as you can. Listen to two friends to check. For you, which was the hardest question?

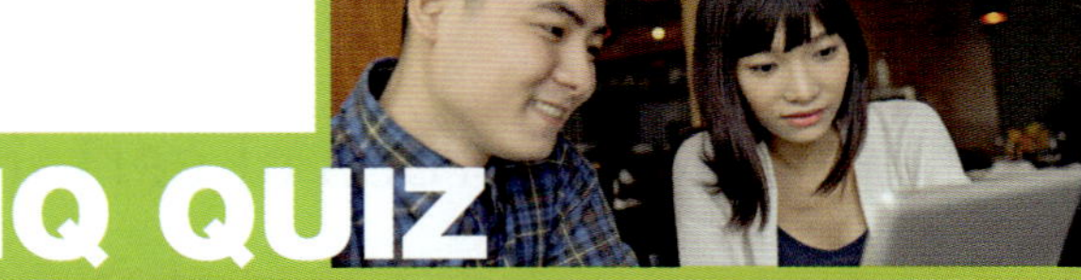

IQ QUIZ

1 Which number should come next in this series: 25, 24, 22, 19, 15 ...?

2 *Library* is to *book* as *book* is to ...
A copy B page C cover D bookshop

3 Mary, who is 16 years old, is four times as old as her brother. How old will Mary be when she is twice as old as her brother?

4 Which of the following diagrams doesn't belong?

B 2.11 Listen to the rest of their conversation. Circle a or b.

1 Carol thinks IQ tests ...
- a are boring.
- b have more disadvantages than advantages.

2 Flavio ...
- a doesn't have strong feelings for or against IQ tests.
- b sees many advantages to IQ tests.

C 2.11 Listen again and complete 1–6 with one to three words.

Advantages	Disadvantages
1 Internet IQ tests are *fun* .	4 They focus on specifics like ________ .
2 They ________ your brain.	5 They pay no attention to your ________ .
3 They can help teens ________ .	6 They might negatively affect your ________ .

D Go online and take an IQ quiz in English and check your score. Is there an argument in **C** you strongly (dis)agree with?

Common mistakes

I ~~made~~ *took* one of those online tests and ~~took~~ *got* a perfect score. IQ ~~signifies~~ *stands for* Intelligence Quotient.

11 Keep talking

A Choose a question 1–6. Note down two advantages, two disadvantages, and your conclusion.

What are the advantages and disadvantages of ...

1 being considered the family genius?
2 getting into college when you're very young?
3 being rich and famous?
4 being extremely good-looking?
5 being very tall?
6 being an only child?

B **How to say it** Share your views in groups using the expressions in the chart. Who has the best arguments?

Advantages	Disadvantages	Agreeing / Disagreeing
One of the best things about ... is (that) ...	The trouble with ... is (that) ...	Absolutely!
Another plus is (that) ...	Another problem with ... is (that) ...	That's one way to look at it.
		I wouldn't be so sure.

I think being an only child has more advantages than disadvantages. For one thing you get a lot of attention.

Well, I wouldn't be so sure. The trouble with being an only child is you're lonely.

12 Writing: A for-and-against essay

A Read this upper-intermediate student's essay. Ignoring the blanks, find two arguments for tests and two against them.

1 Most schools in my country still evaluate students using formal tests. However, more and more schools are beginning to evaluate students based on their performance, instead. This includes essays, projects, presentations, and real-world activities. Some people think tests are a necessary evil, *while (whereas)* others say students need to be evaluated after every class. Personally, I agree with the second group.

2 ______________ tests is that they're objective and easy to grade, which is useful for teachers who teach large classes. ______________ is that students with low scores can be given enough extra help before it's too late.

3 ______________ , I believe ______________ using test scores to evaluate students. First, students who do well might think they're better than everybody else, ______________ students with lower grades might lose confidence and have a poor self-image. ______________ tests is that they emphasize memorization, instead of creativity and social skills. When performance is evaluated continuously, every class is important. Students try harder, and teachers take more interest in every individual.

4 ______________ , I believe formal tests should be replaced by continuous evaluation. This way, students can also evaluate themselves, and this is really the whole point of education.

B Read *Write it right!* Then complete the essay with items 1–8, changing the punctuation as necessary.

Write it right!

In a for-and-against essay, use expressions like these to help readers follow your train of thought.

Listing pros and cons	1 One advantage of ... 2 A further advantage ... 3 There are a number of drawbacks to ... 4 Another disadvantage of ...
Contrasting	5 On the other hand ... 6 While ... / 7 Whereas ...
Reaching a conclusion	8 To sum up ...

C Complete the guide with the numbers of the paragraphs 1–4.

- Present both sides of the question in paragraphs ____ and ____ .
- Give your own opinion in paragraph ____ and summarize it in paragraph ____ .

Common mistake

Some people are in favor of school ~~uniforms, on the other hand~~ *uniforms. On the other hand,* others want to ban them.

D Complete 1–3 with an opinion of your own. Then compare sentences in groups. Any similarities?

1 While it's true that schools ... , personally, I believe that ...

2 Retiring early gives you a chance to reinvent yourself, whereas ...

3 Living in a big city has both pros and cons. On the one hand, ... On the other hand, ...

E **Your turn!** Write a four-paragraph essay (250 words) discussing one of the questions in 11A.

Before

List the pros and cons. Order them logically. Anything you can add?

While

Write four paragraphs following the model in A. Use at least five expressions from B.

After

Post your essay online and read your classmates' work. What was the most popular topic? Similar arguments and conclusions?

Review 1

Units 1–2

1 Listening

R1.1 Listen to Joe and Amy and choose the best inferences A–D. What did they say that supports your answers? Check in AS R1.1 on p.162.

1 When he was a teenager, Joe probably did something ...
   A embarrassing but not serious.
   B dangerous and illegal.
   C motivating and exciting.
   D cool and fun.

2 Joe uses the expression "Need I say more?" because ...
   A he doesn't want to go into details.
   B he's already told the whole story.
   C he might have forgotten what happened.
   D he'd like to continue with his story.

3 Amy keeps the conversation going by ...
   A talking about herself.
   B showing interest.
   C being overly curious.
   D changing the subject.

4 Joe and Amy are probably ...
   A close friends.
   B brother and sister.
   C just getting to know each other.
   D teacher and student.

2 Grammar

A In pairs, rewrite 1–6 about Joe. Begin with the underlined words and use modal verbs.

1 Maybe Joe was arrested when he was 16.
2 I doubt he has a criminal record. He seems like such a nice guy.
3 I'm pretty sure they moved because of something more minor.
4 Maybe his grandparents liked change in general.
5 I'm pretty sure his grandparents had an interesting life.
6 I doubt they made much money, though.

B Role play the conversation between Joe and Amy, changing the details to those of a story you've heard or read about. Act out your conversation for the class. Whose is the most creative?

C **Make it personal** Write sentences with your opinion. Share in groups. Any disagreements?

1 The best thing about moving to a new city is ...
2 A problem with our school is ...
3 One advantage of this city (town) is ...
4 The most difficult thing about getting up in the morning is ...
5 A disadvantage of having a part-time job is ...
6 A good thing about having older parents is ...

3 Reading

Read the title. What do you think the article is about? Skim the article quickly. Were you right?

Science fiction may soon be fact!

Do great new developments in science start as science fiction? And does the creative process of science fiction encourage breakthroughs in science? According to the Center for Science and the Imagination (CSI) at Arizona State University, founded in 2012 to foster cooperation between writers, artists, and scientists, the answer to both questions may be yes.

Science fiction authors have a long history of imagining life-changing technology. Rockets for space travel were popular in science fiction long before they became reality, culminating in the Apollo mission that put a man on the moon in 1969. During the most exciting periods of innovation, science has had many "dreamers."

While space travel is still too expensive, other elements of science fiction stories have become part of everyday life. The "picture phone" of the 1964 World's Fair was a failure initially. For one thing, service was only available in three cities, and customers had to schedule screen time in advance. Calls were prohibitively expensive, with a three-minute call between New York and Washington, D.C. costing $16, or the equivalent of $120 today. By 1968, the project had been judged a failure. Yet today, free video calls over WiFi are a fact of life around the world.

Of course, much scientific innovation happens without science fiction stories. Future computers may be a big theme in science fiction today, but the foundations of modern computing were established in the 1940s and 50s. The most imaginative ideas may lack funding, and surprising innovation may happen spontaneously. Nevertheless, according to CSI, even though failed ideas can be expensive, scientists should be encouraged to keep dreaming.

4 Writing

Using the ideas in the article and three of the words or expressions below, write a paragraph to support the following statement.

Ideas that sound like science fiction today may be real tomorrow, and companies should fund scientists' innovative ideas.

First, To begin with,	→	In addition, Besides, Moreover,	→	Finally, Lastly,

5 Point of view

Choose a topic. Then support your opinion in 100–150 words and record your answer. Ask a partner for feedback. How can you be more convincing?

a You see many advantages to owning a pet. OR
You think pets are a lot of unnecessary work.

b You feel there are far too many rude people using technology inappropriately. OR
You feel technology is a wonderful modern invention.

c You think there's no such thing as types of intelligence, and you can learn anything if you put your mind to it. OR
You think people have unique talents and should spend their time developing those.

d You don't believe what appears in science fiction will ever be real. OR
You think the world is a mysterious place, and it's impossible to know what's true.

3 Do you get embarrassed easily?

1 Vocabulary: Physical actions

A 3.1 Read and match the highlighted verbs in the radio station's countdown to pictures a–g. Listen to check.

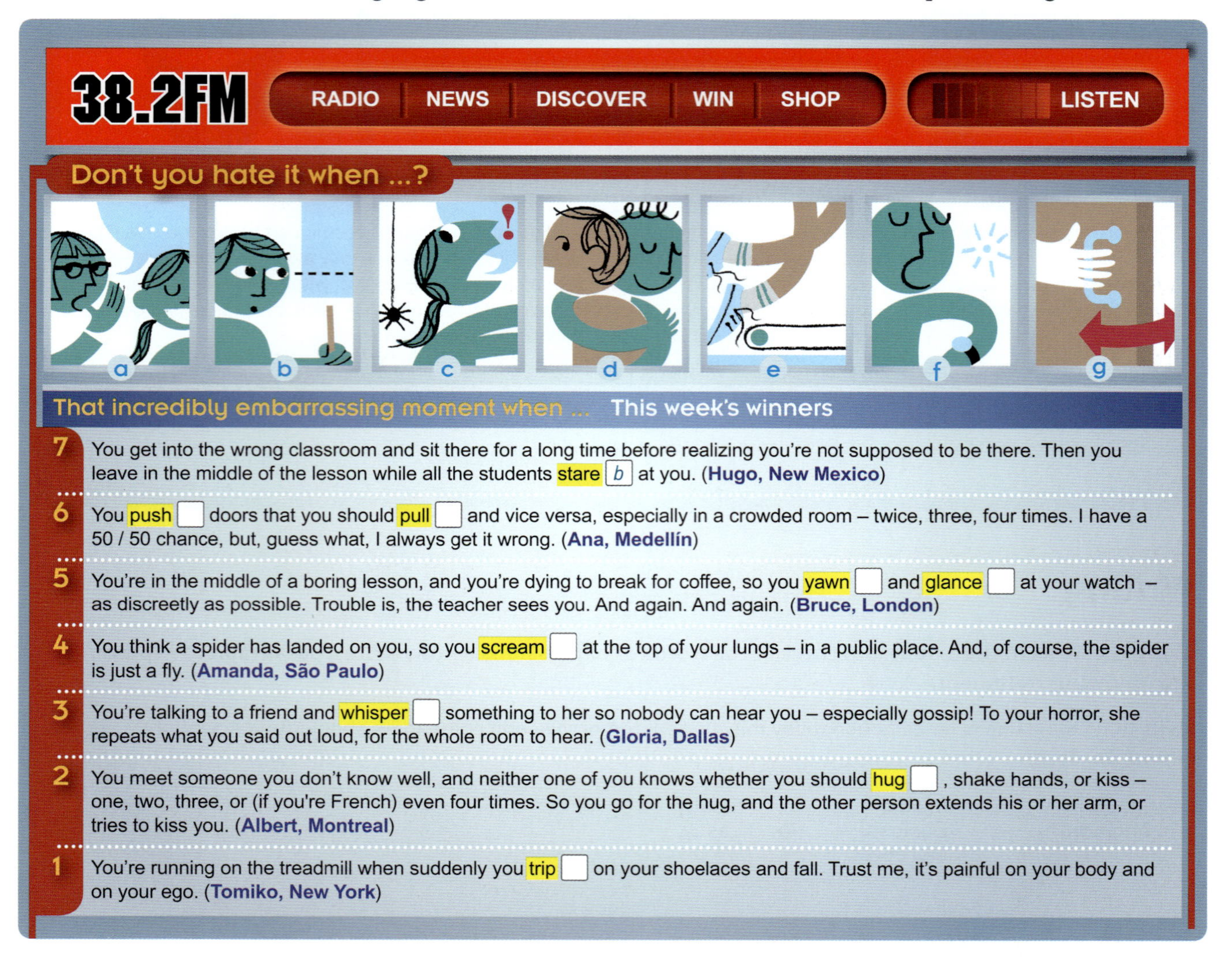

7 You get into the wrong classroom and sit there for a long time before realizing you're not supposed to be there. Then you leave in the middle of the lesson while all the students **stare** [*b*] at you. (**Hugo, New Mexico**)

6 You **push** [ ] doors that you should **pull** [ ] and vice versa, especially in a crowded room – twice, three, four times. I have a 50 / 50 chance, but, guess what, I always get it wrong. (**Ana, Medellín**)

5 You're in the middle of a boring lesson, and you're dying to break for coffee, so you **yawn** [ ] and **glance** [ ] at your watch – as discreetly as possible. Trouble is, the teacher sees you. And again. And again. (**Bruce, London**)

4 You think a spider has landed on you, so you **scream** [ ] at the top of your lungs – in a public place. And, of course, the spider is just a fly. (**Amanda, São Paulo**)

3 You're talking to a friend and **whisper** [ ] something to her so nobody can hear you – especially gossip! To your horror, she repeats what you said out loud, for the whole room to hear. (**Gloria, Dallas**)

2 You meet someone you don't know well, and neither one of you knows whether you should **hug** [ ], shake hands, or kiss – one, two, three, or (if you're French) even four times. So you go for the hug, and the other person extends his or her arm, or tries to kiss you. (**Albert, Montreal**)

1 You're running on the treadmill when suddenly you **trip** [ ] on your shoelaces and fall. Trust me, it's painful on your body and on your ego. (**Tomiko, New York**)

B Are the highlighted verbs a) movement, b) speech, or c) vision? Notice the preposition, if any, that goes with each verb. *stare (at) – vision*

Common mistake

Everybody looked / glanced / stared ~~to~~ *at* me when I fell.

C Do you agree with the station's ranking? Which stories would be in your personal top three?

> Not knowing how to greet people should be Number 1.

D **Make it personal** Embarrassing moments! In groups, use the pictures to ask and answer questions. Any surprises?

> Don't you hate it when you trip on your shoelaces, fall, and the whole room stares at you?

> Oh, yeah, that keeps happening to me. Once I fell down an airport escalator!

2 Listening

A 3.2 Listen to three friends doing activity 1C. Which two stories from 1A are they talking about?

B 3.3 Listen to the rest of the story. Answer 1–3.

1 Where did Marco go and why? 2 Who did he see here? 3 What did he do?

C 3.3 Listen again. What can you infer about Marco? Check (✔) the wrong statement.

- ☐ He sometimes goes to the movies alone.
- ☐ He'd been looking forward to that movie.
- ☐ He and his sister-in-law get along.
- ☐ Marco is a friendly person.

D 3.4 In pairs, how do you think the story will end? Listen to check. How close were you?

E Read *Narrative style*. Then underline seven examples in AS 3.3 and 3.4 on p.162.

Narrative style

When telling stories or jokes, we sometimes use present tenses to create a dramatic narrative effect. Don't mix present and past tenses in the same sentence.

Then I click "send" and ~~realized~~ realize I ~~had~~ 've sent a message to the wrong person, so I start to sweat.

F Make it personal Tell your own "embarrassing moment" story.

1 3.5 **How to say it** Complete these expressions from Marco's story. Then listen, check, and repeat, first at normal speed and then faster. Be sure to use appropriate gestures.

Creating suspense	
After that	**What next?**
1 The ________ thing I know (the woman moves three rows back.)	4 OK, go ________ .
2 You ________ believe what happens next.	5 And ________ what?
3 Before I ________ it, (everybody's staring at us).	6 So what ________ next?

2 Choose an idea below for inspiration, or think of your own.

You're never going to believe what happened to me! Last week ...

a Note down what happened, using the past tense.
b In groups, tell your story. Use the present tense for dramatic moments.
c Use physical action verbs and *How to say it* expressions.
d Write each student's name on the "embarrassment continuum" and compare your rankings!

being caught doing something wrong · breaking something · texting / emailing the wrong person · forgetting your wallet · mistaking people · spilling drinks / food · forgetting appointments

3 Language in use

A 3.6 Guess how these photos are connected. Listen to a radio show to check. How close were you?

Hmm ... Ellen's not a movie star, right? What's she doing there?

Yeah. And I don't think Bradley Cooper has won an Oscar.

Longer numbers

In informal writing, longer numbers are sometimes simplified:
23**k** followers = 23 **thousand**
1.1**m** retweets = 1.1 **million**
2m **plus** views = **over** 2 million

B 3.7 Read *Longer numbers* and listen to the rest of the story. Which two longer numbers do you hear?

C In each paragraph, check (✔) the action that happened first. Did you hear the correct numbers?

DeGeneres then **posted** ☐ the photo online, and it reached nearly 800k retweets in about half an hour, temporarily crashing Twitter®. Before the three-and-a-half hour show **was** ☐ over, it **had become** ☐ the world's most retweeted photo ever, with 2m plus tweets. The selfie had just made history. "We're all winners tonight," said DeGeneres.

Was it 100% spontaneous? No one knows for sure. The photo was taken with a popular phone, so some people say it **was** ☐ a multi-million dollar deal with the phone company, which **had been sponsoring** ☐ the Oscars for years. Others believe it was totally unplanned.

HOW ABOUT YOU? WHAT DO YOU THINK? LEAVE A MESSAGE ON OUR WEBSITE.

D Make it personal In pairs, answer 1–6. Any major differences?

1 Is the word *selfie* used in your language?
2 Should selfie sticks be banned?
3 Are you both into taking selfies? Looking at others' selfies?
4 Where and when was the last one you took?
5 Would you have the courage to ask a celebrity to take a selfie with you?
6 Find the Ellen DeGeneres selfie. Why do you think it was retweeted so many times?

I'd never have the courage. I'm way too shy to ask a celebrity for a selfie!

4 Grammar: Narrative tenses

A Read the grammar box and match examples a–d with rules 1–4.

Past narration: simple, continuous, and perfect tenses

When telling a story, use a variety of tenses to sequence events logically:

a Ellen took her phone out of her pocket and **went** into the audience. (past simple)
b The photo was taken while she **was hosting** the show. (past continuous)
c Later she announced that the photo **had crashed** Twitter®. (past perfect)
d Ellen was tired because she **had been working** really hard. (past perfect continuous)

1 *d* : longer action in progress before the time of a new event
2 ___ : longer action in progress at the same time as a new event
3 ___ : two single or short events that happened at the same time
4 ___ : a single or short event before the time of a new event

Grammar expansion p. 142

B Circle the most logical way to complete five people's reactions to the show.

1 I thought the Oscars were a bit boring, so I [**turned** / **had turned**] off the TV and went to bed.
2 I could hardly recognize some of the actors! They [**had changed** / **had been changing**] a lot.
3 Ellen was the best host I [**had seen** / **had been seeing**] in years! She did a wonderful job.
4 When they took the selfie, I [**hadn't paid** / **wasn't paying**] attention. Too bad I missed it!
5 When the show finally ended, I [**was sleeping** / **had been sleeping**] for hours!

C Read *Spoken grammar*. Then rewrite the underlined sentences in tweets 1–4 to make the grammar traditional.

Spoken grammar

Here are three traditional grammar rules that people sometimes break in informal spoken English:

1 Avoid continuous forms with stative verbs, such as *like*, *need*, and *want*.
2 Use the past perfect after "It was the first second / third / time ... "
3 Use the past perfect continuous for earlier actions when you say how long they were in progress.

1 I bet Ellen had ~~been wanting~~ *wanted* to host the show for a long time. Good for her.

2 Hated the show. It was the first time I saw it. First and last.

3 Ellen said that people were tweeting for half an hour when the site crashed.

4 I was really liking the show at first until I saw that dumb selfie!

D Complete the text with the verbs in the correct tense.

This photo was taken on Einstein's 72nd birthday in 1951, while he [1] __________ (return) from an event that [2] __________ (take place) in his honor.

Einstein [3] __________ (just / get) into his car to go home when photographer Arthur Sasse [4] __________ (ask) him to smile for the camera.

It [5] __________ (be) a long day and Einstein was exhausted. But Sasse wouldn't give up. Einstein finally [6] __________ (agree), but stuck out his tongue. The photo became a cultural icon!

E Make it personal Share a selfie (or recent photo) and tell the story behind it. Which is the class favorite? Think through these three questions:

- The event: When did it happen? Where were you? What were you doing?
- Background: What had just happened? What had you been doing?
- The aftermath: What happened after the event? Why do you think you still remember it?

This is me right here ... This photo was taken in 2014, and I was 17 at the time. I had just graduated from high school.

5 Reading

A 3.8 Read the blog quickly and check (✔) the meaning of serendipity.

- [ ] The ability to make logical connections.
- [ ] Something good that happens by accident.
- [ ] Scientists' ability to create new inventions.

BLOGADMIN **THE POWER OF SERENDIPITY**

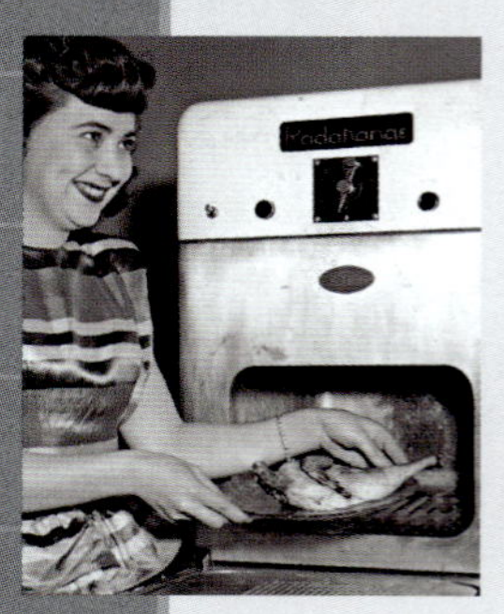

A lot of the things we buy, eat, and drink today were not designed and created step by step. Here are two examples of chance discoveries you might be unaware of.

If potato chips are ruining your diet, blame it on chef George Crum. According to one legend that became popular after Crum's death, in the 1850s, he had an impossible customer who kept sending his French fries back to the kitchen because they were "not crunchy enough." Eventually, Crum got sick and tired of the customer's never-ending complaints and decided to ignore all the dos and don'ts of potato frying: He sliced the potatoes extra thin, fried them in hot oil, and drowned them in salt. To his surprise, the customer, completely unaware of the changes, loved the new recipe and kept going back, again and again. Before long, Crum's fries became the house specialty, changing the history of junk food forever!

Speaking of food ... sometimes all you need to make a groundbreaking discovery is a snack. In the early 1940s, American engineer Percy Spencer was conducting an experiment to generate microwaves – a form of electromagnetic radiation – when he felt an odd sensation in his pants. Spencer reached for his pocket and found out that the chocolate bar he'd been saving for later had melted. He then tried to replicate the same experiment with popcorn – sure enough, it worked. A few years later, Spencer gave us the first microwave oven, which weighed 750 pounds and cost between $2,000 and $3,000. Little did he know that one day, his invention would become one of the most widely used household appliances in the whole world.

Some scientists and inventors are understandably reluctant to report accidental discoveries out of fear that they might appear foolish. Fair enough, but I can't help wondering, though, how many other discoveries and inventions we would have if all of us were more willing to admit that necessity isn't always the mother of invention and that serendipity does seem to play a major role in innovation. What do you think?

B Check (✔) the correct statement in each group. Which story did you enjoy more?

Crum ...

- [ ] was surprised by his customer's feedback on the new chips.
- [ ] invented a very popular story about a customer.

Spencer ...

- [ ] knew the microwave oven would become very popular.
- [ ] suspected that the microwaves might pop the corn.

C What's the writer's main point in the last paragraph? Do you agree?

- [ ] If we were more open-minded about serendipity, we might have many more good inventions.
- [ ] If we focused more on necessity, we would have more good inventions.

D 3.9 Look at the highlighted words in the blog and choose the correct alternatives. Listen to check.

1 *Crunchy* sounds like a [**positive** / **negative**] adjective to describe [**food** / **places**].
2 *Slice* probably describes a way of [**cutting** / **cooking**] food.
3 *Groundbreaking* sounds like a [**positive** / **negative**] adjective that describes [**minor** / **major**] events.
4 *Odd* sounds like a [**positive** / **negative**] adjective.
5 *Widely* is an adverb that probably describes [**frequency** / **size**].

E **Make it personal** Choose one item from each pair that you couldn't live without. Compare in groups. Can you change everyone's mind?

bed / sofa
buses / trains
fridge / air conditioning
fruit / vegetables
microwave / stove
wide-screen TV / tablet

I'd die without a microwave. I don't know how to cook!

6 Vocabulary: Binomials

A Read *Binomials*. Then scan paragraphs 1 and 2 of the blog in 5A and complete the chart with the bold expressions.

Binomials

Remember that binomials are expressions where two words are joined by a conjunction, most frequently "and." The word order is usually fixed. Binomials may have:
1 Repeated words: *I've never met a famous scientist* ***face to face*** (in person).
2 Combined opposites: *What are the* ***pros and cons*** (advantages and disadvantages) *of microwave cooking?*
3 Combined related words: *Creativity is the* ***heart and soul*** (essence) *of successful businesses.*

1 fed up *sick and tired*	3 done in stages ______
2 repeatedly ______	4 rules ______

Common mistake

I'm sick and tired ~~to eat~~ *of eating* junk food.
I need some vegetables for a change!

B 3.10 Use your intuition to complete these song lines. Listen to check.

1 "If you fall, I will catch you. I'll be waiting, **time after** *time*." (Cindy Lauper)
2 "We've had some fun, and yes, we've had our **ups and** ______." (Huey Lewis and The News)
3 "It's not the game; it's how you play. And if I fall, I get up again, **over and** ______." (Madonna)
4 "**Sooner or** ______, we learn to throw the past away." (Sting)
5 "For **better or** ______, till death do us part, I'll love you with every beat of my heart, I swear." (All4one)
6 "Every **now and** ______ I get a little bit tired of listening to the sound of my tears." (Bonnie Tyler)
7 "You've got a friend in me when the road looks rough ahead, and you're **miles and** ______ from your nice warm bed. You've got a friend in me." (Randy Newman)

C 3.11 Listen to two friends and answer the questions.

1 How did Ann start dating her boyfriend?
2 Where did she know him originally?

D 3.11 Listen again. Write down the six binomials Ann uses. Check AS 3.11 on p.162. Do you have a favorite word in English, like Ann?

E **Make it personal** In groups, share good things that have happened to you by accident. Use at least one binomial. Does the whole class believe serendipity is both real and powerful?

winning money unexpectedly
meeting old friends / your soulmate
near misses
a lucky find
an amazing coincidence
an accidental / fortunate discovery
following your intuition successfully

I had an amazing experience last month! I'd just left home for work when all of a sudden ... and ...

7 Listening

A 3.12 Read the webpage and check (✔) the meaning of *fad*. Then listen to a conversation. Which fad from the website are they talking about?

A fad is something that ...

☐ is really fun and enjoyable. ☐ wastes people's time. ☐ is very popular for just a short time.

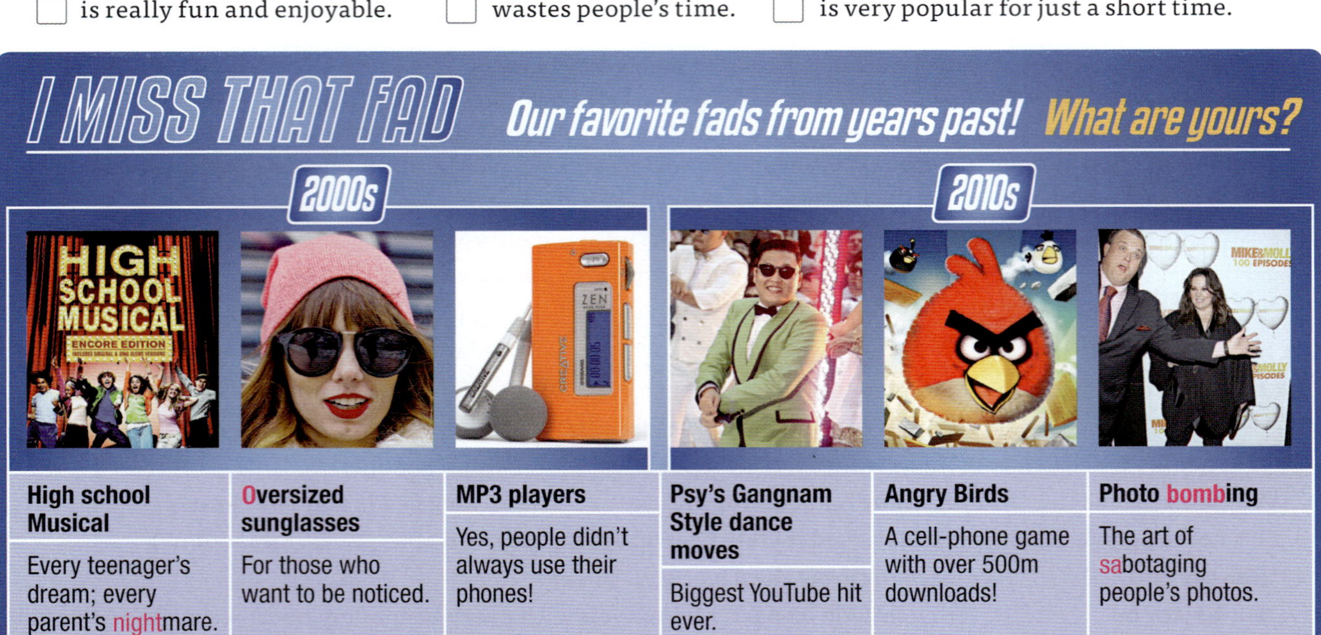

B 3.12 Listen again. T (true) or F (false)?

1 The fad was very popular in Joe's class.
2 He didn't want the teacher to see what he was doing.
3 He never played at home.
4 He usually played with friends.
5 He lost his enthusiasm after a while.

C 3.13 Write the missing letters. Listen carefully. How are the sounds pronounced?

Joe: I was crazy about [beep], you know. Actually, everyone in my class, boys and girls, _sed to love it.
Pedro: Oh, yeah?
Joe: Uh huh. It was such an _bsessi_n. I used t_ sit in the back row so the teacher w_ _ldn't see me. Then I'd get home from school, l_ck myself in my r_ _m, and start again, playing the same game over and over.
Pedro: S_ _nds b_ring.
Joe: No, it was fun, actu_lly, though a bit s_l_tary. I'd spend hours and hours alone, trying to get r_d of the pigs. I j_st kept playing the same game again and again.
Pedro: How good were you?
Joe: I was OK, I guess. Well, eventu_lly I beg_n to use it less and less ... , and then I just del_ted th_ app from my phone.

D Re-read the conversation in **C** and underline the evidence supporting 1–5 in **B**.

E **Make it personal** In pairs, answer 1–4. Anything in common?

1 Are you familiar with the fads in **A**? Which ones are still popular?
2 Can you think of any other fads, past or present?
3 If you could bring a fad back from an earlier time, which would it be?
4 Which would you love to kill off forever?

Oh, I'd get rid of those stupid online contests – like the ice-bucket challenge that was so popular a few years back.

8 Grammar: Describing past habits and states

A Read the grammar box and complete the chart for *used to*.

Past habits and states: simple past, *used to*, and *would*

a Once I **got** a Tamagotchi for my birthday. I **played** with it every single day. I really **liked** it. (simple past)
b **I didn't use to / never used to** collect DVDs. (*used to*)
c I **used to** have really long hair. I**'d** spend hours combing it. (*used to* and *would*)

We often start with *used to* and then continue with *would*. Past tenses can express:	a single action	a habit	a state
simple past	✔	✘	✔
used to			
would	✘	✔	✘

Grammar expansion p.142

Common mistakes

In the 90s, ~~it~~ *there* used to be a show on TV called *Dinosaurs*. It ~~would be~~ *was / used to be* very popular.

B Read about two more fads. Which verbs in **bold** can be replaced by *used to*? Have you ever tried these or similar fashion fads?
In the 60s, straight hair used to be very fashionable.

Don't be alarmed by the photo – there's a logical explanation! In the 60s, straight hair **was** very fashionable. Teenagers all over **would spend** hours and hours ironing their hair, trying to look their best! Thank goodness for modern technology. Today's hair straighteners are much safer!

Bellbottoms **became** extremely popular in the 60s, partly because artists like Elvis Presley and James Brown **would wear** them in their shows, night after night. Also, in the 70s, hippies **saw** bell-shaped pants as a way to rebel against their parents. Bellbottoms **came back** a few years ago and haven't completely disappeared. Are there any in your closet?

9 Pronunciation: Weak form of *and*; *used* vs. *used to*

A 3.13 Listen to 7C again. Notice the links and the pronunciation of *and* (/n/).

boys and girls   over and over   hours and hours   again and again   less and less

B 3.14 Pronounce *used to* with /s/, not /z/. Which do you hear? Write "s" or "z."

1 *s* I used to have an MP3 player.
2 __ We used that book in class last year.
3 __ My mom used to play that game over and over.
4 __ Have you ever used a PlayStation?

C Make it personal Did you have a childhood obsession? In groups, share your stories.

- How old were you at the time?
- How did your obsession start?
- How often did you use to do it?
- How long did it last? When did you lose your enthusiasm?

I used to be crazy about *Friends*. I'd spend hours and hours watching *Friends* reruns.

10 Listening

A 3.15 What do you think makes these people happy? Listen and fill in the missing words.

1 Getting good ________ on my ________

3 Learning how to ________ ________ ________

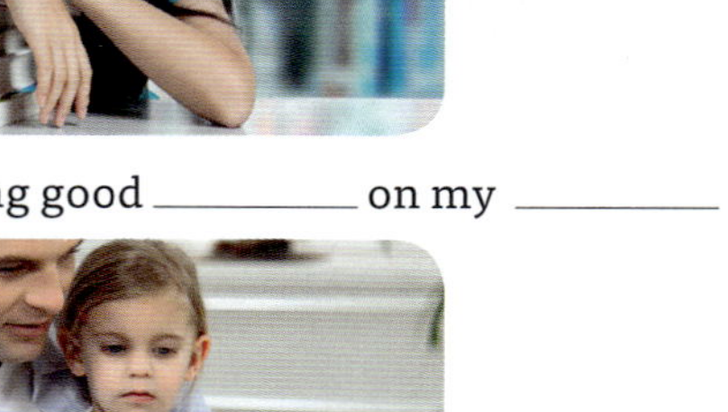

2 Spending ________ ________ with my child

4 Enjoying life's ________ ________

B 3.15 Listen again. Note down one reason for each person's answer.

11 Keep talking

A 3.16 Competition! In teams, complete each quote with one word. Listen to check. Which team guessed the most words correctly?

1 "For every minute you are *angry*, you lose sixty seconds of happiness." (Ralph Waldo Emerson)
2 "Happiness is not something ready-made. It comes from your own ________." (Dalai Lama)
3 "Joy is not in ________; it is in us." (Richard Wagner)
4 "One of the keys to happiness is a bad ________." (Rita Mae Brown)
5 "If you spend your whole life waiting for the storm, you'll never enjoy the ________." (Morris West)
6 "The true way to make ourselves happy is to love our ________ and find in it our pleasure." (Madame de Motteville)

B Which is your favorite quote and why?

I love number 4. If you think about ... too often, you can't enjoy it.

C **Make it personal** In groups, answer 1–5 and compare your choices. You can't say "both" or "It depends." Can you change anyone's mind?

What do you really need to be happy?

1 a very high IQ or very good looks
2 a loving family or a circle of very close friends
3 a well-paid job or a job you love
4 luck or persistence
5 perfect health and not enough money or less-than-perfect health and lots of money

I think a high IQ is much more important. Looks are temporary; IQ is permanent!

D In pairs, complete this sentence in as many ways as you can.

My idea of perfect happiness is ...

My idea of perfect happiness is having a long weekend lunch with my family.

12 Writing: Telling a story (1)

A Read Bob's story and complete the first sentence with a choice from 11C. Do you identify with his story?

WHAT DO YOU REALLY NEED TO BE HAPPY?

This week's winner: Bob Goldman, from Chicago

Last year I made a decision that completely changed my life and taught me that in order to be really happy all you need is ______________________ .

I come from a family of well-respected lawyers who had always expected me to follow in their footsteps. Day after day, Mom and Dad would spend hours talking about cases they'd won, trials they'd attended, and people they'd helped – just to get me interested in law. Eventually, they were able to persuade me to go to law school.

Initially, I enjoyed my classes, but after a while, I realized that law was probably not for me. I started missing classes, and my grades kept getting worse and worse. In the meantime, a friend who had a small band invited me to be the bass player, and I jumped at the chance. We played mostly at weddings and birthday parties, usually on the weekends, but it was wonderful.

One day, as we were packing up after a gig, a man who had come to see us several times introduced himself as an agent. He said he loved our music, and he offered us a record deal – just like that! Suddenly, it all made sense: Music, not law, was my destiny. So I quit law school, got into music school, and continued playing with the band on a part-time basis. I know I might only make half as much money as I would as a lawyer, but I don't care. I followed my heart, and I'm happier than I've ever been.

B Write *Do* or *Don't* at the beginning of guidelines 1–4.

When you write a narrative ...

1 ___*do*___ include at least three paragraphs.
2 ________ try to build suspense.
3 ________ reveal the main event right in the first paragraph.
4 ________ include enough background information.

C Read *Write it right!* Then find and match the highlighted linking words in the story to the synonyms in the chart.

Write it right!

When you are writing a story, use linking words, such as *at first*, *while*, and *immediately*, to make the sequence of events clear and build interest and suspense.

Sequencing		
1 at first	2 some time later	3 finally
a ___*initially*___	b ________	c ________
Simultaneous events		**Interruptions**
4 while	5 meanwhile	6 all of a sudden
d ________	e ________	f ________

D 3.17 Improve these extracts from other competition entries by adding two linking words from 1–6 in C to each. Then do the same for a–f. Listen to some sample answers. Did you choose the same words?

1 We moved to London in 2010. *At first* I hated the neighborhood, our house, and my new school. *Some time later*, I began to change my mind, though, little by little.
2 I was on my way back home from work, my phone rang, and I got the best news ever: My wife had just had twins! I realized that our lives had changed forever.
3 I lost my job last year and spent months looking for a new one. I started learning another language to increase my chances. I found the job of my dreams, but it took a long time.

E Your turn! Write your own competition entry in about 200 words.

Before

Pick an item from 11C and think of a story that illustrates your choice.

While

Check the guidelines in B and use at least four linking words from C.

After

Proofread, especially the tenses. Share your story with the class. Which one should win the competition?

4 Are you ever deceived by ads?

1 Vocabulary: False advertising

A Read the guide. In pairs, share five tips to protect yourself from false ads.

I haven't stayed in a hotel in years. Can you recognize a fake review?

Yes ... if it doesn't give many details, it's probably fake.

Common mistake

Our hotel was filthy!
What a ~~deception~~ disappointment!

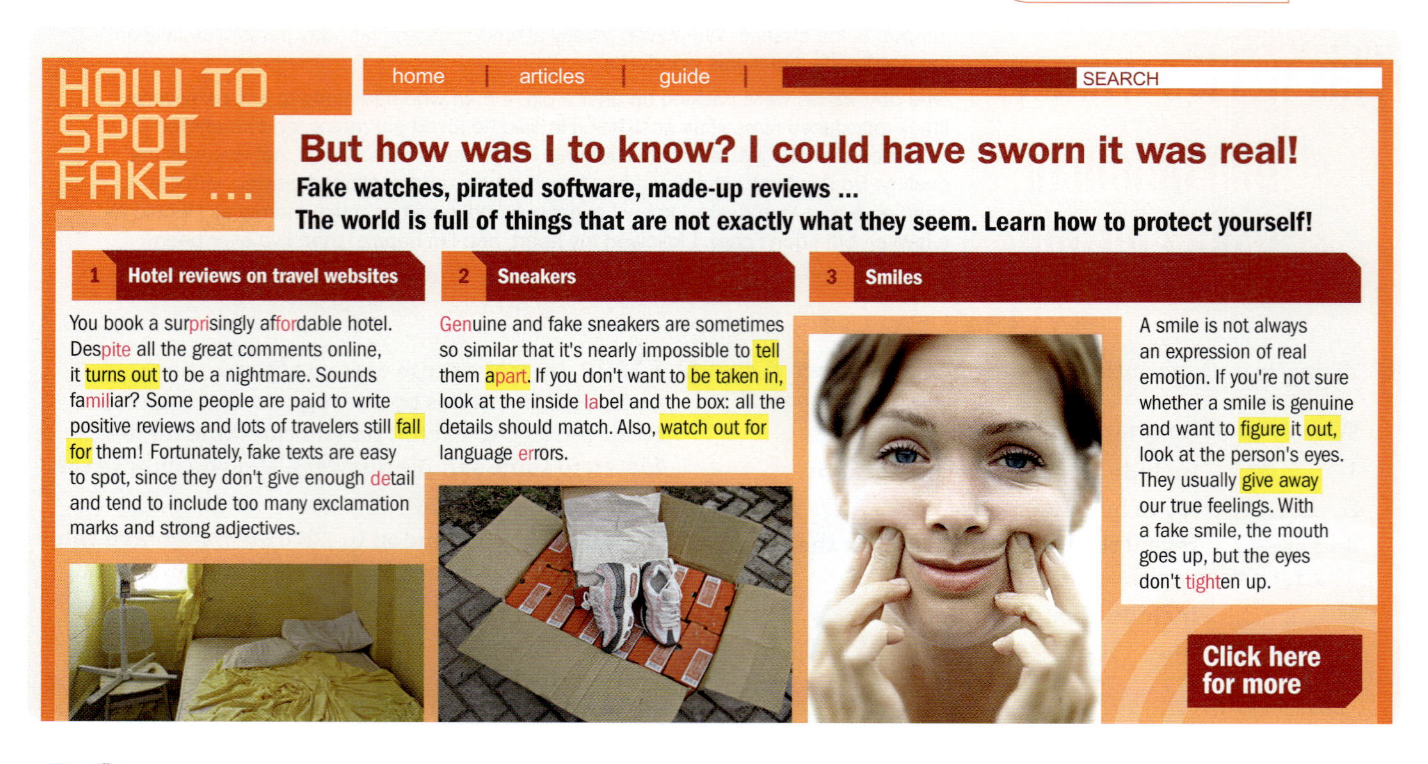

B 4.1 Complete dictionary entries 1–7 with the highlighted phrasal verbs in the correct form. Listen to check.

Separable:

1 reveal something secret: "I can't lie. My voice always _gives_ me _away_."
2 passive when meaning to fool or deceive someone: "I've never ________ by a TV ad."
3 recognize the difference between two people or things: "The twins look so much alike that no one can ________ them ________."
4 discover an answer or solve a problem: "It took me weeks to ________ how to use our new washing machine."

Inseparable:

5 look out or be on the alert for: "What problems should I ________ when buying a used car?"
6 be deceived by something: "I can't believe you ________ that trick!"
7 prove to be the case in the end: "This jacket was cheap, but it ________ to be really warm."

C 4.2 Re-read and listen to the guide in A. Then use only the photos to remember at least three tips. Use phrasal verbs.

If you look at the shoe label, you won't be taken in.

D Complete the next item in the guide with phrasal verbs from **B**.

E **Make it personal** In groups, choose a topic from those below. What information would you include in a "how to spot" guide?

4 Facebook® profiles

Be careful before accepting friend requests from strangers. You might be _________ . Studies suggest that there may be more than 100 million fake Facebook® accounts worldwide. Here are two signs that can _________ a fake profile and help you _________ if you're talking to a real person:

- Pages with few status updates, but lots of "likes," often _________ to be fake.
- You can also _________ real and fake profiles _________ because the average Facebook® user has over 300 friends. An impostor will often have far fewer.

> Let's see ... how about this: Emails from banks sometimes turn out to be viruses.

> Yeah. And watch out for other signs too, like spelling mistakes.

2 Listening

A 4.3 Listen to Kim, Mark, and Linda talking about fake goods. Which ways to identify a fake product can you infer? Check (✔) the correct answers.

Fake goods ...

1 ☐ often come without the original packaging.
2 ☐ are often more affordable.
3 ☐ don't always work well.
4 ☐ can't always be returned.

B 4.4 Listen to the rest of the conversation. What does Mark want to do with his phone? Does Kim agree in the end?

C 4.4 Listen again and order their arguments against fake goods 1–4. Can you think of any others?

Fake goods ...

☐ may harm the environment.
☐ might discourage new products.
☐ could hurt the country's economy.
☐ are made under bad working conditions.

> Fake goods can be expensive. You think you're saving, but they don't last.

D **Make it personal** Try to persuade the class!

1 4.5 **How to say it** Complete the sentences. Then listen to check.

Developing an argument (2)

	What they said	What they meant
1	Just because (it's legal) doesn't _________ (it's ethical).	Being (legal) doesn't make it (ethical).
2	_________ you'd agree that ...	I know you'd also agree that ...
3	You're _________ the point.	You don't understand my argument.
4	Let me _________ it another way.	Let me make the same point differently.
5	Look at it this _________ .	Listen to my (convincing) argument.

2 Choose a dilemma from the list on the right, or think of your own, and note down arguments for or against.

3 In groups, present your arguments. Who was the most convincing?

Is it ever acceptable to ...

- use a radar detector?
- cheat at sports?
- take someone's photo without permission?
- genetically modify food?
- break the law to save someone's life?
- lie on your résumé?

> I think it's wrong to use a radar detector while you're driving. I'm not sure it's illegal, though.

> Yeah, just because you can use one doesn't mean you should.

3 Language in use

A 4.6 Read the homepage. Then listen to / watch a teacher and circle the correct alternatives.

B In pairs, are / were your science lessons like that?

> My physics teacher was horrendous. I used to fall asleep.

C Read the comments on a discussion forum and predict the missing words 1–5 from the box. There are two extra words.

coffee	communication	~~focus~~	grades	language	sleep	smile

1 **Location: Australia** Learning through video at home might be enjoyable. But in spite of all the fun, it would take a lot of self-discipline and *focus* not to check my Twitter® feed or upload a photo to Instagram® every five minutes.

2 **Location: U.S.** I'd definitely miss having live lectures. I think my ______ and test scores might improve, though, since I'd be able to watch all the explanations again and again, go at my own speed, stop, drink coffee, take notes …

3 **Location: Brazil** Despite its advantages, "flipped learning" wouldn't work for me. I need a real live teacher to ______ at me, nod, look me in the eye … you know, just generally encourage me.

4 **Location: Mexico** Although "flipped learning" is becoming very popular and even though it might work well for math and science, I think "hands-on" skills should be taught traditionally. I mean, just imagine what it would be like to learn how to drive like that. Or to learn a ______ !

5 **Location: Canada** Absolutely. Unlike other subjects, languages should be learned through ______ – and preferably in the country where they're spoken.

D Answer 1–4 in groups. Any disagreements?

1 Who do you agree with?
2 Can you think of another (dis)advantage?
3 Do you think there should be a minimum age for "flipped learning"?
4 Would you like to learn English in a flipped classroom?

> I think it would be fun. Plus, we'd have more time to speak in class.

> I don't know … I hate spending too long in front of a screen.

4 Grammar: Conjunctions to compare and contrast ideas

A Read the examples. Then check (✔) the correct grammar rules a–c.

Conjunctions: *although, (even) though, despite, in spite of, unlike, while,* and *whereas*

Comparing	Conceding (but ...)
1 **Unlike** my classmates, I can't stand the "flipped" classroom. 2 My grades improved **while** my sister's stayed the same. 3 Teenagers can learn independently **whereas** small children need more guidance.	4 **Although** / **(Even) though** the students work at home, the teacher is still essential. 5 Learning on your own is practical. It can be a bit lonely, **though**. 6 Some people are still skeptical **despite** / **in spite of** the good results. 7 **Despite** / **In spite of** having a bad Internet connection, I still manage to do my homework.

a **Though** can come at the end of a sentence. ☐
b Use the *-ing* form or a noun phrase after **despite / in spite of**. ☐
c Use a complete sentence after **while** and **whereas**. ☐

Common mistake

Despite ~~it is convenient~~ *the fact that it is convenient*, online learning is not for me.

Grammar expansion p.144

B In pairs, rephrase the examples (1–7) in the grammar box using *but*.

OK, number 1: I can't stand the "flipped classroom," but my classmates like it.

C Read the opinions on comment 5 in 3C. Circle the correct words. Which ones do you agree with?

1 **Location: Peru** I agree you need to spend some time abroad to master a language. Or marry a native! Lots of people, of course, disagree with me, [**though** / **although**].

2 **Location: Colombia** Well, I disagree. Have you heard of that guy who's fluent in 11 languages [**although** / **despite**] he's never left his country? How do you explain that?

3 **Location: India** I'd say he's exaggerating. But I speak fluent French [**even though** / **in spite of**] the fact that I've never been to France or Canada.

4 **Location: U.S.** How about the opposite? Take my grandma. [**Unlike** / **Whereas**] my grandpa, she speaks very poor English [**even though** / **despite**] she's lived in the U.S. for nearly forty years.

5 **Location: Japan** Well, [**while** / **in spite of**] there are exceptions, I still think you need to be surrounded by the language 24/7 to become truly fluent.

Well, I'm not sure. Although some people say you can only learn a language abroad, I actually think ...

D Make it personal In groups, can you think of misconceptions usually associated with the topics below? Search online for "popular misconceptions" for more ideas. Use conjunctions!

controversial celebrities   health and fitness   kids' beliefs   current events   intelligence   sleeping

Although some say we need eight hours of sleep every night, I've read it's not necessarily true.

It really varies. ... whereas ...

Even though some believe ...

Despite what many kids are told ...

People think ... That's not necessarily true, though.

Unlike most of us, I actually think ...

5 Reading

A In pairs, read the first part of the article, a paragraph at a time. Answer the question in bold. Then read the next paragraph to check.

NEW YORK SUBWAY

MY COUSIN'S NEIGHBOR SWEARS HE SAW IT TOO!

1 If you're planning a visit to New York City any time soon, be careful if you use the subway. It's filled with danger. **"What kind of danger?"** you must be wondering.

2 The kind that purses are made of. Apparently, the sewers under the city are filled with mutant alligators, waiting for their next victim. Back in the day, southern migrants moved to New York City and took their pet alligators (!) with them. At first, it seemed like a good idea, but in the end, Manhattan and alligators turned out to be a bad match. So some owners got tired of their pets and simply dumped them into the city's sewers. They started multiplying, of course, and, in no time, formed an underground city of reptiles. **Now, why would anybody fall for a story like that?**

3 Oh, human nature, I guess. Although it seems logical that underground Manhattan wouldn't be hospitable to cold-blooded reptiles, this particular urban legend, like many others, refuses to go away. In the process of writing my latest book, *What if it turns out to be true?* I tried to figure out why these myths persist. But first things first: **What exactly is an urban legend?**

4 It's like a modern-day fairy tale, except it's retold as a true story and usually includes an element of fear. An urban legend tends to spread very quickly. All it takes is one person to share it with someone else and, soon enough, it's all over the Internet. These are some common questions people ask about urban legends.

B Read the second part. Match the questions and answers. There's one extra question.

a Why do people create urban legends?
b How do urban legends originate?
c Are all urban legends false?
d Do all cultures have urban legends?

5 *Are all urban legends false* ?
Nine times out of ten, that turns out to be the case. However, some urban legends are based on actual events that are changed and exaggerated so much that, at some point, they become fictional stories with bits of truth in them – pretty much like some of today's journalism. New versions of classic legends also appear from time to time, which means they're never out of date.

6 ______________________________ ?
Experts think they do, although since urban legends are often passed on as stories that "happened to a friend," it's virtually impossible to trace them back to their original source. Most people, though, tend to enjoy these stories for what they are – stories – and don't ask their origin because they know they're being taken in.

7 ______________________________ ?
To me, this is perhaps the most intriguing question. While we don't know the reasons exactly, we do know that urban legends are an integral part of popular culture. They represent who we are as a society and reflect our own concerns and fears. Plus, as my grandmother used to say, "Life is much more interesting if there are monsters in it." I couldn't agree more.

C 4.7 Re-read and listen to both parts. In which paragraphs (1–7) are these points made? Did you enjoy the article?

- [4] Urban legends spread rapidly and are often meant to make people afraid.
- [ ] Some urban legends make no sense, but they remain popular.
- [ ] Some of today's news stories are not very reliable.
- [ ] Urban legends make our lives more exciting.
- [ ] People like urban legends even though they suspect they might be fake.

D Make it personal Do you know the two urban legends below? Search online for more "urban legends".

There's that one about the hitchhiker that disappears. Or is that a movie?

I heard that if you leave a tooth in a glass of soda overnight, it will completely dissolve!

Common mistake

Last week I ~~listened~~ heard Katy Perry had retired. It turned out to be a rumor.

6 Vocabulary: Time expressions

A 4.8 Listen and match three conversations to pictures a–c. Which was the easiest to understand? Why?

B 4.9 Complete parts of conversations 1–3 with the highlighted expressions in the article in 5A and B. Listen to check.

1 A: _At first_ (= initially), I wasn't sure whether the story was real.
 B: ... So I guess ________ (= it turned out that), Don was lying.

2 A: Well, ________ (= in the past), people used to say that taking a shower after a meal could kill you.
 B: I eat and then shower ________ (= occasionally) – maybe once a month – and I'm still here.

3 A: Try refreshing the page. Maybe it's ________ (= not updated).
 B: Oh, don't worry! ________ (= sooner or later) we're going to find out that the rumors are false.
 A: You post something and, ________ (= very quickly), it's all over the web.

C **Make it personal** In groups, make true statements with four of the expressions in B. Whose were the most interesting?

Last week, I was walking home when ... At first ...

D 4.10 Read *Similes*. Then match the words in the circles. There are three extra words or phrases in circle 3. Listen to check.

Similes

Using a verb + *like* + a noun can make your descriptions more vivid:
I was so scared (that) **I ran like the wind.** (= very fast)
This dress **fits like a glove**. (= fits perfectly)
Remember: These are fixed combinations. You can't change the words!

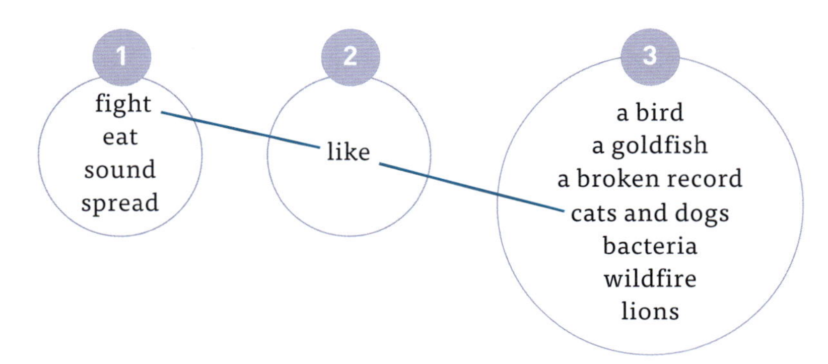

E Using only the pictures and new expressions, improvize and expand the three mini dialogs in B.

Have you lost your mind? You can't throw a coin from here.

Why not? They say it brings good luck ...

F **Make it personal** In groups, answer 1–2. Anything in common?

1 Do you ever check if a news story is true before you share it on social media?
2 Are you into gossip? Have you ever accidentally spread a false rumor?

I'm really into celebrity gossip. I love expressions like "A little bird told me (that) ..."

7 Listening

A 4.11 Listen to Bill and Rachel on a radio show describing an experiment. Order the pictures 1–3.

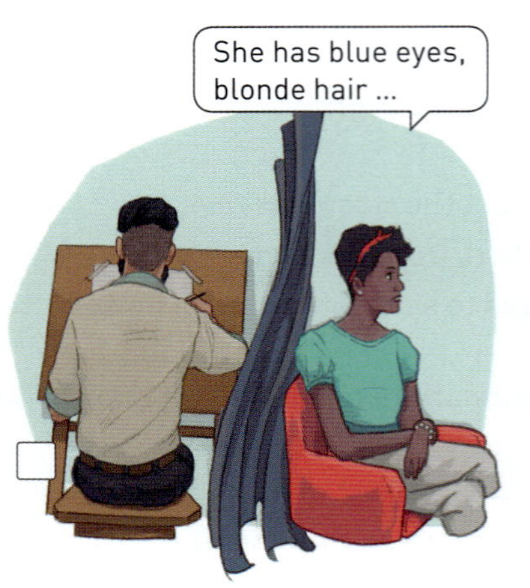

B 4.11 Listen again. T (true) or F (false)?

1 The experiment was designed to sell a product.
2 After each woman described herself, the artist drew her.
3 He then drew a second sketch looking at the woman.
4 The participants had all met before the show.

C 4.12 Guess the experiment results. Circle *more* or *less*. Listen to check. Any surprises?

BILL: As it turns out, the sketches based on self-descriptions were [**more** / **less**] attractive than the other drawings – all of them! In other words, when participants were asked to describe each other, they were [**more** / **less**] positive than when they talked about themselves.

RACHEL: Well, I'm not surprised, really.

BILL: I was a bit puzzled myself, to be honest. Anyway, the moral of the story is that maybe you're [**more** / **less**] attractive than you give yourself credit for.

RACHEL: Yeah. In other words, how we see ourselves is one thing; how others view us, quite another.

D Read *Avoiding repetition*. Then connect the highlighted words in C to their (near) synonyms.

Avoiding repetition

Writers often use (near) synonyms to avoid repetition. When you come across an unknown word, look for related words nearby. They can help you guess the meaning!

This experiment was **conducted** by a New York psychologist. It was **carried out** to change the way people see themselves.

E **Make it personal** In pairs, choose three questions to discuss. Are your answers similar?

1 Do you remember what product was being advertised? Was this a good experiment for it?
2 What do you think might have happened if they'd picked men instead of women?
3 What's your favorite recent photo of yourself? Why? Who has seen it?
4 Do others usually see you the same way you see yourself?
5 Has your personality / self-image changed much as you've grown older?

My friends say I'm really outgoing, but I think I'm a bit shy, actually.

I don't think you're shy at all.

8 Grammar: Reflexive pronouns and *each other / one another*

A Read the grammar box. Then find an example of emphasis in 7C.

Reflexive pronouns with *-self / -selves*; reciprocal actions with *each other / one another*	
When the subject and object are the same person: 1 **We** can be too critical of **ourselves**.	3 To express "all alone" or "without help": **The artist** sketched the pictures (**by**) **himself**.
2 For emphasis: **I myself** was surprised by the results. **I** was surprised by the results **myself**.	4 To express reciprocal actions: **We** were asked to describe **each other / one another**.

B Do a) and b) have the same or a different meaning? In pairs, explain the differences.

» Grammar expansion p.144

1 The two politicians introduced **a) themselves b) each other**.
2 Before the debate, they had really motivated **a) themselves b) each other**.
3 They argued **a) a lot b) a lot with each other**.
4 We taught **a) ourselves b) one another** how to play the guitar.
5 My daughter wrote her name **a) herself b) by herself**.
6 The children drew pictures **a) by themselves b) of themselves**.

In sentence a), the politicians say their own names, but in sentence b), they say the name of the other politician.

C 4.13 Read *Common mistakes*. Then check (✔) the correct pronouns in sentences 1–5 and change the wrong ones. Listen to check.

1 You see ~~yourself~~ in mirrors often, so your minds internalize that image. *yourselves*
2 If you see an ugly angle, you can instantly correct itself.
3 We stand closer to mirrors than to each other, so we see us from the same height.
4 When people see theirselves in a photo, their imperfections are magnified.
5 On some level, we will always be a mystery to ourselves. But maybe not to others!

Common mistakes

You can both put on your shoes ~~yourself~~ *yourselves*.

Sarah and ~~myself~~ *I* are going to the meeting.

I got ~~myself~~ up at six yesterday.

The survivors consider ~~theirselves~~ *themselves* fortunate.

9 Pronunciation: Final /l/

A 4.14 Read about final /l/. Then listen and repeat 1 and 2.

The /l/ at the end of a syllable or word is pronounced with the tongue further back in the mouth.
1 Paul, I don't see myself as a celebrity at all.
2 On some level, we will always be a mystery to ourselves.

B Make it personal In groups, answer 1–5. Then share the most surprising answers with the class. Remember to pronounce final /l/ carefully.

1 Do you like looking at yourself in the mirror, or do you look better in photos?
2 How often do you and your closest friends call / email / text each other?
3 Have you ever tried to teach yourself something? How successful were you?
4 What exactly is your usual morning routine? What are the first six things you do?
5 Have you ever formed a false perception of someone? What made you change it?

Well, when I look at myself in the mirror, I look thin, but in photos I often look heavier.

10 Listening

A 4.15 Listen to Liz talking to her friend Ryan. Answer 1–3.

1 What's special about Liz's glasses?
2 Did she buy them herself?
3 Where were they made?

B 4.16 In pairs, guess six things the X29 can do. Listen and take notes. Any surprises?

I never knew smart glasses could ...

Me neither. And I had no idea it was possible to ...

C 4.16 Listen again. Check (✔) the correct answer.

It can be inferred that Liz ...

1 ☐ speaks good Portuguese.
2 ☐ wishes the X29 was a better translator.
3 ☐ doesn't mind speaking in public.
4 ☐ exercises.

D 4.17 Listen to the end of the conversation. Order Liz's feedback 1–4. Which aspect(s) was she surprised by?

The glasses ...

☐ can be socially isolating.
☐ make multitasking difficult.
☐ are a little uncomfortable to wear.
☐ are kind of unnatural in a way that's hard to explain.

E 4.18 Read *Figurative expressions with 'die'*. Then complete 1–3. Listen to check.

Figurative expressions with *die*

You can use the verb *die* figuratively to emphasize your ideas:

I'm dying for / **to get** a pair of smart glasses. (= I really want ...)
My mother's **scared to death** of technology. (= She's very afraid of ...)
I **wouldn't be caught dead** wearing that thing! (= I would never do it.)

1 I'm ____________ ____ go to Rio de Janeiro.
2 I nearly ____________ ____ embarrassment when my mind went blank.
3 The kids love them ____ ____________ .

F **Make it personal** In pairs, answer 1–3. Any surprises?

1 Would you like to test the X29? Why?
2 What else do you think smart glasses should be able to do?
3 What other products would you volunteer to test?

I'd love to test a 3D printer. I mean, that would be so cool!

I'd never be a guinea pig for anything. I'd be too scared.

11 Keep talking

A Talk about a product that let you down. Think through 1–6 first.

1 Was it (a) a gift or (b) did you buy it yourself?
2 If (b), how did you choose it? Did you fall for a misleading ad / fake reviews?
3 Do you still have it? How much longer do you intend to keep it?
4 What are three things that turned out to be disappointing about this product?
5 Is / Was there anything positive about it? If so, what?
6 Would you recommend this product?

B In groups, share your stories. Who's had the worst experience?

Well, I once bought a new bicycle, and I regretted it immediately!

12 Writing: A product review

A Read Liz's review. Which feedback in 10D has she changed her mind about?

B Re-read the review. Cross out the wrong guideline.

- Use headings to make your review easy to read.
- Start with an introduction.
- Use a very formal style.
- Try to find something positive to say, even if you don't like the product.
- Be careful to include only relevant details and information.
- Finish by saying whether or not you recommend the product.

C Read *Write it right!* Then underline five more similar expressions in the review.

Write it right!

Notice how the bold words and expressions can help you generalize:
As a rule, the product worked well.
Customer support was **generally** helpful.
The experience was, **by and large**, satisfactory.
The battery lasted five hours **on average**.

D Cross out the wrong alternatives, if any.

1 I read the manual and, on the whole, I found [**it complicated** / ~~**a mistake on page 22**~~].
2 Overall, my experience with your new 4D TV [**was disappointing** / **started on Monday**].
3 Generally speaking, the car [**has a sunroof** / **handles great**].
4 As a rule, I [**don't write product reviews** / **didn't write a review of my last phone**].
5 I've had the R34 for a week and, for the most part, [**I'm disappointed** / **it works well**].

E Your turn! Write a review of the product you talked about in 11A in 175–200 words.

Before
Re-read questions 4–6 and think of any details you can add.

While
Check the guidelines in B and use at least four phrases from C to express generalizations.

After
Proofread your review. Share it with the class.

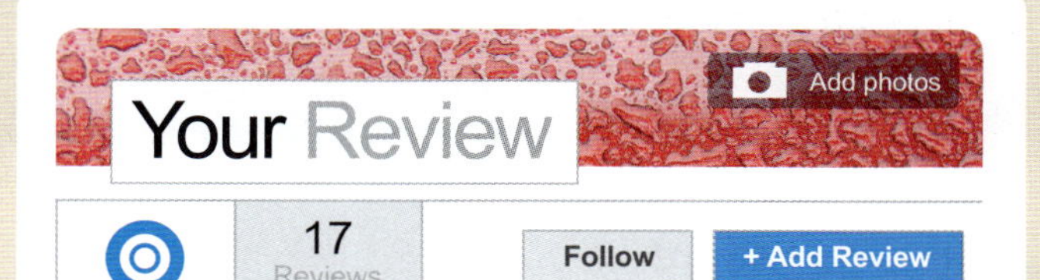

Rate the X29!

I've had the X29 for thirty days and, generally speaking, I find the device well built, reliable, and easy to use. The glasses work well as a translator and mini-teleprompter, and the battery life is better than I expected. I'm not sure, though, if they have made my life easier.

Comfort

On the whole, the glasses are surprisingly comfortable. Even though the first few days were tough, I soon got used to wearing them. My husband, on the other hand, never did – possibly because he wears prescription glasses.

Multitasking

For the most part, it's nearly impossible to carry on everyday activities such as driving – or even crossing the street – while actively using the device, which has often made me wonder what the whole point of the X29 is.

Look

Overall, the X29 is stylish and tasteful. However, the screen is way too big, and the device attracts a lot of stares, which makes me feel really uncomfortable. It's possible, of course, that people are still not used to smart glasses and that this will change in the future.

Conclusion

In general, I believe the X29 is a solid product that people who are interested in technology will enjoy. However, if you're a more casual user like me, stick to your phone – at least until an improved version is available.

Common mistake

I have ^ (had) this product for about a week and I love it.

Review 2
Units 3–4

1 Speaking

A Look at the photos on p.38.

1 Note down two questions for each, using the phrasal verbs below.

be taken in	fall for	figure out	give away	tell apart	turn out	watch out for

2 Take turns giving advice.

A Choose a photo. Ask your questions.

B Give **A** suggestions on how to avoid being taken in.

How can you tell apart fake sneakers and real ones?

Well, if you don't want to be taken in, you should ...

B **Make it personal** Choose three question titles from Units 3 and 4 to ask a partner. Ask at least three follow-up questions for each. What did you learn about each other?

Do you get embarrassed easily?

Yes! The other day, I had just arrived at school when ...

C Search on "common embarrassing moments" and in groups, share a story about someone you know who's experienced one of them, using *used to*, *would*, or the simple past.

My little brother always used to have food in his teeth!

2 Listening

A R2.1 Listen to a radio show on embarrassing incidents. Put the events in order. Write an X for any events that aren't mentioned.

The caller ...

- [ ] complains about her boss.
- [ ] explains how she feels.
- [ ] is thanked by her boss.
- [ ] breaks up with her boyfriend.
- [ ] apologizes.
- [ ] goes to her boss's office.
- [ ] is working on a deadline.

B **Make it personal** In pairs, have you or has anyone you know ever had a similar experience? Share your stories using the expressions below.

all of a sudden	at first	finally	meanwhile	some time later	while

You'll never believe what once happened to me! ...

3 Grammar

A Circle the correct forms of the verbs.

I [1][used to leave / was leaving] work every day at 6:00 p.m., but that day I [2][had stayed / would stay] late to finish a project. So at 8:00 p.m. I [3][just left / had just left] work, but the snow [4][already fell / was already falling]. The buses [5][didn't run / weren't running], so my only choice was to take the subway. But unfortunately, I [6][had injured / was injuring] my ankle two weeks before. Since I [7][wasn't able to / am not able to] walk down stairs, I [8][decided / used to decide] to take a taxi. The snow [9][kept falling / would keep falling], and my feet [10][were freezing / froze]. Finally, a nice taxi driver [11][would stop / stopped]. He [12][had stopped working / was stopping working] for the day, but he [13][took / used to take] me home anyway.

B In pairs, rewrite the paragraph, without changing the meaning, using at least four of these conjunctions. How many verbs can you change also?

although	be taken in	despite	even though	in spite of	though	unlike	whereas	while

Although I usually finished work every day at 6:00 p.m., that day ...

4 Self-test

Correct the two mistakes in each sentence. Check your answers in Units 3 and 4. What's your score, 1–20?

1 Everyone was staring me because I glanced my watch in class.
2 Jean sounded like a broken cassette with that false rumor, but it spread like fire.
3 So then he hear a really loud noise, so he look around and opened the door.
4 Sometimes I'm really tired to study English and hate hearing my accent over and again.
5 I didn't used to like bellbottoms and use to always wear straight pants.
6 That program would be very popular, but personally, I don't like it.
7 They should consider theirselves lucky and do more to help each others.
8 John and myself are planning a trip, and maybe you'd both like to join us yourself.
9 I have this phone for a week, and for and large, I like it.
10 Whereas my little brother, I can't learn to swim, in spite of really trying.

5 Point of view

Choose a topic. Then support your opinion in 100–150 words, and record your answer. Ask a partner for feedback. How can you be more convincing?

a You think false advertising is a serious problem. OR
You think, by and large, companies do a good job of advertising their products.
b You think everyone buys fake goods, and it's nice to save money. OR
You think the purchase of fake items is truly unethical.
c You think urban legends can be fun and persist because everyone enjoys them. OR
You think urban legends can do serious damage when people start to believe them.
d You think "flipped learning" is a wonderful idea. OR
You think "flipped learning" is only the latest fad and just a way for teachers to do less work.

What's your biggest life decision so far?

1 Vocabulary: Adversity

A 5.1 What do you know about these people? Guess the missing words. Then listen to check. Were you close?

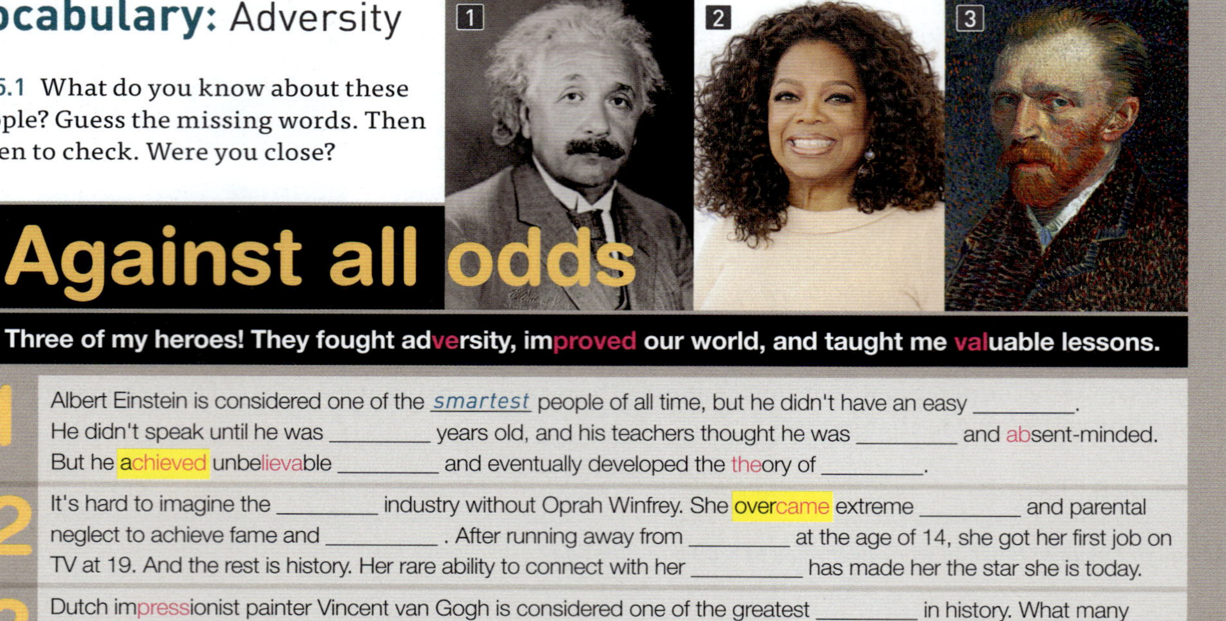

Against all odds

Three of my heroes! They fought adversity, improved our world, and taught me valuable lessons.

1 Albert Einstein is considered one of the *smartest* people of all time, but he didn't have an easy ________. He didn't speak until he was ________ years old, and his teachers thought he was ________ and absent-minded. But he achieved unbelievable ________ and eventually developed the theory of ________.

2 It's hard to imagine the ________ industry without Oprah Winfrey. She overcame extreme ________ and parental neglect to achieve fame and ________. After running away from ________ at the age of 14, she got her first job on TV at 19. And the rest is history. Her rare ability to connect with her ________ has made her the star she is today.

3 Dutch impressionist painter Vincent van Gogh is considered one of the greatest ________ in history. What many people may not know is that he only sold one – yes, one – ________ during his short lifetime. He died in 1890 at the age of only 37. He faced many difficulties, and he made very little ________, but that didn't stop him from painting over 900 works of ________. He was a tortured soul, but he just persevered and pursued his ________.

I don't know very much about ... yet. Was he/she the one who ...

B Read *Collocation*. Then complete the mindmaps with the highlighted words in A.

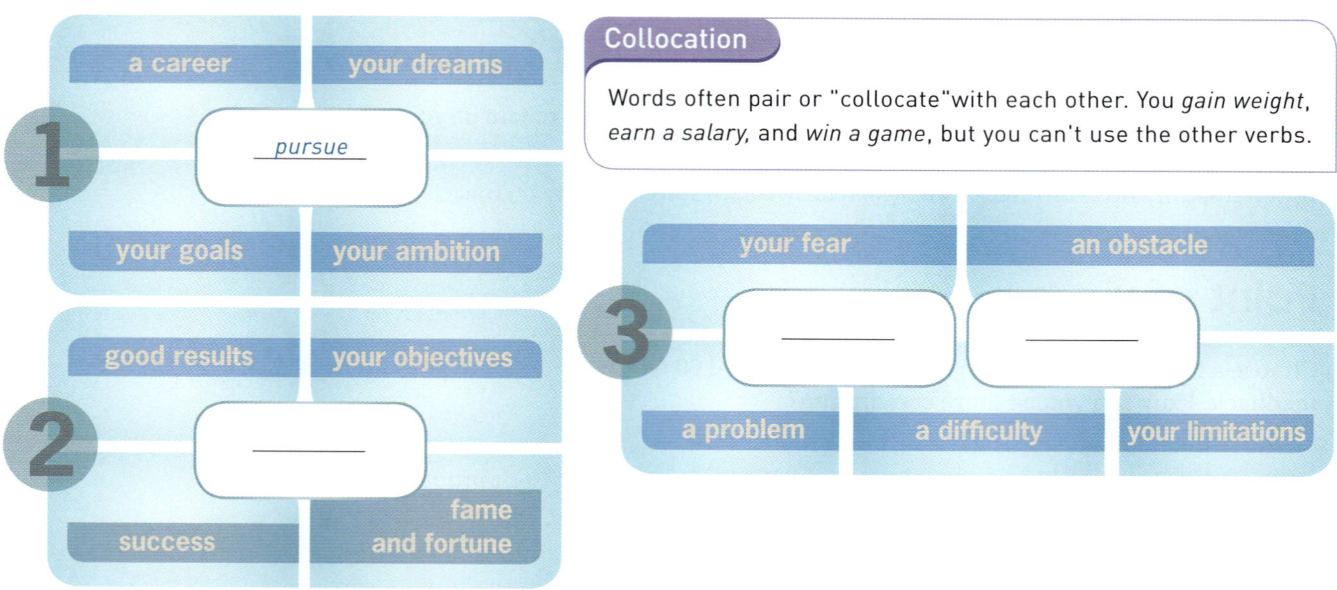

Collocation

Words often pair or "collocate" with each other. You *gain weight*, *earn a salary*, and *win a game*, but you can't use the other verbs.

C Which phrases from B can you use to describe 1) the people in A and 2) famous people from your own country?

Let's see. Despite her family background, Oprah has achieved a lot of success.

2 Listening

A 5.2 Read the webpage, listen to two people's stories, and complete the chart.

Our magazine is looking for heroes.
Who are yours?

They're your friends, neighbors, relatives – maybe even your parents. And their personal stories have inspired you and have had an impact on your lives.

Share your story with us. Three questions to help you get started: Tara

1 Who's your chosen hero?

2 What kind of problem has he / she been able to overcome?
☐ health ☐ relationships ☐ money ☐ other (what?)

3 What did he / she do that so impressed you?

Send us a short video telling us about your hero.

The ten most convincing entries will win a $1,000 gift card.

	Tara	Fernando
Speaker's relationship to ...	*friend*	
Problem(s)		
Most impressive thing		

B 5.2 Listen again. For each person, cross out the incorrect statement.

Tara ...	Fernando ...
couldn't afford her home.	is very close to his grandson.
didn't get along with her mom.	used to lead a stress-free life.
made a fortune on her first book.	had always been in good health.

C In pairs, whose story impressed you more? Why do you feel that way?

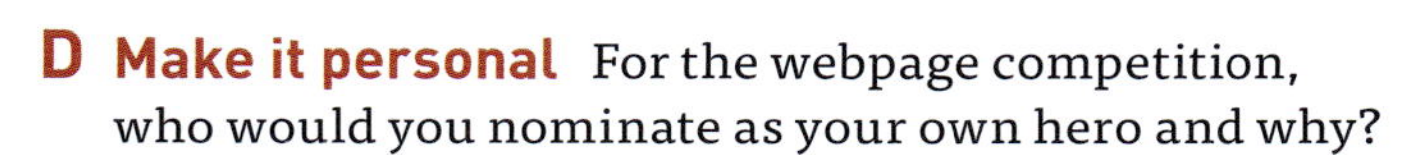

Fernando's story really made a big impression on me because he never gave up.

D **Make it personal** For the webpage competition, who would you nominate as your own hero and why?

1 Think about questions 1–3 in **A** for two minutes. Read *Beginning a narrative*.

2 In groups, share ideas, and then take a vote. Which are the most convincing narratives? Whose story should win the prize?

Beginning a narrative

A good narrative creates suspense and gives only relevant details. Always start by capturing your listener's attention:
My cousin Bruno is amazing / unbelievable / a total inspiration!

My friend Sara is amazing! I'd like to nominate her. She's been in a wheelchair her whole life, but she ...

Common mistakes

My grandmother faced lots of setbacks, but she ~~overcome~~ *overcame* most of her problems and ~~turn~~ *turned* her life around.
Don't forget! When you tell a story, be careful with both tense consistency and, in the present, third person -*s*.

3 Listening

If only I could multitask!

A Which skills (1–9) from the website have(n't) you learned?

NINE LIFESAVING SKILLS YOU'LL REGRET NOT LEARNING BEFORE YOU'RE 18!

1 cooking	4 playing a sport well	7 learning self-defense
2 driving	5 saving money	8 swimming
3 multitasking	6 speaking a second language	9 touch typing

I haven't learned how to swim yet, and I'm already 16!

B 5.3 Listen to two colleagues. Which skill is Anthony talking about?

C 5.3 Listen again. T (true) or F (false)? Guess what they will say next.

1 Anthony was surprised he didn't pass.
2 He's taken the test four times this year.
3 Claire thinks instructors are usually friendly.
4 When Anthony had to turn, he got even more nervous.
5 There was an accident at the end of the test.

D 5.4 Complete the rest of the conversation with the sentences. Listen to check.

I wish she wouldn't do that.	If only I'd started in my late teens.	I wish I knew, though.

CLAIRE: Don't let it get you down. You can do it! You're taking lessons, right?
ANTHONY: Oh, yeah. It's been two years now.
CLAIRE: Two years? Wow! Same instructor?
ANTHONY: Yeah. She's all right. But she keeps yelling, "Watch out!" whenever I do something wrong. [1]____________________. It's really annoying.
CLAIRE: Why do you think you always get so nervous?
ANTHONY: No idea. [2]____________________. If I did, I'd be able to do something about it. But here's the thing … I started taking lessons in my late 20s.
CLAIRE: So?
ANTHONY: Too late, I guess. [3]____________________. For example, I still don't know how to park! Can you believe it?
CLAIRE: Look, just take the test again, and do the best you can. You'll do better next time.
ANTHONY: I don't think there will be a next time. After more than a hundred lessons and eight exams, I'm calling it quits. Enough is enough.
CLAIRE: Oh, no! Keep at it! It's never too late to learn.
ANTHONY: Maybe it's not meant to be.
CLAIRE: Don't be silly! Just stick with it.

E Make it personal Answer 1–4 in groups. Any big disagreements?

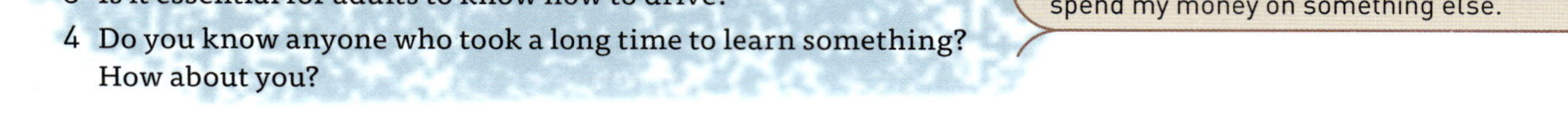

1 Guess how their conversation ends. Will Anthony retake the test?
2 If you were in Anthony's shoes, what would you do now?
3 Is it essential for adults to know how to drive?
4 Do you know anyone who took a long time to learn something? How about you?

Well, if I was Anthony, I'd take a break and spend my money on something else.

4 Grammar: Imaginary situations (1)

A Match statements 1–3 to their meaning (a–c). Then check (✔) the correct rules.

Imaginary situations (1): *wish* and *If only*

1 I **wish I had started** when I was younger.	a ☐ a strong wish for the present to be different
2 **If only I knew how** to park the car!	b ☐ a wish for the past to be different
3 **I wish** my instructor **would give** clearer instructions.	c ☐ a wish for a situation or another person to change

For wishes about the present and future, we use a verb in the ☐ **simple present** ☐ **simple past**.
For regrets about the past, we use a verb in the ☐ **simple past** ☐ **past perfect**.

» Grammar expansion p.146

More about *wish*

Other verbs and tenses can also be used with *wish* to express the present or future:
I can't draw. → I wish I **could draw**.
He's coming with us. I don't like him.→ I wish he **wasn't** / **weren't coming** with us.
The simple past and *would* are often interchangeable for repeated actions:
I wish my mom **listened** to me. = I wish my mom **would listen** to me.

Common mistake

I wish I ~~would~~ could speak French fluently.
Don't use *wish* or *if only* + *would* to talk about yourself.

B Choose the correct ending for sentences 1–3 in A.

1 ... but I [**don't / didn't**]. 2 ... but I [**don't / didn't**]. 3 ... but she [**doesn't / didn't**].

C ▶5.5 Complete six reactions to the website in 3A with a subject and the correct verb form. Listen to check.

1 I wish *I knew* (know) how to cook so I wouldn't spend so much on fast food.
2 I had the best dad in the world, but I wish ________ (teach) me how to save money.
3 Why are languages so hard? If only ________ (be) a magic pill to speak English.
4 Carlos, I wish ________ (miss) so many classes. Please try to come more often!
5 Mom says I'm not ready to get my driver's license yet. I wish ________ (change) her mind.
6 They say you can learn how to multitask at any age. If only ________ (be) true!

D Make it personal Role play "What went wrong?"

1 ▶5.6 **How to say it** Complete the chart. Listen to check.

Expressing encouragement

	What they said	What they meant
1	Don't let it ____ you down.	Don't let it make you sad.
2	You'll ____ better next time.	Your performance will be better next time.
3	Do the ____ you can.	Try hard.
4	Keep ____ it!	Don't give up.
5	Stick ____ it!	Don't give up.

2 Role play in pairs. Explain what went wrong, and tell **B** two things you regret.

A Choose a situation.

an exam a job interview a sports event
a meal you cooked an audition

B Support and encourage **A**, and ask for more details. Use *How to say it* expressions.

So, how did it go?

Terrible. I wish I'd studied more. I mean I couldn't even answer some questions.

5 Reading

A In pairs, what can you learn about Victoria from the photo and title of the article? Then read the first paragraph to check. Were you close?

Up and coming

From dull dinosaurs to glorious Greek food

Meet Victoria Sánchez, the 25-year-old college dropout behind *Fossil*.

We all know the stories – talented individuals who didn't graduate from college, never regretted it, and still managed to make absurd amounts of money despite lots of setbacks. According to a recent survey, 63 of the 400 wealthiest people in the U.S. don't have a college degree. That's about one in six. *Up and coming* spoke to Victoria Sánchez, the archeology dropout behind *Fossil*, elected best Greek restaurant of the year.

Q: *Why archeology* ?

A: Mostly because I had a wonderful archeology teacher as a freshman. So I wanted to follow in her footsteps and pursue a career in science, as well.

Q: ______________________?

A: It took a while. I guess it wasn't until my sophomore year when it just hit me that there was life beyond dinosaurs and fossils and rocks. So at the end of the year, I dropped out, which hardly anyone in my family had done before. Since I knew that eventually I wanted an international career, I decided to spend some time traveling around Europe. That's when I fell madly in love with Greece.

Q: ______________________?

A: My friends couldn't believe their ears when I told them I'd decided to start my own business. But they were generally supportive – most of them, that is. They kept reminding me of all the famous dropouts who'd made a fortune, while secretly wondering, I think, if I had the skills to be my own boss. Mom was cool about it, too. She used to say, "Better to be stressed out and overworked than underpaid and unhappy." Dad wasn't exactly thrilled, though. He still wishes I'd stuck with archeology, even now! He's always had such an interest in it.

Q: ______________________?

A: Europe was great, but after that, being back home was pretty much the same since I had to study again! Before opening *Fossil*, I spent about a year reading about Greek cuisine, learning from experts, seeking mentors, and learning the basics of running a restaurant, which I knew virtually nothing about. Now I'm happier than I've ever been. *Fossil* is winning award after award, and we're opening our first restaurant abroad next month.

Q: ______________________?

A: Well, above all, I've learned that formal education, with its overemphasis on theory, doesn't necessarily lead to actual learning. Learning can take place at work with a boss mentoring you, by going abroad and immersing yourself in a new culture, while starting your own business – or in a million other ways. It's wrong to underestimate the power of practical, real-life experience.

Q: ______________________?

A: Well, I wouldn't go as far as that. For every mega-success, there are a thousand students who drop out of college and, after a few years, wish they hadn't. College can help you develop social skills, self-discipline, and good study habits. So, despite what some people might say, college is anything but a waste of time. In my case, though – and I don't want to generalize beyond my own experience – there were more effective ways to reach my goal.

B 5.7 Skim the interview to put the questions back in the article. Listen to check. Any difficult parts?

1 So are you saying that a college education is a complete waste of time?
2 What was life after college like?
3 How did people react when you broke the news?
4 When did you realize you'd had enough of college?
5 Why archeology?
6 Looking back, what have you learned from the whole experience?

C Read *Expressing negative ideas*. What does Victoria say to express 1–4? Underline the relevant sentences in **A**.

1 There were very few college dropouts in my family. *I dropped out, which hardly anyone in my family had done before.*
2 My father wasn't happy with my decision.
3 I knew very little about how to manage a restaurant.
4 I disagree with those who say college is useless.

Expressing negative ideas

There are many subtle ways to express negativity:
Being a student is **far from** / **anything but** easy. (= very difficult)
I have **hardly any** / **virtually no** free time. (= very little free time)
Some subjects **aren't exactly** interesting. (= They're boring)

D In groups, discuss 1–3. Do you generally agree?

1 How would your parents / friends (have) react(ed) if you('d) dropped out of college for whatever reason?
2 Do you think you have the skills to run your own business?
3 Is it better to be self-employed or to work for somebody else?

I think it's much better to be self-employed, without a boss telling you what to do.

6 Vocabulary: Prefixes *over-*, *under-* and *inter-*

A Look at the highlighted words in the article in 5A and circle the correct answer.

1 The prefix *inter-* means [**"between" or "among"** / **"in the middle"**].
2 The prefix [**over-** / **under-**] means "too much" or "more than necessary."
3 [**Over-** / **Under-**] means "too little" or "not enough."
4 *Under-* and *over-* can be followed by [**only a verb or an adjective** / **a verb, an adjective, or a noun**].

B 5.8 Complete the call-in statements to a radio show about Victoria Sánchez. Use *under-*, *over-*, and *inter-* and the words in the box. There is one extra word. Listen to check.

achiever (n)	act (v)	paid (adj)	perform (v)	privileged (adj)	qualified (adj)	rated (adj)	simplify (v)

THIS WEEK'S HOT ISSUE:

Do you need a college degree to get ahead in life? What some of our callers had to say:

No, of course not!

1 "College education is *overrated*. Intelligence and flexibility are more important. Victoria's living proof of that."
2 "I have an MBA and a PhD, but I'm having trouble finding a job. They say I'm ____________. So, not very helpful!"
3 "Not having a degree doesn't necessarily mean you're going to ____________ at work. Talent and the ability to ____________ with people are far more important."

Yes, absolutely!

4 "We shouldn't ____________ things. For some careers, like engineering and medicine, you do need a college degree."
5 "Not everyone's an ____________ like Oprah Winfrey or Bill Gates. Most people need a college degree to make a decent living."
6 "A college degree is a passport to a better life. The government ought to help ____________ students fund their college education, I think."

C **Make it personal** In groups, answer 1–4. Do you mainly agree?

1 Which statement in B best describes your own views?
2 If you were to start college (again) tomorrow, what would you study?
3 Do you think online courses will replace traditional teaching?
4 Do you think it's a good idea to take a year off before college?

Common mistake

My dad never *went to / attended* ~~did/made/studied~~ college.

I've always thought taking a break after 12 years of school was a good idea, so I agree with ...

7 Language in use

A 5.9 In pairs, imagine the story behind each photo. Listen to a radio show to check. Were you close?

The Beatles

J.K. Rowling

Walt Disney

Well, maybe the first one is an album photo.

B 5.9 Listen again. In groups, share the additional details you understood. Then check AS 5.9 on p.162. Did you miss anything?

Let's see ... the Beatles got that letter in 1962.

C Do the speech balloons 1–3 mean the same as a–c below? Write S (same) or D (different).

1 I bet they wouldn't have sent that letter if they'd had a crystal ball at the time.

2 What a fighter she is. If she didn't have such willpower, she might have given up.

3 Maybe if he hadn't had so much faith in himself, we wouldn't have Mickey Mouse today!

a The executives sent the letter because they didn't have a crystal ball.
b Rowling has a lot of willpower, but she gave up.
c Mickey Mouse might exist because Disney had faith in himself.

D Which of the people mentioned would you most like to meet / have met?

I wish I'd met Walt Disney. I bet he was a lot of fun!

E **Make it personal** Search online for "famous people who weren't successful at first." Find an interesting fact to tell the class.

I bet you didn't know this! Guess what I learned about ...

8 Grammar: Imaginary situations (2)

A Read the example sentences and check (✔) the correct rules.

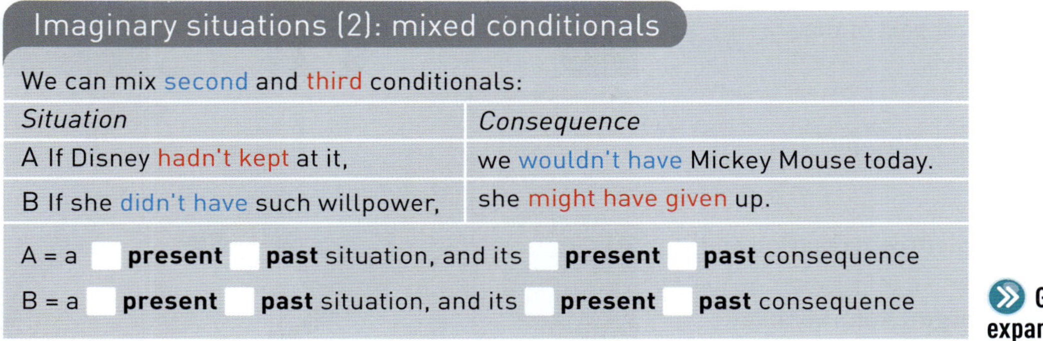

Imaginary situations (2): mixed conditionals

We can mix second and third conditionals:

Situation	*Consequence*
A If Disney hadn't kept at it,	we wouldn't have Mickey Mouse today.
B If she didn't have such willpower,	she might have given up.

A = a ☐ **present** ☐ **past** situation, and its ☐ **present** ☐ **past** consequence

B = a ☐ **present** ☐ **past** situation, and its ☐ **present** ☐ **past** consequence

» Grammar expansion p.146

B ▶ 5.10 What are they saying? Complete 1–3 with the correct forms. Listen to check.

1 We ________ (be) lost now if you ________ (check) the directions.

2 I ________ (maybe join) you last week if I ________ (be) so short on money these days.

3 If I ________ (stay) in my old job, I'm sure I ________ (be) miserable right now.

C In pairs, use only the pictures to expand and role play each situation.

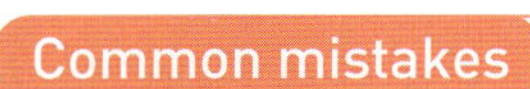

Common mistakes

If ~~you would have~~ *you'd* taken your phone, we ~~would have been~~ *'d be* able to call now.

9 Pronunciation: Sentence stress

A ▶ 5.11 Read about sentence stress. Listen to and repeat the sentences, slowly and then faster.

Auxiliary forms are often contracted, as in these songs, and sentence stress is on a content word.

If I'd /aɪd/ never **met** you.
I would have /ˈwʊdəv/ **loved** you anyway.
You've /yuv/ lost that loving **feel**ing.
I've /aɪv/ been **wait**ing for a girl like you.

B Make it personal Tell a story about a good or bad decision you've made.

1 Choose a topic and think about a–d.

accepting or rejecting advice
adopting or buying a pet
buying an expensive item
getting or quitting a job
changing schools
taking a trip

a When / Where / How did your decision happen?
b What happened afterwards?
c What if something different had happened?
d What have you learned from the experience?

2 In groups, share your stories. Use different conditionals and pay attention to sentence stress. Any similar experiences?

> Last month I adopted a puppy. I'd always wanted to have a pet and ...

10 Listening

A 5.12 Ron is telling his friend Holly about his very unlucky birthday last week. Guess what happened. Listen to the first part of the conversation and answer 1–3.

1 Where did Ron go?
2 What did Ron's boss, Barry, find out?
3 What did Barry do?

B 5.13 Listen to the complete conversation and circle the correct answers.

1 Holly [**remembered** / **forgot**] Ron's birthday.
2 Ron and Aimee are [**just friends** / **a couple**].
3 Ron and Aimee [**had** / **hadn't**] been looking forward to the show.
4 Holly [**approves** / **disapproves**] of the story Ron told Barry.
5 Ron suspects Barry was watching the show [**live** / **on a recording**].
6 Ron is [**worried** / **confident**] about Monday.

C In pairs, answer 1–3. Any differences? Has anything like this happened to you?

1 What do you think Ron's boss wants to talk about on Monday?
2 Do you think Ron's boss really saw him on TV? Is there another hypothesis?
3 If you'd been Ron, what would you have done (a) before the show and (b) when you got the text message?

Well, maybe he just wants to catch up on Ron's work.

Are you kidding!

11 Keep talking

A Read the quotes. How strongly do you agree? Write ++ (= strongly agree) to –– (= strongly disagree). Compare your ideas in groups. Which is the most controversial quote?

1 "Luck is what happens when preparation meets opportunity." (Seneca)
2 "Remember that sometimes not getting what you want is a wonderful stroke of luck." (Dalai Lama)
3 "Luck is believing you're lucky." (Tennessee Williams, *A Streetcar Named Desire*)
4 "I believe in a lot of things ... magic, vampires, and even ghosts, but I don't believe in luck. Good or bad." (Hillary DePiano)

I totally agree with the first one. I mean, without hard work, luck means nothing.

Hmm, I'm not sure. I believe some people are just born lucky.

B **Make it personal** In groups, tell each other about a stroke of good / bad luck you've had. Prepare using 1–5.

1 When / Where did it happen?
2 What were you doing at the time?
3 What is the main event? Why were you so (un)lucky?
4 What if something different had happened?
5 What did you learn from the experience?

Mine is about how I came to live in Lima. I was 12 at the time and had just started high school...

12 Writing: Telling a story (2)

A Read Paul's story. In pairs, how many details can you remember?

Forum BLOG INBOX MEMBERS YOU

What's the best / worst luck you've ever had? Tell us your stories.

1 Last year, after the most stressful three years of my life, I decided that my wife and I deserved at least two weeks away from it all. Amanda was delighted with my suggestion that we go on a trip, so we took our savings and booked a five-star hotel in sunny Rio de Janeiro. If only I'd known what those two weeks had in store for me!

2 The first six days were everything we'd dreamed of. We were amazed by the beauty of the city, especially the gorgeous views. Our nightmare began on the seventh day when I got an email from our neighbor Ed saying that there had been a fire in the house! I was terrified! I wondered if I'd left the toaster on, but I thought that couldn't have caused a fire six days later! We were both devastated and, needless to say, our well-deserved vacation was ruined. Miraculously, Ed, who fortunately had our keys, managed to put the fire out. If he'd arrived five minutes later, our 80-year-old house might have burned to the ground.

3 When we got back home, we discovered that actually the fridge had started the fire – the fridge! The freezer had slowly melted, giving off awful toxic fumes. Everything was black and filthy. The insurance company was as surprised by our bad luck as we were. They had never seen anything like it before. One thing is for certain, though: We will never leave the fridge – or any household appliance – plugged in when we go away for a long break.

SHARE

B Order the events in the story 1–7.

____ There was a fire in Paul's house.
____ Paul found out about the fire.
____ Paul's neighbor put out the fire.
____ Paul wasn't sure if he'd left the toaster on.
____ Paul discovered the freezer had melted.
__1__ Paul spent six days relaxing.
____ Paul went back home.

C Read *Write it right!* Match the synonyms (1–5) to the highlighted adjectives in the story.

Write it right!

When you write a story, use a good range of adjectives, both simple (like *angry*) and more intense (like *furious*), to make your story more vivid and interesting.

1 very happy ________ 4 very surprised ________
2 very dirty ________ 5 very frightened ________
3 very upset ________

D Write the number of the paragraph:

The main event: ____
What was unusual about the event: ____
Background information to create suspense: ____

E **Your turn!** Write a story of 200–250 words about the best / worst luck you've ever had.

Before
Note down the main events and organize them into paragraphs.

While
Use highlighted adjectives from A to make your story vivid. Make sure the first paragraph creates suspense. Be careful with tenses, and use linking words to connect your ideas (Unit 3).

After
Record your story, and ask a classmate to listen and react. Is it what you intended?

6 Have you ever Googled yourself?

1 Vocabulary: Online privacy

A Which of the experiences shown in pictures a–e on page 61 have you had?

Once I bought something online, and my credit card number was stolen!

B Read the article. Guess what text is missing.

- Rule number one: Choose your passwords carefully, and stay away from obvious choices, such as your date of birth. Also, avoid using the same password across lots of different sites. Cyber criminals are everywhere these days, and ______________________.
- How would you feel if you were at the mall and someone followed you around with a camera, writing down every single item you looked at? That's what happens when you shop online. Even if you don't buy anything, the store is keeping an eye on you, which means ______________________.
- Do you have a health concern you need to talk to someone about? Or maybe a family problem you want to get off your chest? Be careful with sites containing discussion forums. ______________________, and this information could be accessed by future employers.
- Well, at least there's Google. Surely running a simple search is pretty safe? Well, no. ______________________, and your search will be kept in Google's files for months or even years.

C Extracts 1–4 are from the article. Match the highlighted words to their meanings a–d.

1 whatever you **look up** may appear in your search history
2 they might **break into** a vulnerable site and steal your password
3 they might sell all your shopping habits to **third parties**
4 they might **keep records** of every status update you post and every *like* you click on

a ☐ people not directly involved in something
b ☐ try to find a particular piece of information
c ☐ save information in order to refer to it in the future
d ☐ access illegally

D 6.1 Put the extracts back into the article. Listen to check. Think of one new way to fill in each blank.

E **Make it personal** In groups, discuss the concerns in the article. Do you think they pose serious dangers? Which of you is the most security-conscious online / in the real world?

I don't understand what's wrong with the last one.

Hmm, I don't know. What if Google remembers confidential information?

I live in a dangerous neighborhood, so I'm always thinking about safety!

2 Listening

A Which problems are shown in pictures a–e?

> In the first one, she's shopping, and someone could steal her personal information.

B 6.2 Listen and match five conversations about online privacy to pictures a–e.

C 6.2 Listen again. T (probably true) or F (probably false)?

1 Rob's mother-in-law likes him.
2 Jerry is Don's boss.
3 Cathy and Daniel are close friends.
4 Lynette worries about her online privacy.
5 Sophie's mother is a frequent online shopper.

D 6.3 Complete 1–5 with *risk* words. Listen to check. Then remember the sentences using only the pictures.

risk (v)	risky (adj)	risk-free (adj)
at risk	at your own risk	

1 Well, OK, whatever. Play it ________.
2 I thought the whole thing was ________. How was I to know they'd use my real name?
3 I don't want to ________ losing her over a stupid Google search.
4 You know you're ________, right? I mean, using the same password.
5 Isn't online shopping a bit ________?

E **Make it personal** In groups, discuss 1–4. Any surprises?

1 Something you did at your own risk, despite your parents' advice.
2 Something risky you do more often than you should.
3 Three things worth risking your life for.
4 The greatest risk to the survival of humanity.

Common mistakes

Parents shouldn't listen ^to / eavesdrop ^on / spy ~~in~~ on their kids' private conversations.

> My parents wouldn't let me ride a motorcycle, but as soon as I got a job, I bought one.

> Mine wouldn't let me skateboard.

> Crazy! Not even walking is risk-free!

3 Language in use

A Read the blog. In pairs, answer 1–4 with A (Andrew) or Z (Zoë), and underline the evidence.

1 Who's afraid of past secrets hurting him / her?
2 Who called someone and demanded action?
3 Whose career is suffering because of online information?
4 Who has been confused with a relative?

The online privacy blog

HOME | BLOG POSTS

There are lots of reasons why you might want to delete yourself from the web: embarrassing photos, opinions you no longer have, fake social media accounts – you name it. Our readers share their stories of how they **attempted** to disappear from the web. Forever.

Sept 14, 10:03 a.m. Reply to post #1

Andrew, Chicago: A distant relative with the same first and last name was **arrested** for tax evasion a while back. He had his sentence **reduced** for good behavior and is now out of jail. So it all **ended** well, right? Wrong. Whenever people Google me, his arrest is the first thing **linked** with my name. I'm unemployed at the moment and, because of this mix-up, I have been **turned** down by three different employers this month, which isn't fair. I shouldn't be **penalized** for something I didn't do!

Sept 14, 10:42 a.m. Reply to post #2

Zoë, Calgary: About ten years ago I wrote a comment on an article in a well-known newspaper in Canada, including personal details about myself. Last year, I Googled myself and, to my horror, saw my response in the archive section of the newspaper. Now, who knows how this information might be **used**? I **picked** up the phone and told them I **wanted** to have my profile **deleted** immediately. So far they haven't been very cooperative.

Reply to Thread

B Make it personal In groups, answer 1–3.

1 Who do you feel most sorry for? Why?
2 Who do you think will have the most trouble in the future?
3 What advice would you give someone whose privacy has been invaded? Online? Offline?

If your identity is stolen, you should contact the bank immediately.

C 6.4 Read "*-ed*" *endings*. Then, in the blog, circle the /t/ or /d/ verbs and box the /ɪd/ verbs. Listen to check, echoing the verbs as you hear them.

"-ed" endings

Remember, "-ed" endings are pronounced either /t/ (*liked, kissed, stopped*) or /d/ (*played, rained, called*). The "-e" is silent. Only pronounce the final "-e" /ɪd/ when the verb ends in "t" (*started*) or "d" (*needed*).

4 Grammar: Using passive structures

A Study 1–3 and complete the grammar box. Then find two examples of each type of passive in the blog.

Using passive structures: *be*, modal verbs, and *have*

1 ***Be*** + past participle: I **have been offered** a job by three different employers.
2 Modal verb + ***be*** + past participle: I **shouldn't be arrested** for something I didn't do.
3 ***Have*** + object + past participle: Tom **had his cell phone stolen**.

a In 1–3, which is more important? ☐ the action ☐ who did the action
b In 3, who stole the cell phone? ☐ Tom ☐ someone else
c When you don't want to emphasize who did the action, you can ________ .

» Grammar expansion p.148

B Rewrite the underlined items in the passive.

Common mistake

My brother is ~~been~~ being bullied on Facebook®.

Seven ways to say good-bye to the Internet – *forever!*

1 First, ask yourself why you're leaving the web. Just fed up, or <u>is anyone bullying you</u>?
2 Stop and think things through carefully. Remember: You <u>can't undo the steps below</u>.
3 Focus on well-known sites first, where <u>you can delete your profile</u> more easily.
4 If you've created sites on the Internet, <u>you must completely remove them</u>.
5 Check all the mailing lists you've subscribed to, and <u>have somebody remove your name</u>.
6 Check with your phone company to make sure <u>they haven't listed you online</u>.
7 Sometimes you'll need help from a real person so <u>you can have him / her erase your identity</u>.

C Make it personal Take part in a discussion about digital technology.

1 Answer A (agree), D (disagree), or NS (not sure).

a Facebook® should be treated like a social network, not a diary.
b You can have your "real" life ruined by too much social networking.
c Teenagers' Internet activity must be closely monitored by their parents.
d Digital technology is beginning to control us.

2 ▶ 6.5 Listen to three friends discussing topic a. Do they all agree?

3 ▶ 6.6 **How to say it** Complete the chart. Listen to check.

Responding to an argument

	What they said	What they meant
1	I ________ agree more.	I agree.
2	I don't ________ it that way.	I disagree.
3	OK, ________ taken.	That makes sense, I admit.
4	Look, here's the ________ .	Listen to what I'm about to say.
5	What's your ________ on it?	What do you think?

4 For two minutes, plan what you can say about topics a–d in step 1. Then in groups, compare ideas. Use *How to say it* expressions. Any disagreements?

Facebook® shouldn't be a diary!

I couldn't agree more.

5 Reading

A Using only the title and photo, guess what the magazine article is about.

Home | World | Business | Sports | Health | Tech | Entertainment   Search

I, the Spy

by Jo O'Donnell

This isn't easy to admit, but I felt slightly embarrassed a while back when I was watching a news report about the National Security Agency's (NSA) surveillance program – the one that allowed the government to spy on its citizens, eavesdrop on phone calls, and monitor Internet traffic. Why? Because over the past decade, I have kept my children under strict surveillance in pretty much the same way: capturing instant messaging logs, eavesdropping on Skype® conversations, and even using spy software to keep tabs on what they typed. I have been the biggest threat to my children's privacy.

A few years ago, when I casually mentioned this to a friend, she was horrified. How could I do this, she asked, when it was such an invasion of my children's privacy? At the time, I made the same argument that generations of parents before me have probably made, which is that my children have no expectation of privacy while they are still living under my roof. If invading their privacy was what it took to protect them, then obviously I had every right to do so. Or did I?

The NSA once stated that what the agency did could be justified on security grounds, since it allowed the agency to identify potential terrorist threats to the U.S. So I made a similar argument to myself about monitoring my sons' online activity – after all, all I wanted was to protect them from the kinds of trouble teens get into, especially drug abuse and bad relationships. Was I right to do so? To be honest, I'm not sure. Yes and no, I suppose. Anyway, it's been quite a while since I last spied on my two sons (the youngest of whom is now turning 17), but looking back, I think I've learned some important lessons.

B Quickly read the article in two minutes to check. Does Jo ...

☐ feel spying on the kids was the right thing to do? ☐ regret it? ☐ have mixed feelings about it?

C 6.7 Re-read and listen. T (true) or F (false)?

1 Jo thinks government / parental surveillance are two completely different things.
2 She told a friend it was OK to spy on the kids until they left home.
3 She used to spy on the kids mostly to keep them safe from cyberbullying.
4 She hasn't spied on the kids for some time.

D What nouns do the underlined words in the article refer to? Draw lines to them.

E 6.8 Listen to part of an interview with Jo. Number the lessons she learned 1–3. Then circle A or B.

Lessons		
☐ I learned my son had impressive talents.	☐ It's important for couples not to have secrets.	☐ None of the dangers I'd anticipated came true.
A He wrote fiction online. B He was leading an online book group.	A My husband already knew I was spying. B My husband was really upset.	A They talked about homework and school stress. B There was very little cyberbullying.

F Make it personal In groups, answer 1–4. Any surprises?

1 Do you think Jo acted appropriately? Are the lessons she learned important?
2 How much freedom do / did you have as a teenager?
3 Do you think teenagers have too much, too little, or just enough freedom these days?
4 What do you think of people who read others' texts or WhatsApp® messages? Is it ethical?

> My parents were too strict, so I'll be easier on my kids. How about you?

> I'm not sure I'll ever have kids, but I wouldn't spy on them.

6 Vocabulary: Privacy words and expressions

A 6.9 Listen to five short conversations between parents and their teenagers. Which two match the pictures? Do any of the people remind you of your parents?

B 6.10 Re-read paragraph 1 in 5A. Match the highlighted words to their meanings. Listen to check.

1 surveillance
2 spy on
3 eavesdrop on
4 keep tabs on
5 threat

a ☐ keep yourself informed about something
b ☐ the act of watching someone who might be doing something illegal
c ☐ listen secretly to a private conversation
d ☐ someone or something that is potentially dangerous
e ☐ watch someone secretly

C In pairs, cover and remember both pictures in A. Then role play the conversations.

> In the first one, the woman was about 50 and she was wearing ...

> Mom, I just can't believe you were using my computer! Are you ...?

> Yes, I am. As your mother ...

D Make it personal Complete 1–4 with a word or expression from B. Answer Y (yes), N (no), or S (sometimes). In groups, compare ideas. After five minutes, take a vote on each question. How many unanimous opinions?

Is it OK for ...

1 employers to ________ their employees' phone conversations when they're talking?
2 parents to install ________ equipment in their children's cars and ________ their driving?
3 the government to monitor people's Internet activity to identify a potential ________?
What do you think of people who expose government surveillance? Is it ethical?
4 couples to ________ each other's text messages and recent calls?

> Hmm ... I'm not sure. Isn't everyone entitled to a little privacy?

> I think employers have a right to eavesdrop on conversations.

7 Listening

A In pairs, answer 1–3. Any surprises?

1 Guess what the people in the photo are doing.
2 Why do some people feel the need to keep tabs on their friends?
3 Do you know any apps that make it easy for friends to spy on each other?

> All of my friends spy on me on Foursquare®, and I hate that!

Common mistake

Facebook® lets your friends ~~to~~ see all the stuff you like.

B 6.11 Listen to James, Audra, and Tom, and match the three columns. There's one extra threat. Do you identify with any of the speakers?

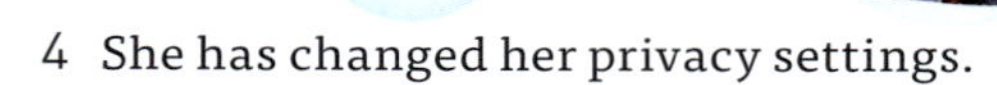

Speaker	App	Privacy threats
1 James	Instagram®	teachers
2 Audra	Foursquare®	friends
3 Tom	Facebook®	boss
		family

C 6.11 Listen again. T (true) or F (false)?

1 James's parents respect his privacy on Facebook®.
2 His friends like Facebook® better than he does.
3 Audra posts photos of where she's been.
4 She has changed her privacy settings.
5 Tom uses Foursquare®.
6 He knows how to use apps correctly.

8 Pronunciation: Blended consonants

A 6.12 Listen to the rule and examples. Then complete 1–4 with the words you hear.

> Two similar consonant sounds are usually pronounced as one.
> Do you have a minute to spare?
> My parents seem totally obsessed with Facebook®.

1 It's ________ ________ ask before you take a photo.
2 ________ ________ app take a picture of you?
3 What if I ________ ________ stay home?
4 ________ ________ addictive.

B Make it personal Draw lines connecting the similar consonant sounds in these questions 1–4. Then ask and answer them.

1 Do your (grand)parents seem to value the Internet?
2 Do you see any future reasons to maintain libraries?
3 How do you think communication will change over the next 100 years?
4 How could the World Wide Web bring more peace to the world?

> My grandparents are amazing. They're really into technology.

9 Grammar: Question words with *-ever*

A 6.13 Match the phrases. Then listen to check. Check (✔) the correct rules in the grammar box.

1 He comments on whatever ...
2 The answer is always the same whoever ...
3 They stop and take a photo whenever ...
4 However you look at this Instagram® craze, ...
5 Wherever you are, ...
6 Whichever app I use, ...

a ☐ I always end up doing something wrong.
b ☐ you just access the app and check in.
c ☐ you talk to.
d ☐ he sees on my newsfeed.
e ☐ they see something "interesting."
f ☐ it's just pointless.

Question words with *-ever*: *how, who, what, which, when* and *where*

1 ***Ever*** means "no matter who, what, or which" in ☐ **all** ☐ **some** of the examples.
2 Question words with *-ever* ☐ **always** ☐ **sometimes** go at the beginning of the sentence.
3 ☐ **Use** ☐ **Don't use** a comma at the end of the clause when an *-ever* word begins the sentence.

» Grammar expansion p.148

B 6.14 James, Audra, and Tom continue the interview from 7B. Complete 1–5 with a question word with *-ever*. Listen to check. How would you answer the reporter's questions?

REPORTER: And what's your favorite social app?
JAMES: I love Vine®. [1] *Whenever* I see something funny, I just video it. I mean, how cool is that? Wechat® is another favorite. I can stay in touch with my friends [2] __________ I am.
REPORTER: And are there any apps you like?
AUDRA: Flickr® is OK for [3] __________ likes photographs. Tumblr® isn't bad, either. I just use [4] __________ I click on first.
REPORTER: OK. What about your favorite app?
TOM: [5] __________ people may say about Facebook®, it's still my number one app. I love it.

C Make it personal Make 1–4 true for you. In pairs, compare. Any similar answers?

Whenever I hear the song *Summer*, I think of my ex. He used to love Calvin Harris.

Yeah, that's a great song. It reminds me of my trip to New York in 2015.

10 Listening

"We no longer look at résumés. We go straight to your Facebook® page."

A In groups, answer 1–2. Any surprises?

1 Why does the interviewer in the cartoon prefer to look at candidates' Facebook® profiles?
2 How can your Facebook® page help you to get a job / stop you from being hired? Think about:

AREAS OF CAUTION

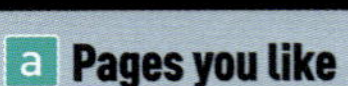

a Pages you like

b Your choice of words

c Photos you post

d Religion and politics

e Photos you're tagged in

The photos you post might make them think you're not serious enough for the job.

B 6.15 Listen to Larry, from the cartoon, talking to his wife about the interview. Which area of caution in A did he ignore?

C 6.15 Listen again and circle the right alternative.

1 The interview was [**short** / **long**].
2 They said they wanted someone [**younger** / **more experienced**].
3 Larry [**worked** / **didn't work**] at Apple®.
4 Larry [**was** / **wasn't**] late for the interview.
5 Larry's photo was taken [**indoors** / **outdoors**].
6 His wife is [**supportive** / **critical**] of him.

11 Keep talking

A In groups, what advice would you give for each area of caution in 10A? Any differences of opinion?

B **Make it personal** What advice would you give for these areas?

be happy   look your best 24/7   spend your money more wisely   impress your English teacher
make a perfect burger   stay out of trouble at college   live to be a hundred   shop online safely

1 Brainstorm as many ideas as you can.
2 Share the best ones with the class.

I think to be happy, it's important not to worry.

Yes, but you should be careful not to spend too much money, though!

12 Writing: A *how to* ... guide

A Read *Watch out!* Write the correct area of caution in 10A for each paragraph.

B Read the guidelines for an effective "how to ... " article. Underline examples in *Watch out!*

1 Create a catchy title.
2 Use section headings.
3 Write a short introduction / conclusion.
4 Add details.

C Read *Write it right!* Write guidelines for email etiquette (1–4).

Write it right!

When writing a "how to ..." guide, it's important to be very specific and tell the reader the dos and don'ts.

Dos	Don'ts
1 Do your best to ...	1 Avoid + noun / *-ing* verb
2 Be sure to ...	2 Whatever you do, don't ...
3 As far as possible, try to ...	3 Never, ever ...

include reply scan write

1 within 24 hours – ✓ [your best]
Do your best to reply within 24 hours.
2 huge attachments – ✗ [avoid]
______
3 your messages for viruses – ✓ [sure]
______
4 in CAPS - ✗ [whatever]
______

D Your turn! Write a "how to ... " article in about 150–180 words.

Common mistake

Try ~~to don't~~ *not to* spend money on things you don't need.

Before
Choose a topic from 11B and in pairs, brainstorm your "Top five guidelines."

While
Pay attention to the guidelines in B, and use at least four expressions from C.

After
Share your work with your classmates. What was the most popular guideline?

Facebook® could be sabotaging your career.

Do the math: If you joined Facebook® in, say, 2010 and have posted an average of two comments every day since then, there are currently more than 4,000 comments floating around the site with the potential to ruin you reputation. Here are five things to keep in mind.

1 *Pages you like*
The pages you're a fan of say an awful lot about you. When you respond to like requests, be selective. Do your best to keep your likes as neutral as possible.

2 ______
Watch out! If you don't want to be seen doing something embarrassing, don't post it on Facebook®. Also, avoid posting inappropriate photos. And whatever you do, don't post pictures of alcoholic beverages.

3 ______
Even if you're careful when posting status updates and photos, other Facebook® users could still get you in trouble. Be sure to keep tabs on the photos you are tagged in, and have them removed if necessary.

4 ______
Never ever – ever – use foul language in a Facebook® post. Period.

5 ______
As far as possible, try to stay away from controversial topics and avoid giving polarizing opinions.

A mantra for you: "Whatever you say leaves a trace in cyberspace!" If you're afraid of being seen, you can bet your life: you probably will be!

Review 3

Units 5–6

1 Speaking

A Look at the photos on p.50.

1 Note down everything you can remember about these people, using these verbs.

achieve face overcome pursue

2 Take turns describing the person who you admire the most.

My hero is ... He / She managed to overcome ...

B Make it personal Choose three question titles from Units 3 and 4 to ask a partner. Ask at least three follow-up questions for each. What did you learn about each other?

What's your biggest life decision so far?

Breaking up with my girlfriend. I had to face ...

2 Grammar

A Rewrite the underlined sentences using the passive.

Even before the Internet, there were many security risks. Once I was in a train station, and I thought (1) someone was watching me. I wasn't sure, though, and I needed to make a phone call, so I took out my phone card. The phones were all in a row, and (2) anyone could see them, but it never occurred to me that might be a problem. Two weeks later, the phone bill arrived. (3) They had charged me $1,200! (4) Hundreds of people had placed calls from all over the world! A police officer explained that (5) they had read my phone card with a pair of binoculars, and (6) they had captured my password as I typed it, too. Even before the technology we have today, (7) criminals victimized many people.

B Make it personal In pairs, use the words below to tell a story about yourself or someone you know. Use at least six passive sentences.

capture eavesdrop on post remove see spy on tag watch

I knew someone who was spied on as he was ...

3 Self-test

Correct the two mistakes in each sentence. Check your answers in Units 5 and 6. What's your score, 1–20?

1 I'm sick of my mom listening my conversations and my dad spying my friends.
2 Jenny has been turn down for the first job, but she been interviewed for another.
3 I had stolen my computer by some thieves, and however I looked, I couldn't find it.
4 It's important to achieve a career and solve any obstacles.
5 My dad face a lot of setbacks, but after he moved to the U.S., he find work immediately.
6 I wish I would speak English better – if only I learn those verb tenses!
7 My job isn't precisely easy, and I have hardly no free time.
8 My mom wasn't able to do college, and it bothers her not to have studies.
9 If I hadn't keep at it, I wouldn't have been so successful now.
10 She's an underachiever, but if she didn't have determination, she wouldn't have win the race.

4 Reading

A Read the title. In pairs, what do you think the article might be about? How many ideas can you think of?

Your Facebook® password and you

You might find this incredibly hard to believe, but more and more employers are asking job candidates for their Facebook® passwords. Get ready. It could happen to you on your next interview. But do you have to agree? Absolutely not! Protect yourself. Never, ever give your Facebook® password, under any circumstances, to a potential or current employer.

Why not? You might think if you're a discreet person and haven't posted anything risky. Be aware. You could still find yourself in legal trouble. First of all, your friends, who have posted on your timeline or written you what they thought were private messages, have not granted permission. They may sue you and your company for invasion of privacy if they find out a company is reading their correspondence. They also haven't given permission for your company to see their photos. And just imagine what might happen if one of your friends applies for a job at the same company and is turned down. You could be in big trouble if your friend suspects discrimination.

And what if you're the employer? You may think your right to information is protected, but you may be wrong. You could be accessing sensitive personal information that would be illegal to ask for in an interview. And again, your candidate's friends have not given you permission for third-party access. Even if you escape legal action, is what you're doing ethical? You wouldn't ask to read through your candidate's personal mail before making a job offer – or would you?

B In pairs, note down reasons not to give your employer your Facebook® password. How many can you remember?

C Fill in the missing words in these actions that may be illegal and write A (Applicant) or E (Employer). Did any of them surprise you?

1 Letting an employer read ________ messages from friends.
2 Allowing an employer to see ________ taken of friends.
3 Allowing access to information if your friend applies for a job and suspects ________ .
4 Gaining access to sensitive information that you could not ask for during an ________ .
5 Not having been given ________ -party access by a candidate's friends.

5 Point of view

Choose a topic. Then support your opinion in 100–150 words, and record your answer. Ask a partner for feedback. How can you be more convincing?

a You think people who overcome illness are more inspiring than those who overcome poverty. OR
You think people who overcome poverty are more inspiring than those who overcome illness.

b You think protecting your online privacy is very important. OR
You're not too worried about online privacy because you have nothing to hide.

c You think college is essential for success. OR
You think college is one option, but there are many other ways to suceed.

7 How important is music to you?

1 Vocabulary: Success expressions

A In groups, share what you know about musicians 1–5. Remember any lines from their songs?

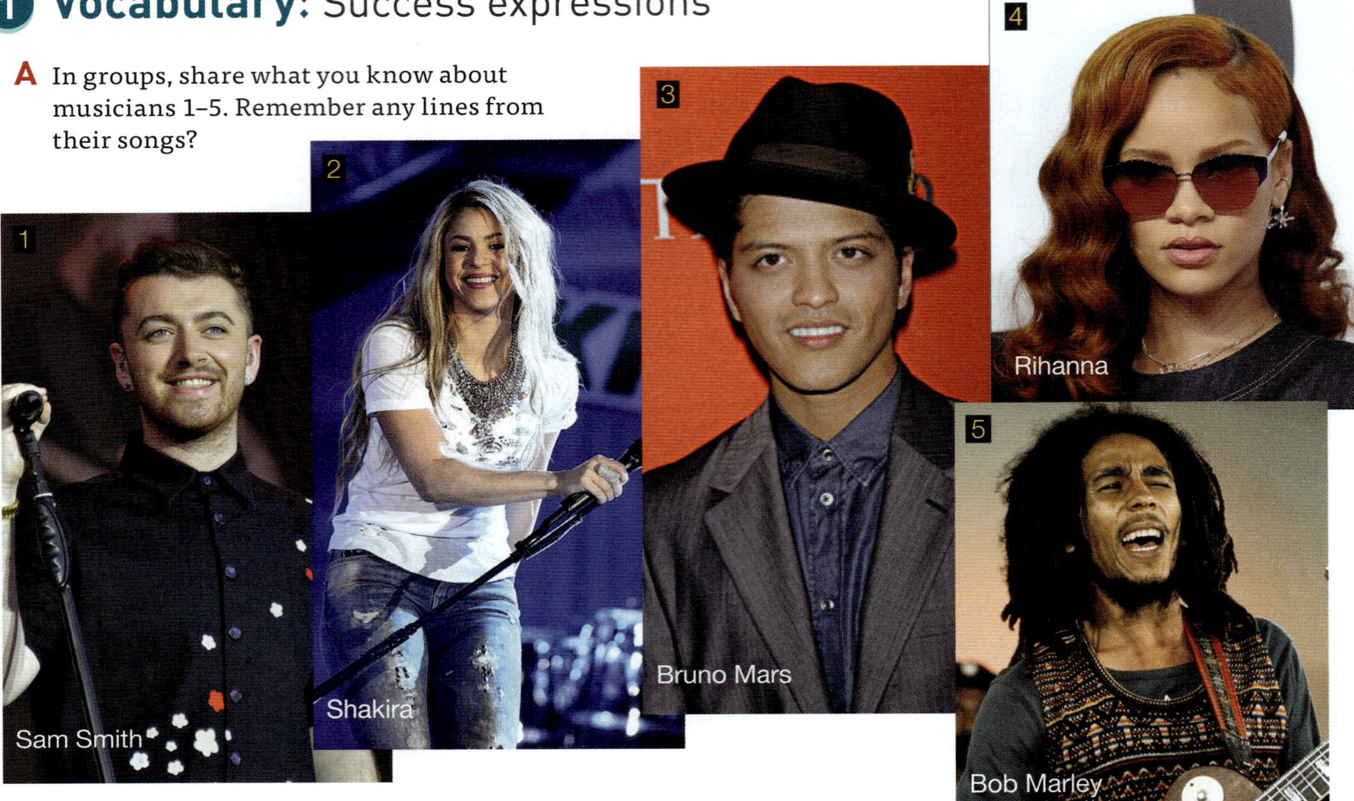

Sam Smith
Shakira
Bruno Mars
Rihanna
Bob Marley

Yes! "Whenever, wherever, we're meant to be together ...". My favorite Shakira song!

B 7.1 Take the quiz. Listen to a radio show to check. Did you get any right?

RU an expert on pop-music trivia?
Try these four tricky questions to find out

1 Sam Smith **rose to fame** in 2012. What was his job before he became a **high-profile** celebrity?
- **a** a taxi driver
- **b** a bartender
- **c** a pet groomer

2 Jamaican Bob Marley (1945–1981) **is** generally **regarded as** the king of reggae. Which is true?
- **a** As a child, he could predict people's futures by reading their palms.
- **b** He only released three albums in his lifetime.
- **c** His biggest hit is *Don't worry, be happy.*

3 Adele's *21*, the best-selling album that **came out** in 2011, topped the charts for nearly six months. What does 21 refer to?
- **a** her lucky number
- **b** the number of songs on the CD
- **c** her age at the time

4 The first U.S. edition of the Rock in Rio music festival **took place** in 2015 and featured the singer behind the smash hits *Uptown funk* and *Grenade*. Was it ...?
- **a** Bruno Mars
- **b** Rihanna
- **c** Shakira

C 7.2 Match the highlighted words in **B** to their definitions. Listen to check.

1 rose to fame
2 high-profile
3 is regarded as
4 came out
5 took place

a ☐ was officially released, became available
b ☐ suddenly became very famous
c ☐ is considered
d ☐ happened, occurred
e ☐ prominent and well known

D **Make it personal** In groups, search online for *music trivia*. Write three questions to ask the class. Try to use some words from **C**. Who are the most popular artists?

OK, Calvin Harris is a high-profile Scottish DJ and singer. Which song did he produce? Was it a) ...

2 Listening

A 7.3 Listen to DJs Tim and Nina after their show. Why is Tim tired of his job?

☐ The pay's not good enough.
☐ His taste in music has changed.
☐ Music has changed.

B 7.3 Listen again. T (true) or F (false)? What do *you* think Tim should do?

1 Tim studied music in college.
2 Nina likes Coldplay.
3 Tim thinks pop songs have predictable melodies, but fine lyrics.
4 Nina seems to dislike the commercial side of pop music.
5 Their station probably has very young listeners.
6 Tim's considering applying for a non-radio job.

I think Tim should follow his heart and just quit.

Definitely, that's what I would do.

C **Make it personal** How have your tastes changed over the last decade?

1 7.4 **How to say it** Complete the sentences from the conversation. Listen to check.

Talking about changing tastes		
	What they said	What they meant
Past	1 I used to be really ______ of (pop music).	I used to like pop music.
	2 I was really ______ (their music).	I really liked their music.
	3 I ______ tired of (playing the same songs).	I lost interest in playing the same songs
Present	4 I'm ______ hooked on (jazz).	I'm becoming fascinated by jazz.
	5 I can't ______ enough of (it).	I really, really like it.
	6 I've had ______ of (this job).	I'm sick of this job.

2 Choose three topics. Note down your tastes under "past" and "present."

clothes exercise food / drink movies music
radio / TV shows reading shopping sports

3 Share your ideas in groups. Use *How to say it* expressions. Many similarities?

I used to be really fond of *The Simpsons* when I was a kid. I wouldn't miss a single episode.

Common mistake

I'm really into / hooked on / tired of ~~read~~ reading gossip magazines.

3 Language in use

A 7.5 Listen to Liz sharing her experience with Josh. Choose the correct headline.

- [ ] MILEY CYRUS CANCELS CONCERT DUE TO SUDDEN ILLNESS
- [ ] DISAPPOINTING TICKET SALES FORCE CYRUS TO CANCEL KANSAS CONCERT
- [ ] CYRUS CONCERT CANCELED BECAUSE OF POWER OUTAGE

B 7.6 Read and predict the missing words. Listen to more of their conversation to check. Do you think Josh is a good listener?

KANSAS CITY, MO

Pop star Miley Cyrus has canceled Tuesday night's concert at the Sprint Center as she had a viral infection.

In a press release, the concert organizers said Cyrus was in a local __________ due to a severe allergic reaction to the __________ she was taking and would not be able to perform.

Ticket holders were told to proceed to the box office so that they could get a __________, but no further information was provided on whether the show would be rescheduled.

Cyrus tweeted a message in order to apologize to her __________: "Kansas, I promise I'm as heartbroken as you are. I wanted so badly 2 be there 2 night." ■

C 7.7 Read four extracts from what Liz said next and guess how 1) her story ends and 2) she feels about Miley now. Listen to check. Were you close?

Since I was on vacation, I thought I'd give her a second chance.

I left home early so I'd have plenty of time to get to the airport.

We nearly froze to death.

In the end, I downloaded the show just to have a taste of what I missed.

I think in the end Liz might not have ...

D Make it personal In pairs, which of these would(n't) you do in order to see and briefly meet your favorite artist(s)?

go into debt | miss school or work | sell something valuable | take an overnight bus | travel abroad | wait in line all day

I wouldn't mind waiting in line all day to meet Leonardo DiCaprio.

I might wait all day for an Alicia Keys concert, but it would depend on ...

E Read *Uses of so*. Then write 1–5 next to the examples in AS 7.7 on p.162.

Uses of so

So is in the top 50 most common words in spoken English. It is used to ...

1. keep the conversation going: ***So**, as I was saying, it was really cold and ...*
2. express a result: *It was a long journey, **so** I'm really exhausted.*
3. avoid repetition: *"Is Metallica playing in Peru this year?" "Yeah, I think **so**."*
4. intensify meaning: *Why do you have to be **so** difficult?*
5. express purpose: *Here's my number **so** you can text me.*

4 Grammar: Conjunctions to express purpose and reason

A Study the grammar box and check (✔) the correct rules.

Conjunctions: *(in order) to, so (that), as, since, because (of),* **and** *due to*

	Purpose	Reason
Neutral	Liz took a day off **to** see her idol. She bought front-row tickets **so** she could be near the stage.	**Because** / **Since** expectations were high, people were very frustrated. She canceled **because of** health reasons.
More formal	Cyrus tweeted **in order to** apologize. We went back **so that** we could get our money back.	**As** Cyrus had a viral infection, she had to take antibiotics. She was hospitalized **due to** an allergic reaction.

Use: a *In order to* + ☐ noun ☐ sentence ☐ verb
b *So (that), as, since,* and *because* + ☐ noun ☐ sentence ☐ verb
c *Because of* and *due to* + ☐ noun ☐ sentence ☐ verb

Grammar expansion p.150

B Circle the correct answers. Then rewrite the text correctly using the incorrect choices.

CANCELED! THREE THAT (ALMOST) DIDN'T MAKE IT!

In 2009, MTV aired *The Osbournes Reloaded* [1]**[so that / in order to]** they could repeat the success of the original reality show. However, it was canceled after only one episode [2]**[because of / as]** it got terrible reviews.

Soccer fan Ric Wee made news in 2014 when he traveled 7,000 miles from Malaysia to the UK [3]**[in order to / so that]** see his favorite team play live. But the game was postponed [4]**[because / because of]** the bad weather.

Eighties British superstar Morrissey, who's a vegetarian, walked off stage a number of years ago in California [5]**[since / because of]** the smell of barbecue coming from backstage. To his fans' relief, Morrissey went back [6]**[to / so]** he could finish the show.

1 In 2009, MTV aired the Osbournes Reloaded in order to repeat the sucesss of the original reality show.

C In pairs, complete headlines 1–5. Use *due to* and your own ideas. Then write one more headline.

1 **SMALL MEXICAN TOWN IN TOTAL PANIC ...**
Small Mexican town in total panic due to water shortage.
2 **ALL NEW YORK-BOUND FLIGHTS SUSPENDED ...**
3 **FINAL GAME MOVED TO (CHOOSE COUNTRY) ...**
4 **FAMOUS RESTAURANT CHAIN (CHOOSE ONE) CLOSES DOWN ...**
5 **MEGA-LOTTERY WINNER FAILS TO COLLECT PRIZE ...**

Common mistakes

The show was postponed because of / due to ~~it was raining heavily~~. heavy rain

D Make it personal In groups, share your stories about events that were canceled, postponed, or that you missed. Use 1–5 to help you. Any happy endings?

1 Remember a(n) show / game / party / date / interview / trip ...
2 What happened exactly and why?
3 Whose fault was it?
4 How did you feel?
5 What happened in the end?

I missed my sister's wedding last year because of a power outage in my neighborhood.

Oh, no! What happened?

I got stuck in the elevator. And they couldn't get me out in time!

5 Reading

A Read paragraph 1 of the article. What do you think *flop* means?

B 7.8 Read and choose the best headings for paragraphs 2–4. There is an extra one. Listen to check.

Risk-taking	Reviews	The cost	Timing

Top of the Flops

– when the best made plans go wrong

1 In 2014, to promote the release of the iPhone 6, U2 made their new album available as a free download to iTunes users worldwide. In theory, a match made in heaven. But thousands of music fans resented the album being added to their libraries! In the end, what looked like a brilliant marketing strategy backfired and became one of the decade's biggest flops. But why? After all, how can anyone say no to a present? This episode shows just how hard it is to predict when something will make millions or flop embarrassingly and go nowhere. Here are three factors that we wrongly assume determine what's hot and what's not.

2 ________________: 2014's *Legends of Oz: Dorothy's Return* had a lot going for it. Loosely based on the *Wizard of Oz* story, it had tons of promotion and featured famous voices such as Lea Michele's, from *Glee*. Yet the movie made only $19 million worldwide – 27% of the production cost. Most people blame it on the critics. But if that's the case, how could a movie like *Teenage Mutant Ninja Turtles*, which critics disliked just as much, make nearly 200 million dollars in the same year?

3 ________________: Unless you were hiding in a cave in the late 2000s, there was no escaping the first *Twilight* movie, a smash hit despite the mixed reviews. Why did it become so massive? Possibly because it hit the screens just four months after the final *Twilight* novel, a cultural phenomenon. But then surely the same formula should have worked for *Joey*, released a few months after the wildly popular *Friends* finale in 2004. Yet *Joey* never caught on and was canceled due to poor ratings. So what did *Friends* have that *Joey* lacked? Maybe the chemistry between the characters, but it's hard to tell.

4 ________________: In the competitive New York theater scene, investors often base their musicals on proven hits. Take *Rocky the Musical*. Based on Sylvester Stallone's Oscar-winning movie, the show couldn't go wrong. It was far from a work of art, but it had an impressive production, masculine appeal, and pleasant songs. But, for whatever reason, *Rocky* failed to impress the public and didn't live up to expectations, running for six months only. Why did it never match the success of *Lion King*?

5 The truth is that no one really knows. Sometimes things just don't work as planned. Even with the most important ingredients in place, there is always an element of luck. C'est la vie!

C Re-read. T (true) or F (false)? Underline all the evidence.

1 iTunes users' reaction didn't come as a surprise.
2 *Legends of Oz* had a lot of potential.
3 The *Twilight* movies were extremely popular in the 2000s.
4 Musicals based on movies tend to be financially risky.
5 Broadway shows are never aimed at men.

D 7.9 Read *Noun, verb, or both?* In which two pairs of underlined words in the article does the meaning change? Listen to check.

Noun, verb, or both?

Nouns and verbs usually have the same meaning: *I sometimes* ***shop*** *(v) for rare CDs in a small record* ***shop*** *(n).*
But sometimes the meaning changes: *I'll be very upset if somebody's phone* ***rings*** *(v) during* ***Lord of the Rings*** *(n).*

Same	answer, cause, delay, damage, email, fight, guess, help, need, offer, practice, promise, rain, request, search, support, tweet, vote
Different	book, rock, show, trip

6 Vocabulary: Failure expressions

A Rewrite 1–5, substituting the bold words with the highlighted words in the article in 5B.

1 I had high hopes for the third season of *House of Cards*, but it **didn't** really **meet** my expectations.
I had high hopes for the third season of House of Cards, but it didn't live up to expectations.

2 The latest Stephen King novel **didn't manage to** generate any interest. Nobody talked about it.

3 I'll never understand why the latest Maroon 5 single **didn't become popular**. It was such a good song.

4 Most critics say the latest Adam Sandler movie **didn't have** "depth and soul," but I thought it was awesome.

5 Brazil was confident of winning the 2014 World Cup, but maybe this confidence **had the opposite effect**. Their team lost to Germany 7–1.

B Make it personal In pairs, share opinions on recent flops you remember. Any surprises?

A Choose two examples in A and replace the underlined words with your own opinions.
B Ask follow-up questions and continue the conversation.

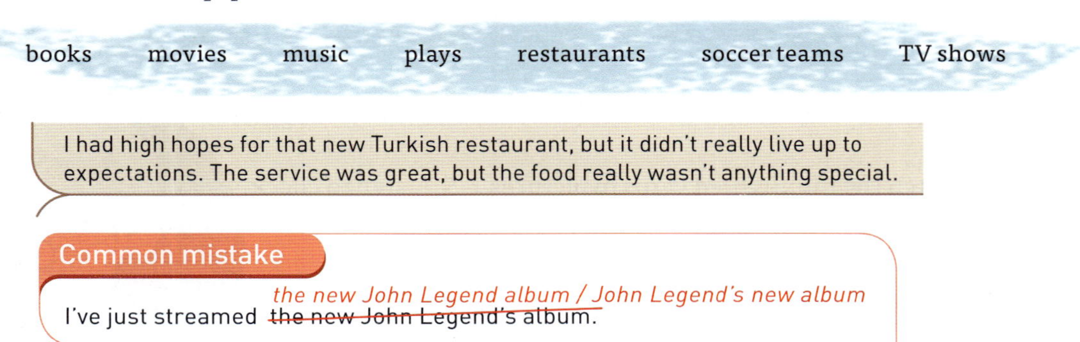

books movies music plays restaurants soccer teams TV shows

I had high hopes for that new Turkish restaurant, but it didn't really live up to expectations. The service was great, but the food really wasn't anything special.

Common mistake

I've just streamed ~~the new John Legend's album~~ *the new John Legend album / John Legend's new album*.

7 Pronunciation: Stress patterns in nouns and verbs

A 7.10 Listen to the examples from the article. Then complete with "verbs" or "nouns."

How can anyone say *no* to a **present**?
Sometimes unexpected problems **present** themselves.

Some words are stressed on the first syllable when they're used as ______ and on the second syllable when they're used as ______ .

B 7.11 Predict the stressed syllable in the bold words. Then listen, check, and repeat.

1 Are you in the middle of an important **project** right now?
2 Have noise, pollution, and traffic **increased** in your city recently?
3 Who's the **rebel** in your family?
4 Do you ever **record** yourself in English?
5 How much **progress** have you made with English this year?
6 When was the last time you got a **refund**?

C Make it personal In groups, ask and answer 1–6 in B. Anything in common?

It's not exactly a project, but I'm midway through my final exams. What a nightmare!

I know the feeling. How's it going?

8 Language in use

A In groups, which of the three paintings do you like most / least? Why?

I'm not sure. The da Vinci is beautiful, but there's nothing to see in the background.

I love Kahlo's hair. But the portrait itself doesn't do anything for me.

I'm not really into modern art at all. The one I like least is ...

1 Pre-impressionism

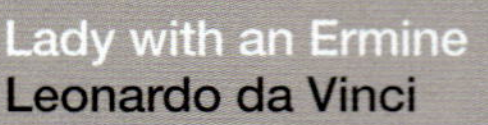

Lady with an Ermine
Leonardo da Vinci

2 Impressionism

Dancers in Blue
Edgar Degas

3 Modern

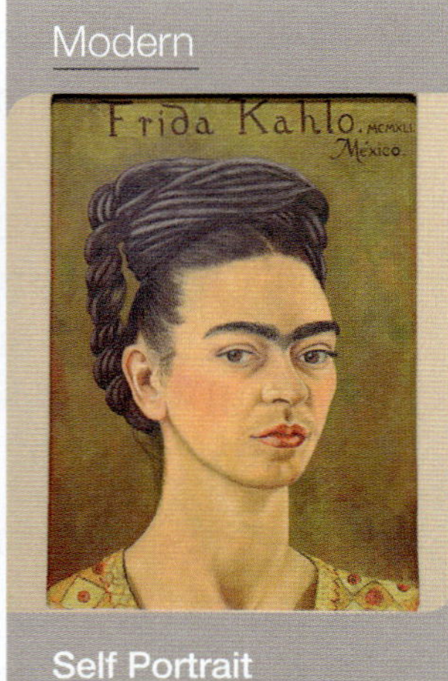

Self Portrait
Frida Kahlo

B 7.12 Listen to Rick and his friend Peter. Why is Rick worried? What does Peter suggest?

C 7.13 Read the guide and match the highlighted verbs to pictures 1–5. Listen to check. When do you do each action?

How to pretend you're ... an art expert

1 Stare thoughtfully, but don't squint as if you need glasses. Act classy.

2 Rub your chin to look intellectual, but don't scratch your head. You'll appear dumb!

3 Examine the piece closely, walk back two steps, and deliver an enigmatic "hmmm." And another one.

4 Listen carefully to the others in your group. If asked a question, frown a little, as if searching your vast mental repertoire.

5 Let the other person do most of the talking by replying with another question.

6 Learn to invent words with the prefix *meta*, meaning "of a higher order." Say, "What an interesting metaperspective!" People may look puzzled, but will probably nod in agreement.

1

2

3

4

5

I scratch my head when it itches, or when I'm thinking.

D **Make it personal** In groups, answer 1–4. Anything in common?

1 What can go wrong when you try to impress people like that?
2 Would you ever date someone with completely different interests from you?
3 Do you have a favorite painting, photo, statue, or museum?
4 Have you ever pretended to be knowledgeable about something?

One day my girlfriend's dad started quizzing me on classical music. Not my specialty!

9 Grammar: Modifying nouns

A Study sentences 1–5 and check (✔) the correct rules. Find three more examples in 8C.

1 Let's look at **another** website.
2 I'd like to find **(some) other** information / opinions.
3 There must be **some other** way to do it.
4 I think **the other** advice / idea / people might be more helpful.
5 I like the first three choices, but **the others** don't appeal to me.

Modifying nouns: *Another, some other, the other,* and *the others*

What follows ...	*another?*	*some other?*	*the other?*	*the others?*
a singular noun	✔			
a plural noun				
an uncountable noun				
no noun at all				

Use ***the*** to refer back to a noun already mentioned. ***One*** is often added when the noun is singular: *Do you prefer this **photo** or **the other** (one)?*

Some in ***some other*** is not optional when nouns are ☐ singular ☐ uncountable ☐ plural.

Common mistakes

I'm sorry, I can't tonight. I have ~~another / others / the other~~ *(some) other* plans. Maybe ~~other~~ *another* time?

Grammar expansion p.150

B 7.14 Complete the extract with *another, other,* or *the others*. Listen to check. Imagine how their date ended.

SUE: This one's nice. I like it better than [1]________ .
RICK: Hmm ... Let me look at it [2]________ time. Yes, I agree. It really captures the essence of passion, conflict, and ... and some [3]________ things.
SUE: I guess.
RICK: And don't you just love his use of color? Experimental, but structured.
SUE: Err ...
RICK: [4]________ artists may try, but nobody comes close to Picasso.
SUE: But that's a Kandinsky.
RICK: Oh, yes, you're right. It's [5]________ metaperspective, isn't it?
SUE: What's that supposed to mean?

C In pairs, find another painting and adapt / role play the conversation in 9B. Role play for the class. Who sounds most like an art critic?

D Make it personal Choose the correct form. In pairs, explain each quote. Who do you agree with most?

1 "Happiness is having a large, loving, caring, close-knit family in [**another** / **other**] city." (George Burns)
2 "Each person must live life as a model for [**others people** / **others**]." (Rosa Parks)
3 "Live rich, die poor; never make the mistake of doing it [**other** / **the other**] way round." (Walter Annenberg)
4 "I believe in living on impulse as long as you never intentionally hurt [**other** / **another**] person." (Angelina Jolie)
5 "Life is what happens while you are busy making [**other** / **others**] plans." (John Lennon)

I think Annenberg is saying we worry too much about the future and don't enjoy the present.

10 Listening

A Do you recognize the musician on the right? His initials are M.D. Guess what the quote refers to, too.

It is one of the single greatest achievements in recorded music.

B 7.15 Listen to two friends talking about *Kind of Blue*. Match the musicians to the comments (1–3). Then search *Kind of Blue* and listen to a few minutes of the album. Do you agree with these quotes?

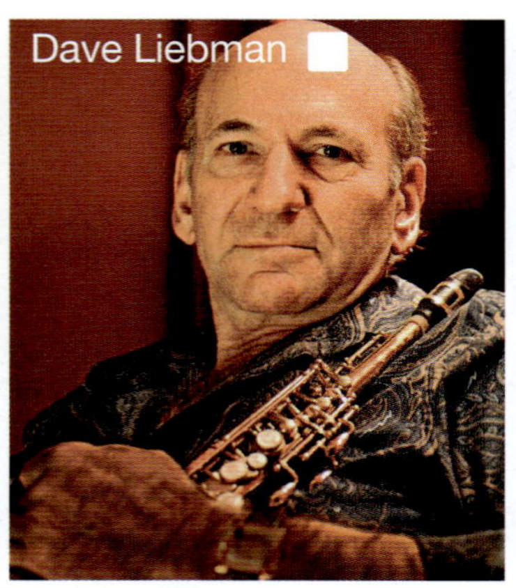

1 How do you go to the studio with minimum stuff and come out with eternity?

2 If there's one record and we've all said it, but it's true, that captures the essence of jazz for a variety of reasons, it would have to be *Kind of Blue*.

3 It's a cornerstone record, not only for jazz. It's a cornerstone record for music.

Definitely. I closed my eyes and started dreaming. Beautiful!

It's a bit slow, with no lyrics. It made me feel kind of lonely.

C 7.16 Listen to the rest of the conversation. T (True) or F (False)? Correct the false statements.

1 In the 1950s, jazz in New York City was played mainly in Harlem.
2 Jazz was so popular that players were in the media regularly.
3 Duke Ellington and Count Basie were popular before Miles Davis.
4 In the 1950s, if you liked R & B (Rhythm and Blues), you couldn't possibly like jazz.
5 Miles was the "essence of hipness" (ultra cool) because he went to Juilliard Music School.

11 Keep talking

A Choose a favorite album. Note down answers to 1–6. Search online as necessary.

1 What's the album called and who recorded it? When?
2 What type of music would you say it is?
3 What makes the music really special?
4 Which is your favorite track? Who wrote it?
5 Are there any tracks that were a letdown? Ones you usually skip?
6 Was the album commercially successful? Locally? Globally?

My all-time favorite is Ivete Sangalo's live album. It came out in 2014. Her music is so easy to dance to.

She's fun, but I'm not really into her music or the lyrics. I prefer songs with a message.

B In groups, discuss your chosen albums. Is everybody familiar with them?

12 Writing: Writing a review

A Read the review on the right and underline the answers to the questions in 11A.

B Read *Write it right!* Underline seven more examples of *-ly* adverbs in the review and mark them a–c.

Write it right!

In a review, use adverbs to make your attitude clear and your ideas more "colorful." Adverbs can modify:

a An adjective or another adverb: She has an ***amazingly*** *good voice. She sings* ***extremely*** *well.*

b A verb: *I* ***highly*** *recommend this album.*

c A whole idea: ***Surprisingly****, sales didn't live up to expectations.*

Common mistakes

Chris Botti plays ~~incredibly well the trumpet.~~ *the trumpet incredibly well.*

I ~~recommend highly his music.~~ *highly recommend his music / recommend his music highly.*

C Complete music review excerpts 1–8 in the most logical way. Check your spelling!

consistent	~~easy~~	unfortunate

1 This is easily their best album in a decade – no doubt about it.

2 This collection is ______ awesome, from beginning to end.

3 ______ , some of the tracks leave you a bit cold.

absolute	wonderful	sad

4 I really wanted to love their live performance. ______ , I didn't.

5 I ______ adored the new CD. It exceeded all my expectations.

6 Throughout, it is fun, romantic, and has ______ written lyrics.

occasional	disappointing	consistent

7 I enjoyed this CD, but, ______ , there are only 10 tracks in the standard edition.

8 It's ______ good, from start to finish, rather than only ______ great.

She rules the world!

I've been a Beyoncé fan since 2003, when *Dangerously in Love* came out. Her last truly great album was the 2008 smash hit *I Am ... Sasha Fierce*, so I was starting to lose hope and doubt that she would ever release another masterpiece like that. Thankfully, her fifth album, *Beyoncé*, released at the end of 2013, proved me wrong.

What I love about this album is the way she cleverly experiments with different genres. There are elements of electronica, hip-hop, disco, and R&B, of course. The album starts off with *Pretty Hurts* (co-written by superstar Sia), a deeply powerful song about the pressure to look perfect. The other 14 tracks will take you on the musical journey of a lifetime, with some of the catchiest melodies you'll ever hear. My personal favorites are *Heaven* and *Rocket*, but, honestly, there's not a single letdown. And *Blue* as a finale is just a great way to end the album.

As everyone knows, *Beyoncé* was a surprise release, with zero promotion other than an Instagram® post. Incredibly, it managed to sell close to a million copies in two weeks, which I bet even *Queen Bey* herself wasn't expecting. But even more impressive is the fact that the album featured 17 music videos – something no one had ever done before.

I'm not a professional critic, but I firmly believe that *Beyoncé* is one of the best albums of the 2010s. It's mature without being boring, courageous without being forced, and entertaining without being silly. It's just the sort of album that both fans and non-fans will fall in love with.

D Your turn! Write your own review in about 200 words.

Before
Order your notes from 11A into three paragraphs, including an introduction. Then think of a conclusion.

While
Use at least four adverbs from 12C.

After
Proofread and then post your review online. Share the link with your class.

8 Has fear ever held you back?

1 Listening

A 8.1 Listen to the ad and remember the seven sound effects. Brainstorm other common fears and add them to the three groups in the ad.

Another real fear is that your boyfriend or girlfriend might meet someone new.

F.E.A.R. = False Evidence Appearing Real

Fear is everywhere!

- **Real fears** (losing your job, getting ill, offending people)
- **Fears we love** (scary movies, theme park rides)
- **Exaggerated or even irrational fears** (flying, public speaking, confined spaces, the dark), which can be really upsetting

Email a video to IQYP TV talking about your worst fear, and you could be invited to our groundbreaking show, *Making F.E.A.R. disappear*.

B 8.2 Listen to the beginning of three stories. What is each person afraid of? Are any of your ideas in **A** mentioned?

1 Lucy

C 8.3 Listen to the full stories. Who answer(s) each question, Lucy, Rob, or Donna?

1. How long have you had this fear?
2. How did your fear begin?
3. Do you experience any physical symptoms?
4. How supportive are your family and friends?
5. What have you done to overcome your fear?

2 Rob

D 8.3 Listen again. In pairs, answer one question for each person.

E **Make it personal** Don't panic! In groups, share your fears.

1 8.4 **How to say it** Complete the sentences from the conversation. Listen to check.

Expressing fears

	What they said	What they meant
1	I'm ______ of (spiders).	I'm really afraid of ...
2	(Clowns) freak me ______ .	
3	I ______ (flying) if I can.	I'm not comfortable with ...
4	(Cockroaches) make me a bit ______ .	
5	(Dolls) don't ______ me.	I'm not afraid of ...
6	I don't ______ (bats) at all.	

3 Donna

2 In groups, answer a–d. Use *How to say it* expressions on p.82. Any surprises?

a What are you / others you know most afraid of?
b What have you / they tried to do about it?
c Would you ever send your own testimonial to a show like this? Why (not)?
d Do you agree with the acronym F.E.A.R.? Are most of our fears false?

2 Vocabulary: Physical symptoms of fear

A 8.5 Match 1–7 to pictures a–g. Listen to check. When do you feel these symptoms?

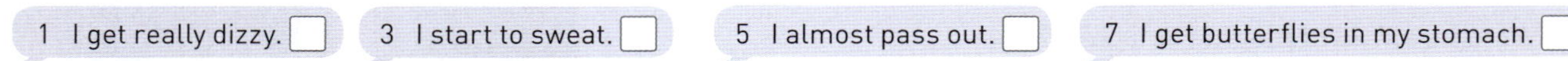

1 I get really dizzy. ☐
3 I start to sweat. ☐
5 I almost pass out. ☐
7 I get butterflies in my stomach. ☐
2 I can't breathe. ☐
4 I burst into tears. ☐
6 My heart starts to race. ☐

My hands start to sweat on a plane when there's turbulence.

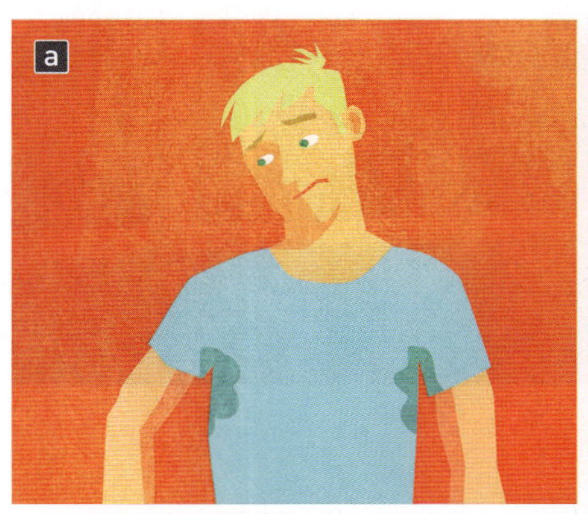

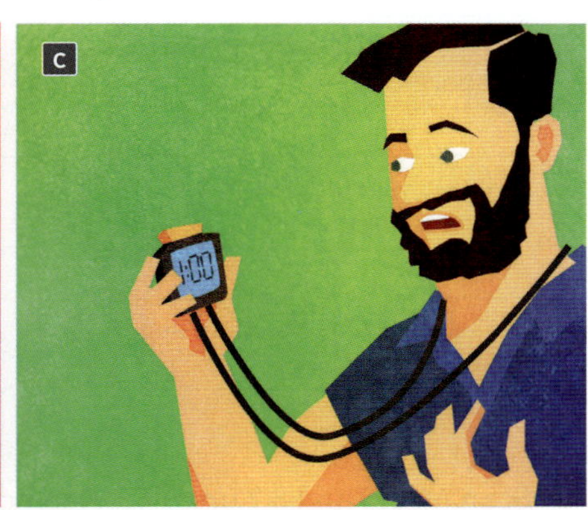

B Make it personal Share your scary experiences!

1 In pairs, share a frightening experience (true or made up!), using three expressions. Guess what is (not) true.

I was walking home alone late one night when I heard footsteps right behind me. My heart started to race ...

2 Take turns role playing the TV show. Who's the best actor?

a Plan what to say using the questions in 1C and expressions in 1E.
b Share your fear and answer the "interviewer's" questions.

So, welcome to *Making F.E.A.R. Disappear.* Please introduce yourself and share your fear with us.

Hi, my name's Dan and, please don't laugh, but I'm terrified of going anywhere without my cell phone. I've felt like this for as long as I can remember, and ...

3 Language in use

A 8.6 In pairs, guess the story behind the photo. Listen to check.

> I have no idea. Maybe her house was on fire.

> But then she wouldn't be smiling, would she?

B 8.7 Listen to the rest of the story. Answer 1–3. Has anything like this ever happened to you?

1 Did Louise try to contact her parents?
2 Was she afraid of heights as a child?
3 Why didn't she enjoy the party?

C 8.6 and 8.7 Who said these lines, L (Louise) or D (Diego)? Order them logically as you think you heard them. Listen again to check.

☐☐ I couldn't find the spare one.

☐☐ So you're telling me you were able to climb the fence?

☐☐ I could climb just about anything.

L 1 I wasn't able to get there until after 10.

☐☐ I think he could see it in my eyes.

☐☐ But you were able to make it to the party ...

D Scan AS 8.6 and 8.7 on p.163. Replace the underlined expressions with 1–6.

1 This might be hard to believe, but ...
2 That's really typical of you.
3 To summarize ...
4 I don't understand.
5 How often does that happen?
6 Why?

E **Make it personal** In groups, answer 1–5. Any coincidences?

1 Would you have the courage to do what Louise did?
2 Have you ever run into someone you didn't want to see at a party?
3 Name three things that are a) essential for b) can ruin a good party?
4 Are there any items you keep losing?
5 What spare items do you keep, just in case? Where do you keep them?

> We keep a spare key hidden outside our apartment, in case we're locked out.

> I thought of doing that, but I'm scared someone might get in.

4 **Grammar:** Describing past ability

A Read the grammar box and *Common mistakes*. Then check (✔) the correct answers.

Describing past ability: *could* and *was / were able to*

General	Louise **could / was able to** climb just about anything, but her friends **couldn't / weren't able to**. They weren't as athletic.
Specific occasion	She **couldn't / wasn't able to** reach her parents. Luckily, she **was able to** climb the fence and get a taxi.
Stative verbs	Her neighbors **could** see her climbing the fence. They **couldn't** understand why.

Can and *be able to* are ☐ **often** ☐ **never** interchangeable. However, to talk about ...

1 a specific past occasion in the ☐ **affirmative** ☐ **negative**, use *be able to*.

2 a past state, with verbs like *see*, *believe*, and *feel*, use ☐ **could** ☐ **was able to**.

Grammar expansion p.152

Common mistakes

The traffic was awful. I ~~wasn't able to~~ *couldn't* believe it. But I ~~could~~ *was able to* get to work on time. Just barely!

B Which *be able to* sentences in **3C** can be replaced by *could(n't)*?

C Correct any mistakes in the use of *could* and *be able to*.

TWO FAMOUS ESCAPES!

Before the Berlin Wall came down in 1989, people from East Germany sometimes tried to escape to the West. In 1979, for example, a man called Hans Strelczyk (1) **could** build a hot air balloon using old bed sheets, and his family (2) **was able to** drift over to the other side! Those who saw it (3) **couldn't** believe their eyes!

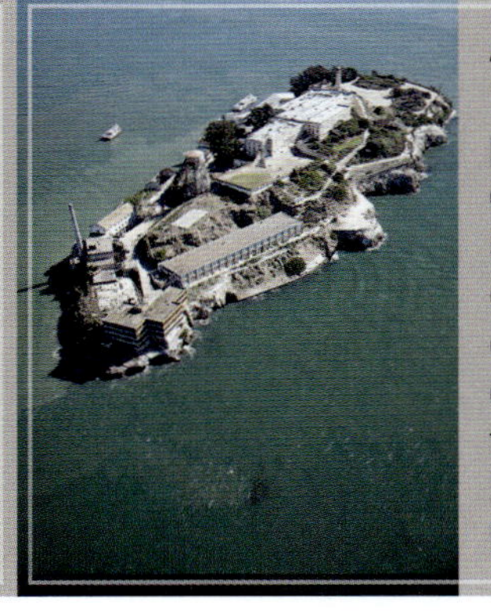

Alcatraz, the most legendary prison in the world, was supposedly escape-proof. However, one day, three inmates disappeared, and Alcatraz officials simply (4) **couldn't** find them. No one knows if the three men (5) **could** escape or if they jumped in the sea and drowned. My grandfather was a guard there, and he told me everything! I (6) **could** spend hours listening to his stories!

D Make it personal In pairs, answer the questionnaire, adding plenty of detail. Use expressions from **3D**. Any coincidences?

R U calm and creative in a storm? | **How well do you improvise?**

Think of times when you ...

1 ran out of gas / money / clean clothes at the worst possible moment.
2 got stuck in traffic and missed something important.
3 got caught doing something you shouldn't.
4 pretended to be enjoying yourself.
5 escaped from a very difficult situation.

We both ran out of gas, and neither of us had a clue what to do.

5 Reading

A Look at the title and choose a meaning for *fear-mongering* (1–3). Read paragraph 1 of the article to check.

1 relevant safety warnings 2 scare tactics 3 strategies to deal with fear

B Guess how Lee will answer his own question at the end of paragraph 1. Then read the rest and choose his most likely answer (1–3). Underline sentences supporting your choice.

1 "No doubt it is." 2 "Not exactly." 3 "To a certain extent."

Be Afraid. Be Very Afraid:
Fear-mongering in the 21st century
By Lee Corelli

1 As part of my job as a freelance reporter, I've been practically glued to the screen lately. Here's a snapshot of my daily routine. Wake up in the morning: "New bomb scare. FBI on the alert." Go to bed: "Unemployment at an all-time high." Wake up: "Broccoli can kill you." The list is endless, and if we took all these scary stories to heart, we might never leave home again. It's no secret that in order to grab the audience's attention and boost ratings, the media rarely fails to make things look worse than they actually are. But is this kind of fear-mongering such a big deal after all?

2 ____. The fear spread by the media shapes the way we think and act, often without us being fully aware of what's really going on. The evening news reports a "worrying increase" in plane crashes, and we rethink our travel plans. It warns of a nasty new virus, and we start to wonder if leaving home without a mask on is worth the risk. We're living as if our lives were in a constant state of imminent danger. But why are we so easily influenced?

3 ____. A number of major studies have examined how our brains cope with all the negativity that surrounds us. A recent one, carried out at Ohio State University, found a significant increase in brain activity when subjects were shown negative images as opposed to positive ones. This is especially frightening in this day and age, when we're bombarded with bad news after bad news, not only on TV, but via social media, too.

4 ____. Back in the day, our grandparents only had about half a dozen TV stations to get their news from, so it was easier for them to see through cheap fear-mongering on the rare occasions they encountered it. But the media has undergone a lot of major changes in recent years, and now, with so many channels and websites, it's much harder to tell fact from fiction. In the end, we're left with a hundred different versions of the same story, wondering which ones to trust.

5 ____. The shocking images we see of war zones and natural disasters can and do inspire fear, of course, but they can also inspire action. For example, would people have mobilized so many resources to help the victims of hurricane Katrina in 2005 if the images hadn't been all over the media 24/7? Probably not. It's up to us, though, to make sure the media does not manipulate our fears in a way that's not proportional to the problem itself.

C 8.8 Match topic sentences a–d to paragraphs 2–5. Listen to check. Did the audio help you understand the text?

a The number of news channels has also greatly increased.
b All this negativity is affecting our thoughts and actions.
c But maybe there's hope, after all.
d One reason might be neurological.

D In which paragraph (1–5) does Lee make points a–f?

a ☐ There is an increase in brain activity when we see bad news.
b ☐ The media knows what kinds of stories will keep people interested.
c ☐ People don't always realize how the media influences their daily lives.
d ☐ People are more likely to help others when they can see the problem.
e ☐ Having access to many different sources of information is not always a good thing.
f ☐ TV stations were more consistent in the past.

E **Make it personal** In pairs, answer 1–4. Any similarities?

1 Besides fear-mongering, how else does the media boost ratings?
2 Did any recent news stories a) scare you b) shock you c) make you laugh out loud?
3 What do you trust more, TV, the radio, the Internet, or the newspapers?
4 What other institutions use scare tactics with you? Do they work?

Oh, my school, for sure. My teachers keep telling me I'll fail this year unless my grades improve.

6 Vocabulary: Common verb + noun collocations

A Read *Noticing collocations*. Then complete the mind maps with the highlighted verbs in the article.

Noticing collocations

It's easy to notice collocations when the words occur together: *We tend to* ***pay attention*** *to bad news.*
But sometimes the words appear far from each other: *This is a key* ***issue*** *that people really need to* ***address***.

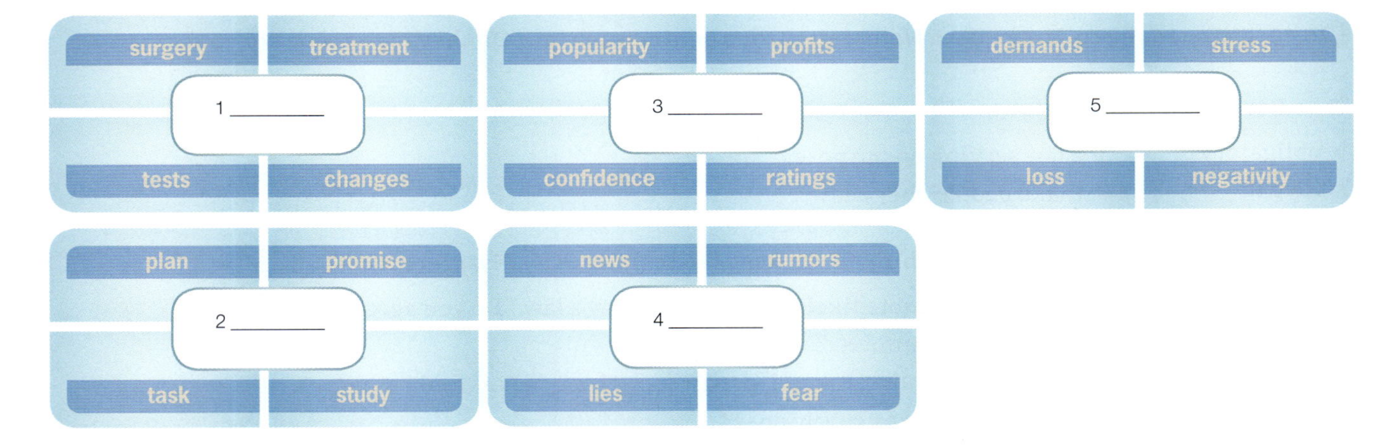

B Complete 1–5 with words from **A** in the correct form.

1 How can children ________ the ________ of a pet when it dies?
2 How different is your neighborhood from ten years ago? Has it ________ many ________ ?
3 Do you always ________ the ________ you make to friends, or do you sometimes find excuses?
4 Have you ever found out that a friend or colleague was ________ false ________ about you? What's the best way to deal with gossip?
5 What successes have you had in life? In what ways did these positive experiences ________ your ________ ?

C **Make it personal** Choose two questions from **B** to answer in groups. Ask for / give more details. Similar ideas?

I guess their parents should simply explain that pets die, just like people.

7 Language in use

A 8.9 Guess the missing words from an interview about the author's recent trip to Europe. Listen to check.

Milan, in northern Italy, is a very happy city. So much so that you're not allowed to frown unless you're at a [1]__________ or at the hospital. Yes – smiling is required by law ... a pointless law, I know! So, if you ever visit, you'd better [2]__________ about your troubles, or else you might have to pay a fine.

In general, tourists are not supposed to eat and drink in [3]__________, but Rome has recently enforced a law banning eating and drinking at all historical sites. The fine? Up to [4]$__________! So maybe you ought to eat an extra slice of bread before leaving the hotel.

In countries like Denmark and [5]__________, driving with your headlights off is considered a violation of the law. You have to keep them on even during the day! This may sound [6]__________, I know, but you've got to obey the local laws.

B 8.10 Listen to the full interview. Note the reasons behind each law. Do they make sense to you?

C Scan **A** to find law expressions with meanings 1–4. Did you know them all?

1 obligatory
2 illegal
3 a law serving no purpose
4 make people obey a law

D Make it personal Crime and punishment! Answer 1–4 in pairs. Any disagreements?

1 "The heavier the punishment, the more likely we all are to obey a law." Do you agree?
2 Where you live, are some laws not enforced?
3 If you could create a new law to legalize, reward, or ban something, what would it be?
4 Search online for "stupid laws." Any funny ones?

Here's one that says it's a violation of the law for French people to name a pig Napoleon!

8 Grammar: Expressing obligation, permission, and advice

A Match meanings 1–5 to the examples in the grammar box on p.89.

1 You (don't) have permission to do it.
2 This is(n't) an obligation. You have a / no choice.
3 My advice or suggestion: (Don't) do it.
4 My strong advice or warning: You *really* should(n't) do it, or else ...
5 People expect you (not) to do it, but it's a rule we often break.

Obligation, permission, advice: *must / have (got) to, had better, be allowed to, be supposed to,* and *should / ought to*

☐	You **must** / **have (got) to** get a visa to enter Russia.	You **don't have to** get one to go to Bermuda. Your passport will do.
☐	You**'d better** pack some warm clothes or you'll freeze!	You**'d better not** forget your coat!
☐	You**'re supposed to** keep your phone off at the theater.	You**'re not supposed to** turn it on.
☐	You **can** / **are allowed to** use computers on a plane.	You **can't** / **'re not allowed to** use them during takeoff.
☐	You **should** / **ought to** visit Times Square.	You **shouldn't** miss it.

Grammar expansion p.152

B Circle the most logical options. Are there any laws in your country you disagree with?

1 In Saudi Arabia, you [**'re not allowed to** / **don't have to**] photograph government buildings. So you [**have to** / **'d better**] leave your camera at home – just in case you forget.
2 In France, between 8:00 a.m. and 8:00 p.m., 70% of radio music [**must** / **ought to**] be by French artists. I don't think the government [**must** / **ought to**] decide what gets played!
3 In 2013, China passed a new law saying adult children [**have to** / **are allowed to**] visit their parents. Hmm ... Maybe I [**ought to** / **must**] call my mom right now!
4 In Victoria, Australia, you [**'re not supposed to** / **'d better not**] change your own light bulbs! There's no need to be afraid, though. I doubt the police will go after you for this one.

9 Pronunciation: *have to, got to, ought to, supposed to* in informal speech

A 8.11 Listen to and repeat the examples. Notice the silent letters and schwas.

1 Tourists are not ~~s~~upposed to eat and drink. /ə/
2 Maybe you ough~~t~~ to eat an extra slice of bread. /ə/
3 You ha~~v~~e to keep headlights on. /f/ /ə/
4 You'~~ve~~ go~~t~~ to obey the laws. /ə/

B 8.12 Read aloud the song lines, using informal pronunciation. Listen to check.

1 "How many times do I have to tell you, even when you're crying, you're beautiful, too." (John Legend)
2 "It's the way I'm feeling, I just can't deny, but I've got to let it go. We found love in a hopeless place." (Rihanna)
3 "Ah, but working too hard can give you a heart attack. You ought to know by now." (Billy Joel)
4 "Make me your selection, show you the way love's supposed to be." (Mario)

C **Make it personal** In groups, take turns personalizing 1–4. Use informal pronunciation. Who feels the guiltiest? Who has the best excuses?

Yeah, I'm guilty, I know. It's not much of an excuse, but ...

1 I know I ought to (do the laundry) more often. What's stopping me is (my dad likes doing it).
2 We have to (keep our phones off) in (class), but sometimes (I check mine quickly under my desk).
3 This week I've got to (change all my passwords). I've been putting it off for (months) because (I'm too lazy to create new ones).
4 I know I'm not supposed to (eat junk food), but I can't help it. I mean, (it tastes so good).

I know I ought to visit my grandparents more often. What's stopping me is ...

10 Listening

A 8.13 Take a test-anxiety quiz. Listen once to note down the key words from the questions. Listen again to answer each question. Then add up your score.

ANSWER ON THE FOLLOWING SCALE:
1 NOT AT ALL LIKE ME — 2 — 3 — 4 VERY MUCH LIKE ME

Conquering Test Anxiety
Dr. Jennifer Price

B 8.14 Listen to / Watch a psychologist's views on test anxiety. Pause at 1.37. In pairs, how accurate is your test anxiety index?

> Very accurate! I scored 17, and I freak out whenever I take a test.

C 8.15 Listen to / Watch the rest and number her recommendations 1–6 in the order she makes them. Which is the most important one for you?

- [ ] Study a little and often.
- [ ] Focus on your breathing.
- [ ] Remind yourself how to succeed.
- [ ] Learn how to relax.
- [ ] Find somewhere quiet to study.
- [ ] Remember: preparation is key.

> My choice would be finding somewhere quiet. It's hard to learn with noise.

D 8.14 & 8.15 In pairs, complete 1–5 with the words in the correct form. Listen to both parts to check. Which ones were easy?

cram	blank (v)	lower (v)	no matter what	way in advance	on a daily basis

1 You studied really hard for a test, but when you got it, you just ______ (= forgot everything).
2 Even if your anxiety was low, these things can be helpful for you ______ (= in any case).
3 The first strategy is just to spend your time preparing ______ (= ahead of time).
4 It really does not work to ______ (= learn too much too quickly) the night before a test.
5 If you practice relaxation ______ (= every day), it ______ (= reduces) your overall anxiety.

11 Keep talking

Read and note down three recommendations. In groups, compare your advice. What would be best for each person?

1 I'm terrified of flying, but in a moment of madness, I bought a ticket to Peru. What should I do?
Mayumi

2 I've always been petrified of public speaking, but I've been asked to give a 20-minute presentation next week!
Roger

3 In three days, I'm supposed to be getting married, but now I'm really not sure I'm ready. What should I do?
Ellen

> The smartest thing for Mayumi to do would be to cancel her flight .

> ______ might want to think about ______ *-ing*.

> If I were in ______'s shoes, I'd probably ______ .

12 Writing: A message of advice

A Read Sonia's message to Cynthia and answer 1–3.

1. Which recommendation(s) in 10C does she mention?
2. Is there anything in Sonia's message you disagree with?
3. Which paragraph includes her most important recommendation?

B Read *Write it right*! Then match the highlighted expressions in Sonia's message to their uses 1–6.

Write it right!

When writing to someone close to you, use a variety of friendly comments to sound natural:

You shouldn't take an exam on an empty stomach. **Trust me**, it's not good for you. I did it once and almost fainted. **I mean**, I didn't literally pass out, but I came close. **Thank goodness** there was a doctor on campus.

1. Most of all, you should remember this.
2. I'm using a metaphor. Don't take my words literally.
3. Besides what I've just said ...
4. This is the first item on a list.
5. This is obvious.
6. In a way, I'm contradicting what I've just said.

C Circle the correct options in Sonia's next message.

Oh, I almost forgot. On the day of the exam, here's what you should keep in mind. [1][**For starters / Other than that**], make sure your head is in a good place, [2][**other than that / so to speak**]. Think positive thoughts, relax your muscles, and watch your breathing – your brain needs enough oxygen to work well. [3][**That said / For starters**], don't breathe too deeply or you may feel dizzy. Remember to read the instructions very carefully and [4][**so to speak / above all**] trust your instincts – you know your stuff! Oh, and [5][**needless to say / that said**], keep your phone off! But I'm sure you know this. [6][**Above all / Other than that**], I can't think of anything else to tell you; you'll be fine!

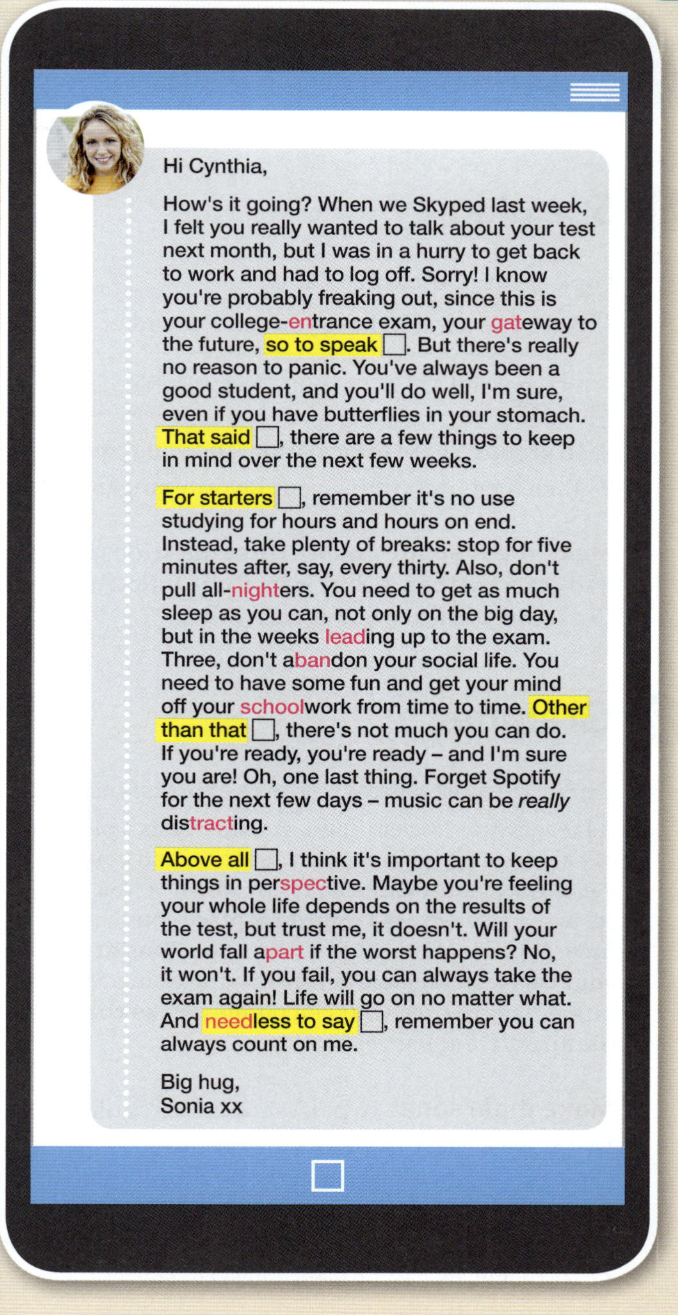
Hi Cynthia,

How's it going? When we Skyped last week, I felt you really wanted to talk about your test next month, but I was in a hurry to get back to work and had to log off. Sorry! I know you're probably freaking out, since this is your college-entrance exam, your gateway to the future, so to speak ☐. But there's really no reason to panic. You've always been a good student, and you'll do well, I'm sure, even if you have butterflies in your stomach. That said ☐, there are a few things to keep in mind over the next few weeks.

For starters ☐, remember it's no use studying for hours and hours on end. Instead, take plenty of breaks: stop for five minutes after, say, every thirty. Also, don't pull all-nighters. You need to get as much sleep as you can, not only on the big day, but in the weeks leading up to the exam. Three, don't abandon your social life. You need to have some fun and get your mind off your schoolwork from time to time. Other than that ☐, there's not much you can do. If you're ready, you're ready – and I'm sure you are! Oh, one last thing. Forget Spotify for the next few days – music can be *really* distracting.

Above all ☐, I think it's important to keep things in perspective. Maybe you're feeling your whole life depends on the results of the test, but trust me, it doesn't. Will your world fall apart if the worst happens? No, it won't. If you fail, you can always take the exam again! Life will go on no matter what. And needless to say ☐, remember you can always count on me.

Big hug,
Sonia xx

D Your turn! Choose a person from 11. Imagine you are close friends. Write him / her a three-paragraph message in about 250 words.

Before

Rank your recommendations from most to least important.

While

Follow the model in A. In paragraph 1, introduce the problem. In paragraph 3, give your most important advice. Use at least four friendly comments.

After

Share your message with classmates. Who has the most original suggestions?

Review 4

Units 7–8

1 Speaking

A Look at the photos on p.72.

1 Note down everything you can remember about the people, using these words and expressions.

be regarded as	come out	high-profile	rise to fame	take place

2 In groups, share information. Did you remember everything?

3 Take turns describing your favorite singer and explaining why.

I used to be really hooked on ..., but now I'm into ...

B Make it personal Choose three question titles from Units 7 and 8 to ask a partner. Ask at least three follow-up questions for each. What did you learn about each other?

How important is music to you?

Very! I look for new songs on Spotify every day so I can keep up.

2 Grammar

A Circle the most logical words or expressions to complete the paragraph.

As recently as 20 years ago, air travel was a pleasure. But things have changed [1][**because** / **because of**] the number of passengers and increased security, and you [2][**have to** / **'re supposed to**] expect delays. Now you [3][**'d better** / **can**] get to the airport three hours in advance [4][**be supposed to** / **in order to**] catch your flight. When you go through security, you [5][**must** / **ought to**] place your carry-on liquids in a plastic bag, and in some countries, you [6][**'d better** / **have to**] take off your shoes, too. You [7][**ought to** / **'re not allowed to**] take any sharp objects on the plane, so check your carry-on luggage before leaving home. [8][**Since** / **Because of**] even a dead cell phone might be a weapon, you might have to turn your cell phone on [9][**so that** / **as**] it can be inspected. I know I [10][**'d better** / **should**] be calm at the airport, but I never am!

B Make it personal In pairs, are there regulations at school or at home that you disagree with? Use at least three of these expressions.

above all	for starters	needless to say	other than that	thank goodness	trust me

My roommate has too many rules. For starters, when I come in the house, I'm supposed to ...

3 Point of view

Choose a topic. Then support your opinion in 100–150 words, and record your answer. Ask a partner for feedback. How can you be more convincing?

a You think popular music used to be better: better lyrics, better melodies, better performers. OR
You think music is always changing, and today's popular music is very good.

b You think culture is important, and everyone should keep up with music, art, and literature. OR
You think people have different interests, and culture is just one of them.

c You think everyday fears can really hold people back. OR
You think everyone is afraid of something, and it's usually no big deal.

d You think the news, for the most part, is accurate and well researched. OR
You think the news is often influenced either by politics or business considerations and may not be accurate.

4 Reading

A Read the title and first sentence of the article. Choose the best answer. Then read the rest to check.

"The jazz age" probably refers to ...

1 the 1950s. 2 a time before the 1950s. 3 a time after the 1950s.

The jazz age and beyond

By the 1950s, when Miles Davis was performing in Harlem, jazz had already come into its own. The birth of jazz is generally credited to African Americans, who began migrating to the American north in the 1920s and brought their music with them to the large cities of New York and Chicago. The "roaring 20s" or "jazz age," which ended with the Great Depression, was a period characterized by rebellion. Traditions were questioned, women got the right to vote and began to work in large numbers, and a new and innovative style of dress emerged. The improvised rhythms and sounds of jazz went hand in hand with the new age.

The spread of jazz was encouraged by the introduction of large-scale radio broadcasts in 1932. From the comfort of their living rooms, Americans could now experience new and different kinds of music. Originally, there were two types of live music on the radio: concert music and big band dance music. Concert music was played by amateurs, often volunteers, whereas big band dance music was played by professionals. As commercial radio increased, big band dance music took over and was played from nightclubs, dance halls, and ballrooms. Musicologist Charles Hamm, who studied American popular music in the context of its complex racial and ethnic dynamics, described three types of jazz on the radio: black music for black audiences, black music for white audiences, and white music for white audiences. In urban areas, African American jazz was played frequently and its popularity spread.

In the early 1940s, bebop emerged, led by Charlie Parker, Dizzy Gillespie, and Thelonius Monk. This was a more serious art form that moved jazz away from popular dance music. Other types of jazz followed, including cool jazz, a melodic style that merged the traditions of African American bebop and white jazz traditions. The original cool jazz musican was Miles Davis, who released *Birth of the cool* in 1957. Jazz had reached maturity, soon to have an international following.

B In pairs, complete the word web on the kinds of jazz played on the radio.

concert music

- [1] ______ ______ **dance music**
- **nightclubs,** [2] ______ ______ **, and** [3] ______
- **black music for** [4] ______ **audiences; for** [5] ______ **audiences**
- **white music for** [6] ______ **audiences**

C Put the events in order.

- ☐ Radio helped to spread jazz in urban areas.
- ☐ Jazz gained popularity along with the innovative style of the decade.
- ☐ Miles Davis released *Birth of the cool*.
- ☐ Jazz was played down south before the migration to the north.
- ☐ Bebop, a more serious kind of jazz, developed.

5 Writing

Write a paragraph about a type of music that's important to you or a musician that you admire. Include *-ly* adverbs, such as *amazingly*, *surprisingly*, and *extremely*.

9 How much time do you spend on your own?

1 Listening

A 9.1 Listen to Angela and Marco. Match them to a photo 1–3. Who's more like you?

B 9.1 Match the sentence halves and write A (Angela) or M (Marco). Listen again to check. Which opinions do you agree with most?

1 People who talk the loudest ...
2 Group work is better than ...
3 All my good ideas ...
4 Most great leaders ...
5 Introverts ...
6 The people I work best with ...

a [ ] happen when I think things over.
b [ ] haven't been outgoing at all.
c [1] always get their ideas accepted! A
d [ ] love talking.
e [ ] should be valued more.
f [ ] working alone.

I definitely think it's introverts who ...

2 Vocabulary: Interacting with people

A Take the quiz. Don't check your score yet! Which situations 1–6 have you been in recently?

ARE YOU MORE OF AN INTROVERT OR AN EXTROVERT?

1 At a party, you ...
A mingle as much as possible.
B talk to and stick with just one person.

2 On a long plane or bus trip, you ...
A reveal personal information to strangers.
B stick to small talk.

3 When you're upset, you ...
A open up to a friend.
B keep things to yourself.

4 When making a hard decision, you ...
A think out loud and ask for advice.
B sit by yourself to think things over.

5 In a group meeting, you ...
A suggest lots of ideas.
B say little and think up ideas on your own.

6 When people discuss politics, you tend to ...
A give your opinion.
B keep quiet.

B 9.2 In pairs, put the highlighted words in **A** into three categories. Listen to check. Which are phrasal verbs?

Socializing	Sharing	Thinking

C 9.3 Read *Word order*. In pairs, decide which of 1–5 are correct. Rephrase the wrong ones. Listen to check.

1 I don't mind revealing people my phone number, but not my address.
2 I'm not really very good at thinking new ideas up. I guess I'm not very creative.
3 Whenever I have things bothering me, I always open my friends up.
4 I guess I'm more likely to keep to myself things.
5 I tend to keep quiet my opinions. I hate disagreements.

Word order

1 Some verbs only allow indirect objects with *to*: I **revealed** the answer **to him**. (Not: ~~I revealed him the answer~~.)
2 Pronouns must go between the verb and the particle in many separable phrasal verbs: I thought **it** over for a long time. (Not: ~~I thought over it~~.)
3 Objects go between the verb and the adverb: She raised **her voice** angrily. (Not: ~~She raised angrily her voice~~.)

Common mistake

on my own / by myself
I like to solve problems ~~by my own~~.

D **Make it personal** Find out how introverted you really are!

1 In groups, using your quiz answers, share your own preferences.

When I'm at parties, I really like to mingle. You never know who you'll meet!

2 How would you react in these situations?

a You're at a wedding where you know no one.
b A new neighbor moves next door.
c You go to a cooking class alone.
d You're sitting next to a stranger on a long bus trip.
e You go to a cafeteria for lunch, but there are no free tables.

I'd smile and speak to the first person who smiled back. But it's still hard to open up to strangers.

3 Do you agree? Who are most alike? Check your quiz score below.

QUIZ SCORE – WHAT IT MEANS

Mostly As: You're the type who has to tell people what you're thinking. You don't like spending too much time alone, either. A true extrovert.

A balance of As and Bs: You're happy being alone, but also like to socialize. You prefer to think things over before expressing your opinions. Public speaking makes you nervous, but it excites you, too.

Mostly Bs: You're a classic introvert, a "strong silent type." At social events, you look for chances to be alone. You like intimate conversations and love to read.

9.2 What behavior is rude in your culture?

3 Listening

A 9.4 What do you know about China? Look at 1–6. T (true) or F (false)? Listen to / Watch the travel advice to check.

1. You can eat before a senior person if you're told to start.
2. Don't leave a business card on the table in front of you in a meeting.
3. It's OK to hold hands, but don't kiss your wife in public.
4. China and Japan have a positive history together.
5. If you invite a translator to dinner, you don't have to pay.
6. At someone's home, your host will give you slippers that are your size.

B 9.4 Listen / Watch again. In pairs, remember the 11 behaviors to avoid. Did any surprise you?

C **Make it personal** In groups, answer 1–3. Any surprising stories?

1. How (im)polite are people from your country? What customs might be rude somewhere else?
2. When was the last time you were mistreated in a store / restaurant? What happened?
3. What is the rudest thing anyone has ever said to you? Use "bleep" for any words you don't want to repeat.

I used to work part-time in a supermarket. And one day, a woman pointed at me and told her son, "This is why you have to stay in school!"

4 Language in use

Read the discussion forum. Underline six expressions to show annoyance or anger. Do you agree with the opinions?

It really gets to me when I'm shopping and the employee at the checkout counter doesn't smile. I don't mean saying "thank you" or even "please," **which most of them manage to do**. I'm talking about trying to be genuinely friendly, **which is the most important thing of all**. Ji-min, Seoul

I hate it when I'm watching a movie and the people around me start talking – even if they're just whispering. It drives me insane! Or, eating! The noise! And don't get me started on the smell of popcorn, **which literally makes me sick**, especially if there's butter on it. Diego, Bogotá

It gets on my nerves when I'm riding on the bus or subway next to people whose headphones are so loud I can hear the music from several meters away. I tell you, it drives me up the wall. So I just stare at the person and start singing along, **which, strangely enough, usually does the trick**. Birgit, Munich

Loud headphones don't bother me at all.

Really? They drive me crazy, especially when people are singing, too. You have no idea!

5 Grammar: Uses of *which*

A Complete rules a and b with the sentence numbers (1–4). Then write a or b next to the bold examples in the discussion forum on p.96.

Uses of *which* in non-restrictive clauses

Non-restrictive clauses often reveal the speaker's opinions and feelings, as well as give information.

1 My new ringtone, **which** I love, is driving all my colleagues crazy!
2 Judy has unfriended me on Facebook®, **which** means she's probably mad at me.
3 My boss is always taking credit for people's work, **which** I think is really unfair.
4 Most of my friends like hip hop, **which** personally I can't stand.

a In sentences ______ and ______ , *which* refers to the noun before it.
b In sentences ______ and ______ , *which* refers to the whole idea before it.

Grammar expansion p.154

B 9.5 Read *Common mistakes* and correct 1–7. Listen to check. Notice the pause and the slight drop in intonation between the two clauses.

1 My car is always breaking down, this drives me up the wall.
My car is always breaking down, which drives me up the wall.
2 My WiFi signal keeps dropping every five minutes that is getting on my nerves.
3 Whenever I'm sad, my mom says "life is too short" which usually makes things worse.
4 I've been thinking of moving abroad, my friends say it's a bad idea.
5 I can't stop biting my nails what is a terrible habit, I know.
6 Yesterday, my supervisor told me to shut up that was very rude of her.
7 Today is Thursday what means I have to help with the housework.

Common mistakes

My boss is always whistling ~~what / that~~ *, which* really ~~get~~ *gets* on my nerves.
I hear message tones constantly, ~~it~~ *, which* really gets to me.
Use a comma before *which* in non-restrictive clauses, but not to separate sentences.

C In pairs, change the underlined words in **B** to make 1–7 true for you. Any unusual stories?

My cell-phone case is always coming off, which drives me up the wall.

Maybe it's time to buy a new one. Mine never comes off.

D Make it personal Complete the "Makes me mad!" chart. In pairs, compare ideas using *which*. Do you get annoyed by the same things?

Place / situation	Annoying habit	Your reaction
eating out	*People speak too loud.*	*It drives me insane.*
shopping		
school / work		
public transportation / driving		
home with my family		
telemarketers and call centers		

Whenever I'm eating out, people always speak too loud, which drives me insane.

Yeah, I hate that, too.

6 Reading

A Read the introduction and paragraph 1 in 6B. Then complete the dates for Generation Z. Search online to complete the chart. Which generations are the members of your immediate family from?

Generation Z: ________ to present
Millenials (Generation Y): ________ to ________
Generation X: ________ to ________
Baby boomers: 1946 to ________

My parents were born in ... , so they must be Generation ...!

B Read the article. Complete the introduction with *better* or *worse*. Did you enjoy the interview?

THE Z FACTOR by Gloria Blanco

Already the largest generational group in the U.S., Generation Z-ers are forming a demographic tsunami that will change the country forever – and probably for the _____. Adam Smith, author of *Generating generations*, tells us why.

1 **Q:** *Why Z? I don't remember hearing that term before.*

A: It's just an arbitrary label to describe children who were born after 1997. I know that these terms don't always mean much – especially outside the U.S. – so let's call them *Screenagers*, a word coined by writer Douglas Rushkoff, which I myself [**also like better / tend to avoid**].

2 **Q:** *Interesting term.*

A: It makes perfect sense, since Generation Z kids spend over 40% of their time staring at different screens. But unlike us, *screenagers* have been using computers, tablets, and phones practically since they were born, which means that, to them, multitasking across devices [**is as natural as breathing / takes a lot of effort**]. These kids have a totally different outlook on technology than you and I do.

3 **Q:** *What else makes them unique?*

A: *Screenagers* are growing up in an unpredictable world filled with danger: extreme weather, massive poverty, endless wars and financial crises. Because of all these threats, they've developed a different attitude to risk-taking, which means they will probably seek [**more / less**] stability as adults. Also, they're fully aware of how interconnected the world is, take an interest in all kinds of social issues and are far more tolerant of diversity than I ever was. These are all very encouraging signs.

4 **Q:** *It seems they have very different priorities.*

A: Yes. In a recent study, thousands of kids were asked whether they'd rather be smarter or better looking. Nearly 70% chose "smarter," which means they seem to value [**intelligence over beauty / beauty over intelligence**] – a very welcome change, in my opinion. Just ask my thirteen-year-old! She couldn't care less about fashion, brands and accessories – unlike her older brother, who spends the whole day at the mall. No wonder they don't see eye to eye on anything!

5 **Q:** *One last question, what kind of employees will they be?*

A: Resourceful and creative, I'm sure, but with alarmingly short attention spans because of the number of distractions from their many devices, which means they'll find it [**easy / hard**] to keep focused. I'm under the impression they'll prioritize self-fulfillment over financial gains and will have a strong preference for green, socially responsible companies. Whether they'll find it easy to deal with hierarchy is hard to tell, but my philosophy has always been "rebelliousness is better than blind adherence to authority."

C Re-read. T (true), F (false) or NS (not sure)? Underline the evidence in the interview.

1 "Generation Z" is a carefully chosen term.
2 *Screenagers* will only feel comfortable with people like themselves.
3 Adam's son probably likes to wear what's in fashion.
4 Adam thinks *Screenagers* will want to have meaningful jobs that make them happy.
5 *Screenagers* will have trouble dealing with people in positions of power.
6 Adam believes authority is very important.

D 9.6 Circle the most logical option in the *which* clauses in the interview. Listen to check. Notice we stress the third syllable from the end in words ending in *-gy*, *-ty*, and *-phy*.

Pronunciation of *-gy*, *-ty*, and *-phy*

Notice we stress the third syllable from the end in words ending in *-gy*, *-ty*, and *-phy*.

psychology   curiosity   biography

E Make it personal In groups, answer 1–5. Similar opinions?

1 How accurately does Adam describe the *screenagers* you know?
2 Are older people necessarily wiser? Why (not)?
3 Which problems from paragraph 3 do you worry about most?
4 Do you agree with Adam's philosophy in paragraph 5?
5 Will *screenagers* have an easier life than their parents? Why (not)?

Well, I think life will be more difficult. Everything is more unpredictable and …

7 Vocabulary: Describing attitude

A 9.7 Listen to Adam and Gloria from 6B. Label the women in her family photo a–d. In Gloria's opinion, which is more important – generation or personality?

a environmentally-aware
b happiness-seeking
c conservative
d technology-minded

B 9.8 Use the correct form of the highlighted expressions in 6B to complete 1–6. Listen to check.

1 My younger sister ______________ (= is not interested in) what's going on in the world.
2 Grandma ______________ (= knows) all the latest technology and enjoys using it.
3 Sometimes I ______________ (= believe) that I have more in common with my grandma than with my parents.
4 My parents and I don't really ______________ (= agree on) lots of things. My ______________ (= attitude to) life is totally different from theirs.
5 I don't ______________ (= give importance to) money and status as much as my parents do.
6 I wish my mother ______________ (= open to) other people's lifestyles.

C Make it personal In pairs, modify 1–6 in B to describe people you know from different generations. Many similarities?

Most of my friends couldn't care less about politics or green issues.

Unlike me! Call me a nerd, but I watch the evening news every day!

Common mistake

~~Not like~~ *Unlike* you, I'm really interested in politics.

8 Listening

A 9.9 Listen to the start of an interview with a police officer. Check (✔) the correct option.

The officer thinks the robbery suspect ...

- ☐ was watching TV.
- ☐ may have hurt someone.
- ☐ was at the crime scene.
- ☐ worked at a store.

B 9.10 Listen to the rest. Number the actions (1–3) in the order you hear them. There are two extra pictures.

a ☐ b *1* c ☐ d ☐ e ☐

C 9.10 Listen again. Match the officer's explanations to the correct pictures. Which explanations might explain the extra pictures, too?

The suspect ...

1 ☐ wanted to run away.
2 ☐ didn't want to fall asleep.
3 ☐ was lying.
4 ☐ was making up a story.
5 ☐ was embarrassed.

D 9.11 Complete 1–6 with words from the interview, without changing the meaning. Then listen to check.

1 I questioned someone believed to have taken part in a robbery. = I questioned someone s*uspected of* taking part in a robbery.
2 A guy saying he was at home was the key suspect. = A guy c______ he was at home was the key suspect.
3 He said he wasn't involved. = He d______ being involved.
4 He said it was true, but it wasn't. = He wasn't t______ the t______ .
5 What showed the most that he was lying was ... = What g______ him a______ the most was ...
6 It's a story you're inventing. = It's a story you're m______ u___ .

E Make it personal Crime time! Work in pairs.

1 Use only the pictures and the words in D to remember the lies.
2 Are you good at spotting a liar? What unusual crime stories have you heard?

I once heard a story where a guy was suspected of ... He claimed ...

9 Grammar: Reduced relative clauses

A Study the sentences and complete the rules. Then find an active and a passive example of reduced relative clauses in 8D.

Reduced relative clauses: active and passive

Relative clauses can be reduced:

Active	Students	who cheat / cheating	on their final exams will not graduate.
	A passenger	(who was) riding	on the train robbed the conductor.
Passive	Anyone	(who is) caught	cheating will be suspended.
	The conductor	(who was) robbed	last night is very upset.

1 If a relative clause refers to a subject, you can delete ☐ only the pronoun ☐ the pronoun and *be*.

2 A(n) ☐ active ☐ passive verb in a reduced clause is always an *-ing* form and a(n) ☐ active ☐ passive one is always a past participle.

Grammar expansion p.154

B Rewrite these signs with reduced relative clauses to make them more natural. Where might they appear?

1 LUGGAGE THAT'S LEFT UNATTENDED WILL BE REMOVED AND DESTROYED.

2 $20,000 REWARD FOR INFORMATION THAT LEADS TO AN ARREST.

3 ANYONE WHO IS SUSPECTED OF ENTERING WILL FACE SERIOUS CONSEQUENCES.

4 THOSE WHO ARE CAUGHT LITTERING WILL BE FINED.

5 CARS THAT ARE MOVING AT EXCESSIVE SPEEDS WILL BE IDENTIFIED BY RADAR.

6 PROTESTERS WHO ARE HOLDING UP TRAFFIC WILL BE ARRESTED.

7 ANYONE WHO SWIMS HERE WILL BE IN FOR AN UNPLEASANT SURPRISE!

1 Luggage left unattended will be removed and destroyed. You might see it in an airport or a bus station.

C Cross out all optional words in these relative clauses. If no words can be crossed out, write "none."

1 The man who was sitting next to me on the bus was very suspicious-looking.
2 People are always pushing against my seat in airplanes, which is incredibly annoying.
3 That's the place that I told you about that said "No pets or children allowed."
4 The girl who was accused of taking my notebook totally denied it.
5 I'm always stepping on gum, which drives me up the wall.

D Make it personal You're under arrest! In groups, role play a trial.

1 List five behaviors you'd like to change or ban. Use ideas from 5D on p.97 or think up others.
2 Create signs for each one. Include the penalty.
3 **A** You're a police officer. Accuse **B** of violating the law.
B Defend yourself. Explain why you did nothing wrong.
C You are the judge. Guilty or innocent? Make a fair decision.

But Officer, I was only making a left turn ...

SCHOOL

THOSE CAUGHT SPEEDING IN FRONT OF THE SCHOOL WILL DO 500 HOURS OF COMMUNITY SERVICE!

10 Listening

A 9.12 In pairs, explain the cartoon. Then listen to two students and choose the correct option.

Laura [**agrees** / **disagrees**] with Alfredo that consumerism is a serious problem.

B 9.13 Listen to and order Alfredo's ideas 1–5. Which one(s) do you agree with?

Consumerism is a problem because ...

- [ ] it has an impact on the planet's resources.
- [ ] it affects people's relationships.
- [ ] people end up overspending.
- [ ] people buy things just to feel better.
- [ ] buying things doesn't bring long-term happiness.

I definitely agree that ...

C 9.14 Listen and note down two solutions to **B**. Any other possible ones?

D 9.15 Listen again to excerpts from the conversation. Number them 1–4.

Alfredo's purpose is to ...

- [ ] begin to build an argument.
- [ ] explain an idea in a different way.
- [ ] try again to persuade Laura to accept his point of view.
- [ ] tell Laura she doesn't understand his argument.

11 Keep talking

A 9.16 **How to say it** Complete the chart. Then listen, check, and repeat, copying the intonation.

Developing an argument (3)

	What they said	What they meant
1	That's a ______ question.	It's hard to answer that question.
2	Why (people think it's a problem) is ______ me.	I don't understand why ...
3	There's ______ to it than that.	It's not so simple.
4	Wouldn't you ______ that (it's just a quick fix)?	Don't you think that ...
5	I know what you're ______ at.	I know what you're trying to say.

B **Make it personal** Choose a problem from the survey. Note down (a) why it's serious and (b) what could be done to solve it.

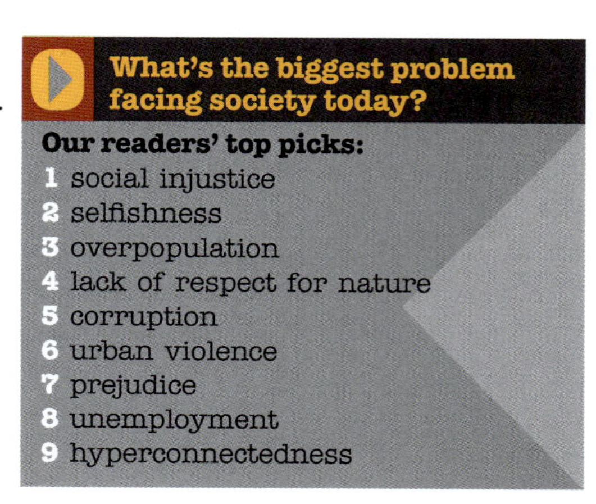

C In groups, compare ideas. Use *How to say it* expressions. Where do you (dis)agree?

Hmm ... that's a tough question, but to me, the biggest problem we face today is corruption.

What makes you say that?

Well, for one thing ...

12 Writing: A problem-solution essay

A Read Alfredo's essay. Which ideas in 10B and C are mentioned?

B Read *Write it right!* Then put a–h back into the essay. There are two extra words or phrases.

Write it right!

In essays, use a variety of conjunctions to connect your ideas well. Refer back to lessons 4.2 and 7.2, too.

Purpose: (a) *in order to*, (b) *so that*

Comparing: (c) *while*, (d) *unlike*

Conceding (*but* ...): (e) *although*, (f) *despite*

Reason: (g) *as*, (h) *due to*

C Which conjunctions (a–h) could be replaced by these?

1 as opposed to *unlike*
2 since ________
3 because of ________
4 so ________
5 even though ________
6 to ________
7 in spite of ________
8 whereas ________

D In which paragraph (1–5) does Alfredo ...

☐ define the problem?
☐ offer more supporting arguments?
☐ conclude his argument?
☐ put the problem in a historical perspective?
☐ propose possible solutions?

E Your turn! Choose a problem from the survey in 11B and write a five-paragraph essay in about 280 words.

Before
Note down problems and solutions. Follow the structure in D to order them logically.

While
Write five paragraphs following the model in A. Search online for facts, as necessary. Use at least four conjunctions from B and C.

After
Post your essay online and read your classmates' work. What was the most popular problem? Similar solutions?

1 Think about the last time you wanted something *badly* – say, new designer sunglasses. When you got them, you felt great. As time went on, the sunglasses probably lost most of their initial appeal. And then you lost them and regretted spending so much in the first place! Sound familiar? Blame it on consumerism, a cultural phenomenon that encourages us to find happiness by buying what we don't need. In other words: "Buy, use, discard, buy more."

2 Consumerism is not a new phenomenon. It had its origins in the Industrial Revolution. What's new is that in today's world, partly ________ globalization, whole societies are organized around the need to consume. Some studies, for example, have found that, ________ the recent bad economy, people in the U.S. spend 100 billion dollars every year on shoes, jewelry, and watches – more than what they invest in higher education.

3 It's a mistake to believe that material possessions can make us feel better. Many studies show that focusing on owning things can lead to anxiety and even depression. Also, consumerism can affect our self-esteem, ________ it encourages us to compare ourselves with others. Finally, the worst environmental problems we face have been caused by consumerism. ________ solve them, we must confront consumerism whenever we can.

4 It's hard to escape materialism, but it's not impossible. Here's a small first step: The next time you buy something, ask yourself "Do I need it?" rather than "Do I want it?" Also, be clear about what *really* matters to you. In other words, concentrate on the things that, ________ shopping, can bring long-term happiness – your family? your career? an important cause? a new challenge? Then, instead of going to the mall, focus your energy on those things.

5 Having a less materialistic lifestyle – and ultimately saving the planet – doesn't mean giving up on life's pleasures. It simply means giving less importance to material possessions ________, over time, they become less and less important to you.

10 How do you like to get around town?

1 Listening

A In pairs, read the ad and take turns guessing the problems. Then add four more.

A Mime a problem.
B Guess what it is.

> From your expression and gestures, that must be annoying kids!

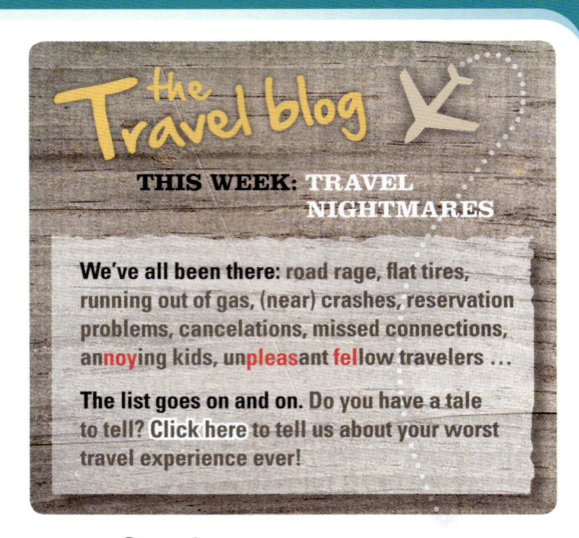

B 10.1 Listen to three friends, Joel, Ana, and Ian. Which travel nightmare in A is each talking about?

C 10.2 Guess how each story ends, picture A or B. Listen to check. Did you get them all right?

Story 1 Story 2 Story 3

D 10.2 Listen again. T (true), F (false) or NI (no information)? Whose story was the most surprising?

1. John was afraid at first that Barry couldn't be trusted.
2. John and Barry didn't talk about work.
3. When Ana saw the twins on the plane, she was sure they'd misbehave.
4. She asked them not to kick her seat, several times.
5. The conductor left the train to get something to eat.
6. Ian says he was never in real danger.

E Make it personal Which quotes 1–5 are good advice for Joel, Ana, or Ian? Which ones do you like best?

1. "Once a year, go someplace you've never been before." (Dalai Lama)
2. "Everything is funny as long as it's happening to someone else." (Will Rogers)
3. "You get educated by traveling." (Solange Knowles)
4. "When traveling with someone, take large doses of patience and tolerance with your morning coffee." (Helen Hayes)
5. "Wherever you go becomes a part of you somehow." (Anita Desai)

> Ana seems to work hard. Maybe the first one is good for her.

> And me! I wish I had the money to travel, though!

2 Vocabulary: Phrasal verbs

A 10.3 Read the definitions and complete 1–6 with the correct phrasal verb. Listen to check. Then, in pairs, use only the pictures in 1C to remember each story.

dawn on: To begin to be perceived or understood. *It only dawned on me that I could actually speak English when I finally went abroad.*

end up: Eventually arrive at a place or situation. *When shopping, I always end up spending more than I ought to. My parents say I'll end up with a huge credit card debt.*

get away: To escape. *College is driving me crazy. I wish I could get away for a week or so.*

get through: To manage to deal with or survive a difficult experience. *If I lived in Canada, I'd find it very difficult to get through winter there. I hate the cold!*

look forward to: To await eagerly or anticipate with pleasure. *I'm really looking forward to (watching) this year's Super Bowl.*

mix up: To confuse two people or things, or spoil the arrangement of something. *My closet is a mess! My winter clothes are all mixed up with my summer clothes.*

1 I was really ________ relaxing after a long flight.
2 How did you manage to ________ a whole week with that guy?
3 The poor man probably got ________ and pulled the wrong switch.
4 When it finally ________ the passengers that they were in trouble, everyone started screaming.
5 It'd been a rough year and all I wanted was to ________ from it all for a few days.
6 The woman got really mad, and we ________ arguing.

Joel had just flown from Washington to London, and he was really looking forward to relaxing after a long flight ...

B In pairs, modify the examples in A so they are true for you. Anything in common?

It only dawned on me how hungry I was when I ...

Common mistakes

I'm not really looking forward to ~~meet~~ *meeting* my in-laws. What if they end up ~~dislike~~ *disliking* me?

C **Make it personal** Describe your worst travel nightmare ever.

1 10.4 **How to say it** Complete the sentences from 1B and C. Then listen to check.

Talking about unexpected events

	What they said	What they meant
1	It ________ out (the hotel had made a mistake).	In the end, it proved to be true that ...
2	I ________ to (know who the man was).	By chance, I ...
3	For whatever ________, (the conductor stepped off the train).	No one knows why ...
4	As ________ would have it, (they were able to stop the train).	Luckily, ...
5	In the end, strangely ________, (it wasn't nearly as bad as I thought).	It may seem strange, but ...

2 Plan or make up your story. Use the travel nightmares in 1A to help you.

a Note down the main events. Ask yourself *what*, *when*, *where*, *why*, and *how*?
b Include three or more a) phrasal verbs and b) *How to say it* expressions.
c In groups, tell your stories. Whose experience was the most unpleasant?

I've got to tell you what happened on my vacation last year ...

3 Listening

A 10.5 Marty Falcon is on vacation. Listen and match the start of three conversations to three of the pictures (a–d). How does his tone suggest he is feeling?

To me, it sounds like he wants to go home!

B 10.6 Listen to the full conversations. Check (✔) all the statements that can be inferred. Have you ever had / heard of a tourist experience like this?

1 Marty ...
- [ ] wants to leave the hotel and go straight to the airport.
- [ ] won't take no for an answer.

2 The salesperson ...
- [ ] has no idea if the pants will shrink.
- [ ] agrees they're expensive.

3 Marty ...
- [ ] hasn't used the app before.
- [ ] stopped the car as soon as he noticed the light.

Well, it didn't happen to me personally, but a friend of mine went to ... and ...

Common mistake

a friend of ~~me / him / her~~ *mine / his / hers*

4 Pronunciation: Word stress in nouns and phrasal verbs

A 10.7 Read *Nouns from phrasal verbs* and listen to the examples. Check (✔) the correct rule.

Nouns from phrasal verbs

Some nouns formed from phrasal verbs are hyphenated; others are written as one word.
- I was wondering if I could get a late **checkout** (n) tomorrow. I need a **wake-up call**, too.
- Sorry, you need to **check out** (v) by noon. Just dial 00. The system will **wake** you **up**.

The stress in most phrasal verbs is on the [ ] **verb** [ ] **particle**.
The equivalent nouns are usually stressed on the [ ] **first** [ ] **second** part of the word.

B 10.8 Underline the stressed syllables in the bold words. Listen to check. Then find three comments in AS 10.6 on p.163 that show Marty is an inexperienced traveler.

1 Almost 100 dollars? That's a **rip-off**! Aren't these things supposed to cost about 20 bucks?
2 My car **broke down** and I don't know what to do! I'm lost in the middle of nowhere.
3 The fastest way to report a car **breakdown** is via our app. Do you know whether you have it installed on your phone?
4 Yeah, but I don't have a **login** or a password. Can't you help me over the phone?
5 It seems there's been a **mix-up**. Let me see if I can correct it and **fix** things **up**.

C Make it personal Complete 1–3 with words from B. Then ask and answer in pairs. Any good stories?

1 When was the last time you said, "I got confused. Sorry for the ________"? What happened?
2 Is 500 dollars for a watch a fair price or a ________? How much would you be willing to pay? Do you ever feel you're being overcharged when you shop?
3 What would you do if your car ________ late at night and your phone was dead?

I'd be terrified if there was no one around! I guess I'd lock the doors and wait until it got light.

5 Grammar: Negative and indirect questions

A Read the grammar box and check (✔) the correct rules 1–3. Then in 4A and B, underline two indirect questions and circle two negative questions.

Negative questions; indirect questions: *Wh-* and *yes-no*

Use negative questions when you expect a positive answer:
Isn't there free WiFi? Yes, the network name is "guest123."
Don't I have until noon to check out? Well, no, actually, check out is at 11:00.

Use indirect questions to soften the tone of your questions or requests:
Where**'s** the nearest ATM? → **Do you (happen to) know** where the nearest ATM **is**?
What time **does** the gym **close**? → **Could you tell me** what time the gym **closes**?
Did anyone **leave** me a message? → **I'd like to know if / whether** anyone **left** me a message.

1 Use ☐ **full** ☐ **contracted** forms to start negative questions. Answer yes to confirm them.
2 Indirect questions ☐ **have** ☐ **don't have** the same word order as statements.
3 The word *If* ☐ **can** ☐ **can't** be replaced by *whether*.

Common mistakes

Do you know how long ~~does it take~~ *it takes* to get there?
Could you tell me where ~~are the restrooms~~ *the restrooms are*?

B 10.9 Correct the mistakes in 1–5. Listen to check. Then, in pairs, use only the pictures in 3A and questions to role play each dialogue in 3B.

1 Can you tell me what time will she be back?
2 Would you happen to know are these machine-washable?
3 Cannot you help me over the phone?
4 Do you remember did any warning lights come on?
5 Do you know what is your exact location?

C Annoying questions! Turn 1–5 into indirect questions. Then complete the follow-up negative questions.

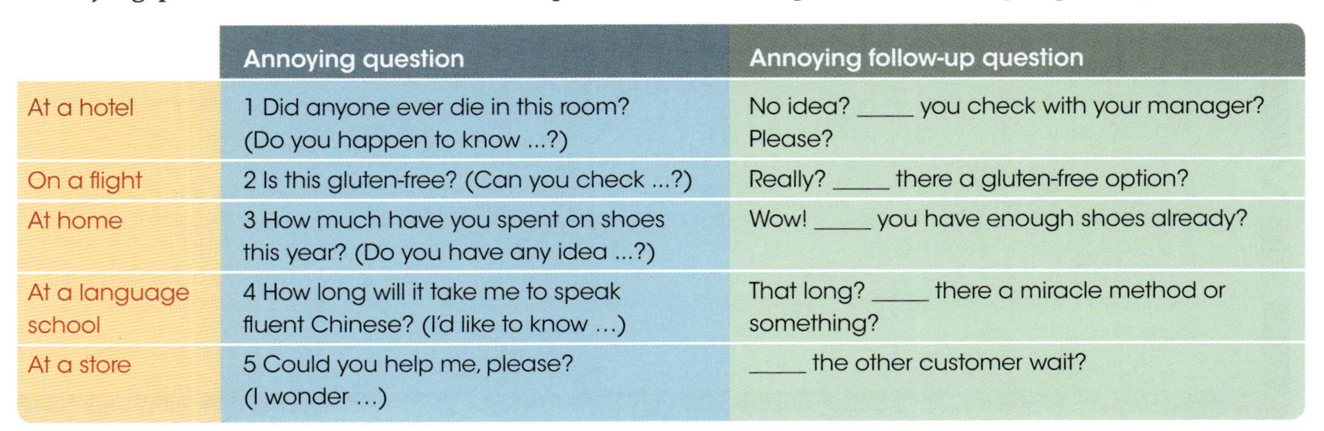

	Annoying question	Annoying follow-up question
At a hotel	1 Did anyone ever die in this room? (Do you happen to know ...?)	No idea? _____ you check with your manager? Please?
On a flight	2 Is this gluten-free? (Can you check ...?)	Really? _____ there a gluten-free option?
At home	3 How much have you spent on shoes this year? (Do you have any idea ...?)	Wow! _____ you have enough shoes already?
At a language school	4 How long will it take me to speak fluent Chinese? (I'd like to know ...)	That long? _____ there a miracle method or something?
At a store	5 Could you help me, please? (I wonder ...)	_____ the other customer wait?

D Make it personal Be annoying! In pairs, role play and expand two situations in C. Include indirect and negative questions. Then present one to the class and vote on the funniest.

Can't the customer wait? I'm important, too!

Please be patient, sir ... what can I do for you?

This phone is driving me nuts. Could you tell me how I turn it on?

6 Reading

A Read paragraph 1 of Arturo's blog. Use the photo to guess his nationality and answer 1 and 2.

1 Was the party in the U.S. or his country of birth?

2 Which five habits did he change when he went abroad?

B Read paragraph 2. Check (✔) the true statement(s). Is the story interesting so far?

Arturo ...

- [ ] got a degree abroad.
- [ ] was starting to lose touch with friends.
- [ ] found it easy to adjust when he returned home.
- [ ] sometimes questions his decision to live abroad.

C Read the rest. How would he answer the last question in paragraph 2?

- [ ] absolutely
- [ ] not really
- [ ] not at all

WINDS OF CHANGE

HOME | ABOUT | ARTICLES | CONTACT

1 Two years ago I was at a birthday party when an old friend called my name. It went in one ear and out the other. "Arturo? Are you deaf?" he repeated. For a split second, I didn't recognize Arturo as my name! I'd grown so used to being called Art by my American friends that now, back home, my birth name sounded as if it belonged to somebody else. That was the first time I'd experienced reverse culture shock; that is, culture shock not from going abroad, but from coming back. Other symptoms followed, of course: being more punctual than anyone else, driving more slowly, eating earlier, giving better tips, telling fewer jokes – you name it. What was going on with me?

2 I'd just returned from doing an MA in San José, CA, in information technology. I was thrilled to see my family and reconnect with all the friends I'd left behind and was beginning to drift apart from. I was also looking forward to going back to work so I could put all the theory I'd learned into practice. I wanted to get on with my old life in Madrid, but something was missing and I couldn't put my finger on what. Strangely enough, after all this time, I still can't. My time in the U.S. is still a powerful magnet that constantly pulls me back to all the sights, the smells, and the little joys and annoyances of the life I left behind. I think I'm finally coming to terms with the fact maybe I'll never have a clear sense of home again, which sometimes makes me wonder: was my time abroad worth it?

3 Studying or working abroad, trying to express your personality in another language, and fitting into a different culture can be frustrating, especially at first. You have to get used to both being and sounding foreign, and you have to grow to like your new self – your new identity. But here's the good news: Your self-awareness develops, and your outlook on life changes. Many of your old pre-conceived ideas crumble like buildings in an earthquake. You learn that "normal" means socially acceptable in different cultures – nothing more than that. And, most of all, you finally begin to remove all the labels that had come to define you. At home, people always thought of me as the family genius, but back in California I was just "the nice guy from Madrid," which means I can be whoever I choose to be.

4 When you move abroad, you're forced to abandon your roots and take a leap into the unknown. Things can and do go wrong, but you learn that you can get through the rough times without your family. You also realize that the ugly haircut or the wrong meal you got because of your limited vocabulary, at the end of the day, mean absolutely nothing. And, most of all, you realize that – pardon the cliché – you become a better person. Not better than those around you, but definitely better than your former self, no matter where you are – "home" or otherwise.

D Does Arturo make these points in paragraph 3 or 4?

When you live abroad, you ...

- [ ] become more accepting of diversity.
- [ ] learn to rely more on yourself.
- [ ] can reinvent yourself.
- [ ] don't get bothered by small problems.

E ▶10.10 Try to pronounce the pink-stressed words. Listen to check. Did you get all the vowels right?

F **Make it personal** In groups, answer 1–5. Any surprises?

1 Which benefit(s) of living abroad in 6D would be most important to you? Can you think of any others?
2 If you could spend a year abroad, where exactly would you go and why?
3 Would you prefer to move abroad or to another place in your own country? Why?
4 If you moved abroad, would it bother you having a foreign accent?
5 Which aspects of your identity might be hardest to abandon?

> I think I'd miss my hometown most of all. After all, I've lived here since I was born. It's part of my identity.

7 Vocabulary: Words with literal and figurative meanings

A Match the words to the pictures 1–6.

crumble	fit	label	leap	magnet	root

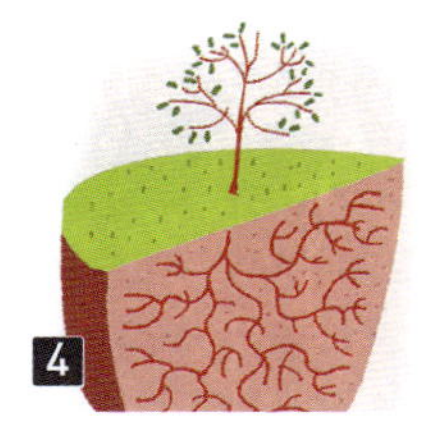

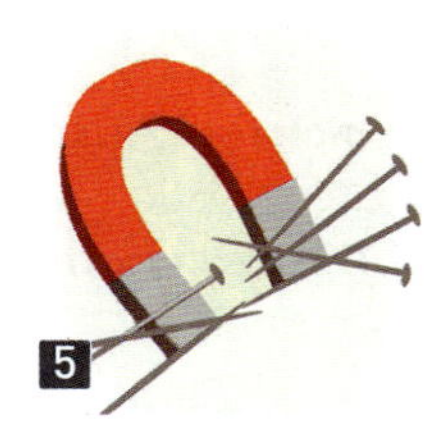

B Read *Literal or figurative?* Then match the highlighted words in Arturo's blog to the definitions 1–6. Do you know any other words with figurative meanings?

Literal or figurative?

Words can have literal (concrete) or figurative (abstract) meanings. Knowing a word's literal meaning can help you guess what it means when it's used figuratively:
My older sister was scared to **dive** into the pool (literal) / into a new relationship (figurative).

1 *fitting* : being in harmony with or belonging to
2 ______ : origins or source
3 ______ : arbitrary description or identifying words
4 ______ : make a sudden change or transition
5 ______ : fall apart or break down completely
6 ______ : a force that attracts

C Complete 1–6 with the correct form of the words in A.

1 Think of a ______ often attached to your country or city. Do you think it's a fair description?
2 How's the economy doing in your country? Is it in good shape, so-so, or ______ ?
3 "Money is the ______ of all evil." Do you agree?
4 Some people seem to be a ______ for bad luck or trouble. Do you know anyone like that?
5 Can you think of an artist that successfully made the ______ from music to movies?
6 At school, how hard do / did you try to ______ in with the "cool kids" in your class?

D **Make it personal** In pairs, choose three questions in C to answer. Any surprises?

> Well, Montevideo is known as "a culinary paradise" because our meat and fish are so good. Of course!

8 Language in use

A 10.11 Listen to the start of a podcast. Who is being interviewed and why?

B 10.12 Listen and order the photos 1–5. Who do you think is having the hardest time?

C 10.12 Listen again. T (true) or F (false)?

1 Mariana had a sedentary lifestyle in Venezuela.
2 Ignacio mostly blames his roommate for their cold relationship.
3 Ines says she lacks self-discipline.
4 Diego found it hard to adapt to life in the U.S.
5 Elena's parents are going to take her back home.

D Match the highlighted words in podcast excerpts 1–5 to definitions a–f. Which feelings and opinions can you relate to?

1 I was born and raised in Caracas, so I kind of miss the **hustle and bustle** of life there. ... I'm sure I'll get used to the peace and quiet eventually.
2 I'm not used to sharing a room with anyone – **let alone** someone I **barely** know.
3 Here we have regular assignments, quizzes, projects, and exams, which can be a little **overwhelming**. I wonder if I'll ever get used to working this hard.
4 When I came here, I was used to life in the States. I mean, there was less of a culture **clash** than I'd anticipated.
5 I started to feel terribly **homesick**. I wasn't used to being away from my parents for more than a couple of days.

a a conflict ____________
b much less, not to mention ____________
c noisy, energetic activity *hustle and bustle*
d scarcely, hardly ____________
e sad because you're away from home and family ____________
f so confusing and difficult, it's hard to deal with ____________

I can definitely relate to the last one. I felt so homesick when I ...

E Make it personal How would you feel about leaving home to study or work?

1 Do you make new friends easily?
2 Are you a good roommate? How many people have you shared an apartment or dorm with? Have you had good experiences?
3 Would you mind sharing a kitchen and a bathroom? Is there anything you couldn't share?
4 How badly would you miss your family? How often would you contact them?
5 How often do you need peace and quiet? What do you do to find it?

Well, I actually went away to school. The first year was a nightmare because ...

9 Grammar: Talking about acquired habits

A Read the grammar box. Check (✔) T (true) or F (false) in rules 1 and 2.

Talking about acquired habits: *be* and *get used to*

be used to **(the state)**	***get used to*** **(the process)**
Ignacio **isn't used** to sharing his room.	He'll have **to get used to** it.
Diego **was** already **used to** living abroad.	He still **hasn't gotten used to** the weather.
Ines **is** still **not used to** college life.	She**'s** slowly **getting used to** doing more homework.

1 ***Be used to*** means *be accustomed to* and ***get used to*** means *become accustomed to.* T F
2 After ***be / get used to***, you can use a verb in the *-ing* form or a noun. T F

Common mistakes

I ~~use to wake~~ *'m used to waking* up early. But I'll never ~~used to go~~ *get used to going* to bed late.

How often did you ~~used~~ *use* to go skiing when you lived in Argentina?

» Grammar expansion p.156

B 10.13 Correct the mistakes in 1–3. Listen to check. Notice the /s/ sound in *used*.

1 Mom says we'll get used to live together.
2 I'm not used to been treated as an adult.
3 It took me a while to used to the weather.

C In pairs, use only the photos in 8B to remember all you can about each person. Check in AS 10.12 on p.163. Anything you missed?

D Complete 1–4 with *be* or *get* in the correct tense. Then complete 5–7 with a form of the verbs in parentheses.

TOUGH CHANGES!

	Marco, from Colombia: moving out of your parents' house	Kathleen, from Denver: selling your car and buying a bicycle
a Was it tough at first?	I come from a large family, so at first I (1) _____ used to the silence. I found it really weird.	Not as hard as I thought. I used to (5) _____ (ride) my bike everywhere when I lived in Amsterdam, which certainly helped.
b Any other problems?	It took me a long time (2) _____ used to doing all the housework by myself because I (3) _____ used to having a housekeeper.	Not really. I don't mind the effort. I go to the gym every day, so I'm used to (6) _____ (work) out.
c How are things now?	I guess I'm slowly (4) _____ used to being on my own, and I kind of like it.	I've gotten so used to (7) _____ (go) to work by bike, I don't think I'll ever need a car again.

SEARCH OUR ARCHIVE:
changing schools / getting into college / getting married / moving to a new city / becoming a vegetarian / starting an exercise program / switching from iOS to Android (or vice versa!)

E **Make it personal** Choose a topic from the website in D, answer questions a–c mentally, and make notes. Then, in pairs, interview each other. Who had the hardest time adapting?

I started college last year, and it was a bit of a shock at first.

What was hard about it?

Well, I was used to smaller classes and ...

10 Listening

A 10.14 Take the quiz. T (true) or F (false)? Listen to check. How many correct guesses?

How much do you know about Istanbul?

1 Istanbul is one of the five largest cities in the world.
2 Two-thirds of the city is located in Europe and one-third in Asia.
3 Istanbul's subway is the oldest in the world.
4 As the city is surrounded by water, it doesn't snow there.
5 Over time, it has been the capital of three different empires.
6 The Grand Bazaar is the world's most visited tourist attraction.

B 10.15 Listen to Bill and Gail's first impressions of Istanbul and answer 1 and 2.

1 List three reasons why Bill loves Istanbul.
2 List three things you can do there. Would you like to visit the city?

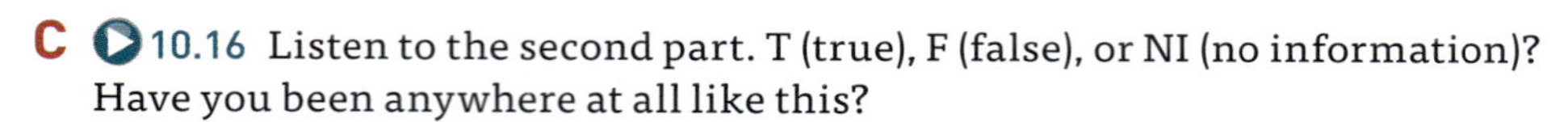

C 10.16 Listen to the second part. T (true), F (false), or NI (no information)? Have you been anywhere at all like this?

1 The Grand Bazaar is smaller than a city block.
2 Bill thinks The Grand Bazaar is still getting bigger.
3 You can buy rugs, slippers, and jewelry.
4 According to the conversation, you can also buy live animals.
5 It's less crowded early in the morning.

D 10.17 Complete 1–5 with the correct prepositions. Use your intuition! Listen to check. Any surprises?

1 I can't wait to explore the city ___ the next few days.
2 We should definitely stock up ___ these for an afternoon snack or two.
3 And then we can go ___ some Turkish ice cream.
4 Istanbul is love ___ first sight, isn't it?
5 It [the Grand Bazaar] is one of the largest markets ___ the entire world.

11 Keep talking

A What's the most amazing place you've ever been / imagined going to? Think through 1–7. Search online, if necessary.

1 What's it called and what country is it in?
2 Is it historically significant in any way?
3 When did you first go (first imagine going) there?
4 What was your first reaction to the place?
5 What are the highlights? What else is there to do?
6 Did you need to take any precautions?
7 Have you been back there since (or in your dreams)? How many times?

B In groups, describe the places. Be sure to answer 1–7. Which sounds the most irresistible?

I think Rio is the most unbelievable place I've ever been.

Oh, I'd love to go. What's so special about it?

Well, as you know, it's famous for Sugarloaf Mountain ...

12 Writing: A travel report

A Read Lucy's travel report. Does it make you want to visit both places? How many times has she been there?

B Write the question numbers 1–7 in 11A next to each paragraph A–E.

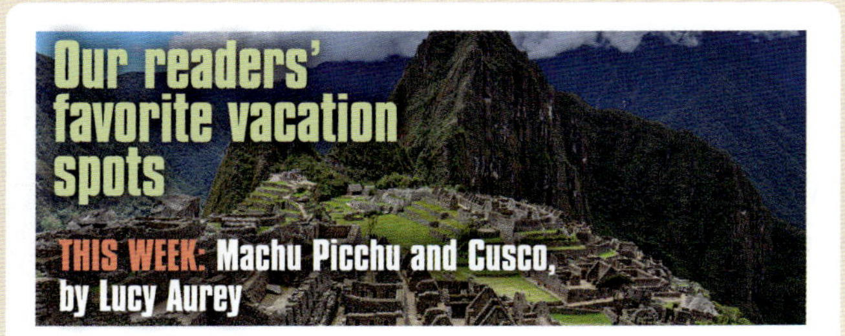

A I was twelve when I first learned that Machu Picchu, which means "old mountain," is Peru's most popular tourist attraction and one of the world's most famous archeological sites. The textbook images of that isolated stone city, built by the Incas more than 550 years ago, **set my imagination on fire** ☐. I had so many questions: Why was it built? Why was it abandoned? I convinced myself that I had to go there one day.

B That day finally came. Last year my fiancé and I spent a week in Peru, and all I can say is that Machu Picchu exceeded my expectations in every possible way. When I saw the Inca ruins for the first time, I was **blown away** ☐ by the perfection. Was it the giant stones, so well preserved? The extraordinary temples? Maybe the **stunning** ☐ views? It's hard to tell.

C Machu Picchu lies just fifty miles from Cusco, the starting point for any visit. It's an amazing city with colorful markets, fine restaurants, and **gorgeous** ☐ monuments. If you have a sweet tooth, check out the ChocoMuseo, where you'll eat the best chocolate in the country. Plus, it'll give you the energy you'll need to climb up the Inca trail. Once in Machu Picchu, don't miss the Temple of the Sun – it's truly **awe-inspiring** ☐.

D Machu Picchu is located nearly 2.5 kilometers above sea level, so it'll **take your breath away** ☐! Take it easy and drink plenty of water so your body can get used to the altitude. As a rule, the best time to visit Machu Picchu is between May and August, outside the rainy season. But, beware! Daily visitor numbers are strictly controlled, so be sure to book your trip way in advance.

E Machu Picchu is magnificent **beyond your wildest dreams** ☐. No wonder it's been named one of the New Seven Wonders of the World. I'm already looking forward to going back next year!

C Read *Write it right!* Then scan the report and write 1 or 2 next to the highlighted examples.

Write it right!

Two ways to make your description come alive are:

1. Avoid the word *nice*, and try not to overuse *beautiful*. Use more "colorful" synonyms:
   The place was absolutely **breathtaking**.
2. Use figurative expressions:
   It was a gorgeous beach spoiled by **a sea of tourists**.

D Read *Common mistakes*. Then correct six mistakes in the paragraph.

Common mistakes

The place was ~~very~~ *abolutely* stunning.

New York is one of the most multicultural ~~city of~~ *cities in* the world.

I'~~ve been in~~ *went to* Bangkok in 2010.

Don't use *very* with extreme adjectives, and be careful with plurals and tenses!

If you never went to Cartagena, located on Colombia's northern coast, you don't know what you're missing. It's a very gorgeous city and one of the most popular tourist attraction of the country. My favorite place is the Café del Mar, a great spot to watch the sunset over the old city walls. It's very amazing! I've been there last December and it was very crowded, so I suggest you go in October or November.

E Your turn! Describe the place you talked about in 11B. Write about 200 words.

Before
Organize your notes into five paragraphs to answer the questions from 11A.

While
Use colorful and figurative expressions from Lucy's report and *Write it right!* Check your grammar, too, for common mistakes.

After
Proofread carefully. Email your text to a classmate before sending it to your teacher.

Review 5
Units 9–10

1 Speaking

A Look at the photos on p.94.

1 Note down your impressions of the people using these expressions:

keep quiet mingle open up reveal small talk think out loud think over think up

2 In groups, share information. Who seems introverted? Who seems extroverted?

3 Take turns describing how you usually react in these situations.

At parties, I like to mingle and get to know new people.

Really? I hate small talk.

B Search "extrovert or introvert" and take a new personality quiz. Then share something new you learned about yourself.

I learned a new word. I'm an "ambivert." I really like to socialize, but I also like time by myself.

2 Listening

A R5.1 Listen to a conversation between Daisy and an employee of a car rental company. Number the problems in the order mentioned.

- [ ] The employee doesn't know much about the device.
- [ ] The only office is at the airport.
- [ ] Daisy can't hear a voice on the GPS.
- [ ] Refunds are only given through the website.
- [ ] The boss is away.
- [ ] The directions are wrong.

B **Make it personal** In pairs, discuss these questions.

1 Describe a specific travel problem that you've had. What happened in the end?

2 Was anyone able to help you?

Once I was locked in the bathroom of a hotel, and I couldn't get out ...

3 Grammar

A Eileen would like to take a study-abroad vacation. Change her questions to a program director to indirect questions, using the words in parentheses.

1 Are there any two-week Portuguese programs in Salvador Bahia? (Do you happen to know ...?)

2 Where do students stay? (Do you have any idea ...?)

3 How many hours a day are classes? (I wonder ...)

4 Is there a placement exam? (Could you tell me ...?)

5 What methodology does the teacher use? (I'd like to know ...)

6 Are there organized social activities? (Can you ask someone ...?)

B Make it personal Note down four indirect questions a visitor to your town or city might ask. In pairs, role play helping the "tourist."

C Complete Eileen's reactions to her vacation (1–5) with a form of *be used to* or *get used to*. Then combine the sentences using *which*.

1 In the beginning, I had some trouble _getting used to_ the food. It was very spicy.
I had some trouble getting used to the food, which was very spicy.
2 I ______________ speaking Portuguese, either. It was overwhelming at first.
3 But it was easy to ______________ early morning classes. It was great because I had the rest of the day to sightsee.
4 I also ______________ singing in Portuguese every day because my teacher loved music. It was amazing.
5 And now I ______________ living with a family and speaking Portuguese at breakfast. It's such a great way to improve my language skills!

4 Writing

Write a paragraph about a problem you may encounter when you move abroad and offer a solution. Include at least four of these words or expressions.

in order to	while	although	as
so that	unlike	despite	due to

5 Self-test

Correct the two mistakes in each sentence. Check your answers in Units 9 and 10. What's your score, 1–20?

1 I'd like to live by my own, but I might have trouble get used to the quiet.
2 I was claiming the truth, but the police thought I was making the story.
3 Students cheat on their exams will end being expelled.
4 People are always chew gum in class, that drives me up the wall.
5 If you raise a lot your voice, it doesn't make people see eye and eye with you.
6 I'm really looking forward my trip with an old friend of me.
7 You have to checkout by 11, so you'd better ask for a wakeup call.
8 I'd like to know did anyone call and where is the nearest bank.
9 I miss the bustle and hustle of city life, and I can't used to the country.
10 The view was awe-inspire and it took my breath.

6 Point of view

Choose a topic. Then support your opinion in 100–150 words, and record your answer. Ask a partner for feedback. How can you be more convincing?

a You think small talk is a total waste of time. OR
You think small talk is a good way to meet new people and feel comfortable with them.
b You think social injustice is the worst problem facing society. OR
You think a lack of respect for the environment is far worse.
c You think living abroad is something everyone should do. OR
You think living abroad is very difficult and not for everyone.
d You think a foreign accent is something people should try to get rid of. OR
You think a foreign accent is like a foreign culture and should be respected.

11 What recent news has caught your eye?

1 Listening

A 11.1 Listen and match news items 1–6 to photos a–f. Then decide the section each is from.

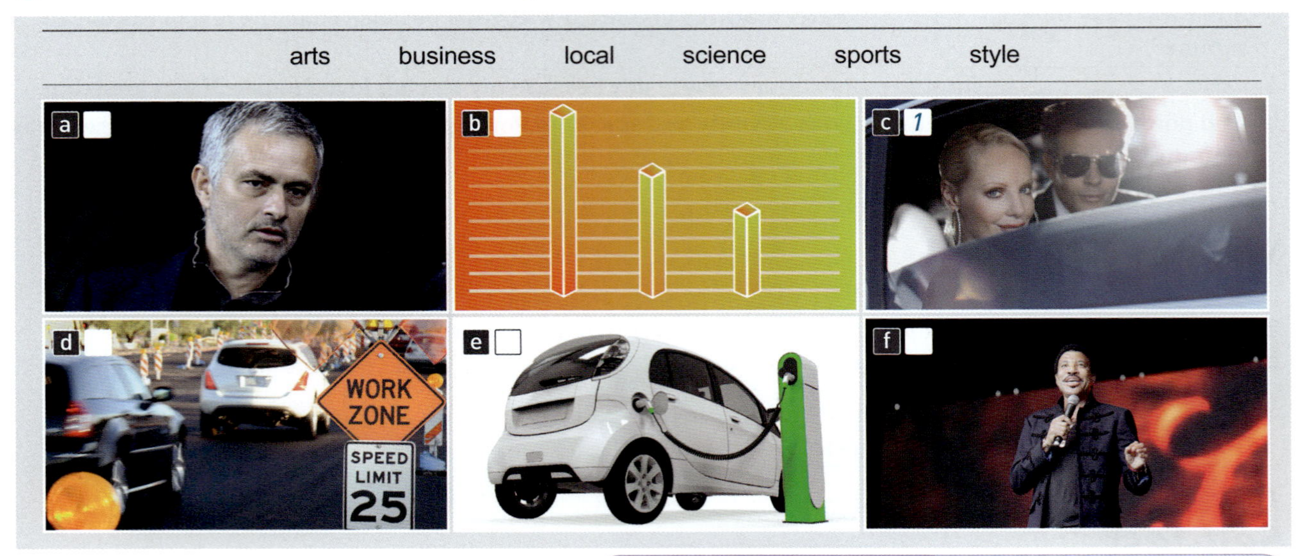

News story 1 must be the style section. That's where they talk about celebrity gossip.

Talking about the news

News is singular and uncountable.
I read **some** news that **was** shocking.
I'm interested in business **news** / **the** arts.
I enjoy reading **the** science **section**.

B 11.2 A reporter from **A** is doing a survey. Listen and note down Jack's answers in 1–3 words.

1 Favorite news topic?	
2 How often?	
3 In print or on digital media?	
4 Favorite news source?	
5 News alerts?	

C 11.2 Memory test! Try to complete 1–5. Listen again to check. Anything in common with Jack?

1 Jack follows the news so he won't seem ________ in front of his friends.
2 He is also interested in ________ , but he doesn't follow this area.
3 He only watches ________ when he's away from home.
4 He likes the ________ in his online magazine, but he would like to see more ________ and ________ .
5 He looks at his news feed on ________ and ________ .

Call me old-fashioned, but I still read a printed newspaper almost every day.

D **Make it personal** Choose a news story you've followed. In groups, share and ask follow-up questions. Any surprises?

Well, I'm studying politics, so I've been following the news story about ...

Oh, I didn't hear about that at all. When did it happen? ...

2 Vocabulary: The news

A 11.3 Circle the choice that is closest in meaning to the highlighted words. Listen to check.

1 I try to **keep up with** what's going on.
A stay informed
B tell people

2 It's such an **accurate** source of information.
A free from error and true
B with errors or not true

3 I wish they'd post more **behind-the-scenes** stuff.
A official
B usually hidden

4 They're **not biased** in favor or against any particular artist.
A neutral
B unfair

5 I tend to **skip** most stories.
A read in detail
B maybe glance at headlines, but not read

6 If a headline **catches my eye**, I click on the link.
A attracts my attention
B worries me

B Complete 1–5 with items from A. Then, in pairs, change the underlined words to make them true for you.

1 The evening news is usually ________ , but not always. Sometimes they don't seem to check their facts .
2 I always try to ________ the latest news about sports.
3 Our main TV network is ________ against the government.
4 When presidents get together, it would be fascinating to know what actually happens ________ .
5 When I check the news, I ________ most of it and move straight to the horoscope section.

3 Pronunciation: Question intonation

A 11.4 Listen to and repeat the examples. Then check (✔) the correct rules.

1 Do you have a favorite news source?
2 What does that include?
3 Can I pick several topics or only one?

> 1 *Yes / No* questions usually have a ☐ rising ↗ ☐ falling ↘ intonation.
> 2 *Wh*-questions usually have a ☐ rising ☐ falling intonation.
> 3 Questions with *or* have a ☐ rising ☐ falling intonation on the first choice(s), but a ☐ rising ☐ falling intonation on the last one.

B 11.5 Listen to 1–5 and write a ↗, b ↘ or c ↗ ↘. Then listen again, copying the speaker's intonation.

1 ________ 2 ________ 3 ________ 4 ________ 5 ________

C Make it personal Give your opinions on the news!

1 Interview a new partner to complete the survey in 1B. Ask for lots of detail. Use words and expressions from 2A.

OK. What's your favorite news topic?

Well, I really like to keep up with sports, but I usually skip the style section.

Do you mainly follow local teams or international ones?

2 Search for and read a news story about your city or country in a well-known English-language newspaper. Discuss 1–3.

1 Was it easy to understand, or were some parts difficult?
2 Was everything included, or were some important parts left out?
3 Overall, did the English version seem fair or biased?

4 Language in use

A 11.6 In the news, a "blooper" refers to a mistake made in public. Guess bloopers 1–3. Then listen and fill in the blanks. How close were you?

B 11.6 Listen again. T (true) or F (false)?

1 The dog had been behaving strangely.
2 Viewers had no idea whether the reporter was OK.
3 The news anchor woke up by himself.
4 He made a joke about his mistake.
5 The candidate lost her temper during the interview.

C Write R (relaxed) or VN (very nervous) for the highlighted expressions. Which ones were you familiar with?

1 No one really knows why the dog lost it like that. The reporter himself **claimed** that everything had been going well behind the cameras.
2 He kept his cool, though, and **reassured** viewers that he was fine.
3 The news anchor was woken up by his colleague, who stayed calm and **reminded** him he was on live TV!
4 He was able to keep it together and simply denied that he had fallen asleep. Then he **admitted** he was just kidding, of course.
5 Instead of freaking out, the candidate **warned** them they'd made a mistake, then she calmly got up and left the studio!

D Make it personal In pairs, answer 1–4.

1 Which story did you like best?

> The last story was great. I would have totally lost it, but she really kept her cool.

2 Can you recall any "bloopers," either by famous people or in comedy?
3 Have you ever made a "blooper" of your own, or been caught on camera at the wrong moment? How did you react?
4 What kinds of things make you laugh? Have you ever laughed at the wrong time?

cartoons   Internet memes   animals doing silly things
comedy shows / funny movies   people falling   stand-up comedians

5 Grammar: Reporting what people say (1)

A Read the grammar box and check (✔) the correct rules 1–3.

Reported statements and questions

The news anchor said, "You're right, I'm exhausted. I went to bed late last night."	The news anchor **admitted** (to us) (that) he was exhausted. He **said** (that) he'd gone to bed late the night before.
She asked, "Can I have a day off?"	She **asked** her boss if she could have a day off.
The announcer asked, "What are you doing here?"	The candidate **explained** (to the announcer) what she was doing there.

In reported speech:
1 You often move one tense ☐ **back** ☐ **forward**.
2 You ☐ **can** ☐ **cannot** omit *that* after a reporting verb.
3 Pronouns, time, and place expressions often ☐ **change** ☐ **stay the same**.

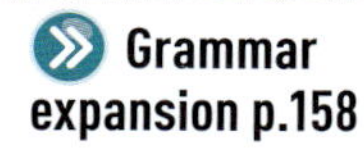
Grammar expansion p.158

B Read *Reporting verbs and indirect objects*. Put the bold verbs in 4C and 5A in the chart.

Reporting verbs and indirect objects

Memorize which reporting verbs are followed by indirect objects!
*He **told me** he was tired.* *She **said** she was fine.* *He **explained (to us)** he was tired.*

Indirect object required	No indirect object or, for some verbs, optional
tell	*say*

C Report the dialogue between a news anchor (Andy) and co-host (Sam). Do you think Andy's right?

Sam: Did you really fall asleep?
Andy: Of course I didn't fall asleep! Erm ... Well, actually, I did.
Sam: Everyone is probably talking about you.
Andy: Really? Well, that doesn't worry me.
Sam: Erm... The video has already been posted online.
Andy: Yeah, but it will create a lot of positive buzz.
Sam: Hmm ... How can you be so sure?

1 Sam asked Andy ...
2 First he denied ... Then he admitted ...
3 Sam warned ...
4 Andy reassured ...
5 Sam reminded ...
6 Andy explained ...
7 Sam asked ...

Common mistakes

I asked him whether ~~he's~~ *he was* OK. He ~~explained / admitted / said me~~ *explained / admitted / said* that he was sick.

D Make it personal Choose a situation and think through 1–3 to prepare. Share your stories in groups. Anything in common?

1 What was the situation?
2 What questions did you ask? What was the response? Use a variety of reporting verbs.
3 What happened in the end?

> I told my boyfriend that he needed to save money, but he didn't listen and ...

When was the last time you ...?
had a small / big disagreement denied you'd done something reminded someone of a promise
tried to get out of doing something boring explained something again and again
were warned about something

6 Reading

A Read the title and questions 1–4, and imagine the answers. Then read the text and put the questions back into the interview. There is one extra question.

1 What kind of content do people tend to connect with?
2 Are there dangers involved in posting a video that goes viral?
3 Are there specific things I can do to make my video go viral?
4 Can viral videos be created? Or do they happen by chance?

How to make your video go viral

"We've postponed the wedding until we come up with something we can do at the ceremony that will become a viral video."

Of the many millions of videos posted online every day, why do some clips stand out from the crowd and go on to attract millions of viewers – sometimes in a matter of hours? Media experts Stacey Wright and Kevin Murray explain to our readers why some videos go viral.

Q: ____________________?

Stacey: Basically, the latter. Having a video go viral is like winning the lottery. It's incredibly hard – though certainly not impossible – to achieve. For every success story out there, there are thousands of flops.

Kevin: Stacey's answer got me thinking about what our goal should be when we create a video. It's important to catch people by surprise. As a rule, I think we should try to leave them speechless. Whether our content will go viral is another story – it may or may not happen. But we shouldn't focus on that goal right from the beginning.

Q: ____________________?

Stacey: People's brains are wired to pay close attention to anything that goes against their expectations. This means that a video that contains an unusual image, a bold statement, or some sort of unexpected turn of events tends to strike a chord with viewers, otherwise it may do nothing for them.

Kevin: The most shareable videos convey strong emotions. In a world obsessed with money and deadlines, people want to get in touch with their humanity. They want romance, entertainment, anger, and joy. They want to burst out laughing. They want to be moved to tears. So, the more intense a video is, the more likely it is to be passed along.

Q: ____________________?

Stacey: The first thing most people do before they decide whether or not to watch a video is check how long it is, so the main thing is to keep it short and sweet. When your video is ready, cut it in half, and then cut it in half again. Keep in mind that you're creating content for the 140-character Twitter® generation – people with increasingly short attention spans.

Kevin: Recent evidence actually suggests nearly one fifth of your viewers will leave your video after ten seconds. By a minute in, nearly half will have clicked away, so you can't save the best for last, really. One more thing, people can be incredibly cruel online! You can't let their comments get to you.

B 11.7 Listen to check. Notice the /eɪn/ sound in the underlined words.

C Who made points 1–6? S (Stacey), K (Kevin), B (both), or N (neither)?

1 It's no use trying to make a video go viral.
2 People tend to share content that moves them.
3 People tend to share content that surprises them.
4 Twitter® is not a good platform for sharing videos.
5 You have to grab the viewer's attention from the beginning.
6 If your video goes viral, you can't be too sensitive.

D Make it personal In groups, answer 1–4. Similar opinions?

1 Who do you think made the best points, Stacey or Kevin?
2 Why else might a video go viral? Would you like one of yours to go viral? Why (not)?
3 How often do you leave a comment on a video? Do you tend to say mostly positive or negative things?
4 Have you ever posted a video yourself? Were you happy with the reaction?

7 Vocabulary: Emotional reactions

A 11.8 Review the highlighted expressions in 6A, then complete expressions 1–7 with the correct form of these verbs. There is one extra. Listen to check. Which expressions do you already use?

burst	catch	do	get (two expressions)	give	leave	move

My favorite viral videos of the past few years!

Emotional baby This one will **(1)** _get_ you thinking, I'm sure. A ten-month-old baby gets teary-eyed as she watches her mother sing an old Rod Stewart song. This video **(2)** _____ me to tears when I first saw it, and it still **(3)** _____ to me whenever I play it again.

Sneezing baby panda A baby panda sneezes and the mother panda is **(4)** _____ by surprise. No big deal, right? Wrong. This clip is hilarious. When I first watched it, I **(5)** _____ out laughing so loud my family came running.

***Friday* by Rebecca Black** *Friday* is about a girl who's bored Monday through Thursday, but cheers up, well, guess when. When the video took off, people either loved or hated the clip. Nobody said, "It **(6)** _____ nothing for me." Did I like *Friday*? Well, let's just say it **(7)** _____ me speechless.

B In pairs, take turns miming and guessing the expressions in A (1–7).

> You're scratching your head. That must be "It gets you thinking."

C Make it personal Talk about viewing tastes!

1 In groups, search online for the videos in A. Vote for your favorite.
2 Share impressions of other clips you've seen. Use expressions in A. Any similar reactions?

music video movie sitcom episode soap opera amateur video documentary

> What was the last documentary you watched?

> I saw a terrifying one on forest fires a few weeks ago. It really left me speechless.

8 Language in use

A Read the website. In pairs, answer 1–3.

1 What's the difference between gossip and news?
2 Which of the three types of gossip might the worker be? Which do you think is most common?
3 Rank the three gossip types most to least harmful.

HERE SHE COMES WITH THE ONE O'CLOCK NEWS

Three types of gossip we've all met!

1 **The forwarder** Forwarders don't start rumors. They simply pass on gossip that comes to them.

2 **The seeker** Seekers are always on the lookout for gossip. They're always seeking someone to fill them in on the latest "news."

3 **The creator** Creators are the ones that start gossip and pass it on, even if they're not 100% sure.

Well, to me, the forwarder is the worst. If you just pass the news on, you're gossiping behind someone's back.

B 11.9 Listen to three conversations taking place in an office. Identify the gossip types.

1 ________ 2 ________ 3 ________

C 11.9 Listen again. M (the man), W (the woman), or N (neither)? Who do you think Truman is?

Who seems ...

Conversation 1	Conversation 2	Conversation 3
1 jealous of Lorrie?	3 to have trouble keeping a secret?	5 sure two people are dating?
2 to dislike gossip?	4 concerned about inconvenience?	6 most worried the rumor might spread?

D 11.10 Complete 1–4. Listen to check. Which expressions describe a) gossip? b) secrecy?

between you and me | my big mouth | keep it to myself | spread it around

1 I asked Truman for a raise last week, but he **refused** to even listen. By the way, this is ________, OK?
2 Truman **made** me swear I'd ________ .
3 If this leaks, Truman will kill me. Once he **threatened** to fire me because of ________, remember?
4 I **begged** him not to ________, and I'm sure he won't. Well, at least, I **expect** him not to.

E **Make it personal** Read the quotes. How strongly do you agree? Write ++ (strongly agree) to - - (strongly disagree). Then compare in groups. Which is the most controversial quote?

1 "I get accused all the time of having a big mouth. But if you ask me, guys gossip way more than girls do." (Meg Cabot)
2 "Whoever gossips to you will gossip about you." (Unknown / graffiti)
3 "Show me someone who never gossips, and I'll show you someone who isn't interested in people." (Barbara Walters)
4 "There is only one thing in the world worse than being talked about, and that is not being talked about." (Oscar Wilde)

Gender terms

Use *woman* and not *girl* to refer to someone who's not a child. Using "girl" can easily offend.

I disagree with the first one. My experience is that women find it harder than men to keep things to themselves.

Hmm ... I don't think gossip has anything to do with gender, actually. It has to do with personality.

9 Grammar: Reporting what people say (2)

A Read the grammar box. Then fill in the blanks with the bold verbs from 8D.

Reporting patterns with the infinitive and base form

1 Verb + (not) + infinitive	She **agreed to tell** me a secret. I **promised to keep** it. Other verbs include ______ and ______ .
2 Verb + object + (not) + infinitive	I **persuaded him to reveal** what he knew. He **urged me not to spread** it around. Other verbs include ______ and ______ .
3 Verb + object + base form	I tried to talk about something else, but she didn't **let me change** the subject. ______ follows the same pattern.

Grammar expansion p.158

B Julia couldn't keep Truman's secret! Complete 1–6 using the verb given and a pattern from the grammar box. Then take turns reporting the whole conversation.

ANN: What were you two gossiping about?
JULIA: Erm ... Nothing.
ANN: (1) I'll keep it to myself. I promise!
JULIA: We weren't gossiping.
ANN: Well, I heard Truman's name. And Lorrie's.
JULIA: Hmm ... (2) I can't tell you. Sorry.
ANN: It must be something big. (3) Don't leave me in suspense!
JULIA: (4) Promise you won't say a word.
ANN: I swear.
JULIA: (5) I'll unfriend you on Facebook® if you do!
ANN: You have my word.
JULIA: (6) All right. I'll tell you.

1 Ann promised *to keep it to herself.*
2 Julia refused ...
3 Ann begged ...
4 Julia made ...
5 Then she threatened ...
6 She finally agreed ...

Ann asked Julia what she and her friend had been gossiping about.

Common mistake

He made me ~~to~~ promise to keep it to myself.

C Make it personal Gossip!

1 11.11 **How to say it** Complete the chart. Then listen, check, and repeat.

Gossiping

	What they said	What they meant
1	You'll never ______ (who I ran into at the mall).	You have no idea (who ...)
2	My ______ are sealed. I won't tell a ______ .	I won't tell anyone.
3	Promise you'll ______ it between the two of us.	Promise you won't tell anyone.
4	You have my ______ .	I promise.

2 Choose a situation, imagine the details, and tell a partner. Ask him / her to be discreet! Use *How to say it* expressions.

You've won a small fortune on the lottery.
Someone in class is actually a secret agent.
You're dating a celebrity.
You've discovered a secret about a classmate.

3 Form new pairs and spread the news. Use reporting verbs. Who's the best gossip?

You'll never guess in a million years who I ran into at the mall over the weekend!

10 Listening

A 11.12 Listen to Rita Sycamore, a young actress, complaining to her friend, Jeb, about a news story. Note down three facts that were wrong.

B 11.13 Listen to the rest of the conversation. Check (✔) the correct answers.

1 Rita is bothered most by the ...
- ☐ invasion of her privacy.
- ☐ inaccuracies in the story.

2 Jeb's main point is that ...
- ☐ fame has more advantages than disadvantages.
- ☐ fame comes at a price.

C 11.13 Listen again and try to complete the sentences. Then check your answers against the definitions. Did you catch all the words and expressions?

1 You'll be ________________ for a day or two. And you know what they say, "Bad publicity is always better than no publicity."

2 Well, if you ask me, celebrity gossip is as ________________ as other more "serious" topics.

3 When you're a celebrity, there's no such thing as privacy. You're ________________ 24/7, and that's exactly the way it should be.

4 I think newspapers are ________________ to publish whatever they like.

entitle (v) (often passive): give someone a legal right or just a claim to receive or do something

in the spotlight (idiom): receiving public notice or attention

newsworthy (adj): important or interesting enough to report as news

the talk of the town (idiom): someone or something everyone is talking about

D **Make it personal** Choose a statement 1–4 in C you (dis)agree with, and share your opinions in pairs. Any major differences?

> I don't agree with the last one. Newspapers should try to be selective about what they publish.

11 Keep talking

A Check (✔) the problems you've experienced for 1–4. Then add one more problem to each group.

1 A TV channel you watch ...
- ☐ presents news that's biased or inaccurate.
- ☐ shows endless reruns of sitcoms.
- ☐ shows content inappropriate for children.

2 Your phone, cable, or Internet company ...
- ☐ keeps sending wrong bills.
- ☐ has terrible customer service.
- ☐ has lots of coverage and stability problems.

3 A recent documentary or news story about your country ...
- ☐ had wrong factual details.
- ☐ made too many generalizations.
- ☐ exaggerated small problems.

4 Your favorite online store ...
- ☐ makes it difficult to find what you want.
- ☐ has security problems.
- ☐ doesn't give enough product information.

B In groups, compare your ideas. Add more details and examples. Which are the most common complaints?

> WEID seems really biased. They only present one side of a story!

> Yeah, I know what you mean. The news just isn't accurate these days.

Common mistakes

There's too ~~many~~ *much* violence on TV.

There's not *enough* educational content ~~enough~~.

12 Writing: A letter of complaint

A Read Rita's letter to the editor of an online newspaper. Which wrong fact from 10A is not mentioned?

Rita Sycamore
101 Maryland Avenue
Pittsburgh, PA 15212

Mr. Jerome Sacks
ID News and Views

May 23, 2016

Dear Mr. Sacks:

I am writing in regard to the photo and the article published in the entertainment section of your home page this morning ("TV star Rita Sycamore spotted with new boyfriend"). I happen to be the woman in the photo and I would like to call your attention to a number of inaccuracies in your article.

You claimed that the man in the photo was my new boyfriend, when, in reality, he is my vocal coach, and our relationship is strictly professional. To make matters worse, my age was incorrect, which shows a lack of attention to detail.

Above all, I am very surprised that a reputable newspaper like yours would even consider publishing stories like this one. It is my belief that celebrities are entitled to the same level of privacy as the general public.

I would like to ask you to remove the photo and article from your website in the next few hours. Tomorrow I will check to confirm that these steps have been taken. Thank you very much for your attention to this matter.

Sincerely,

Rita Sycamore

Rita Sycamore

B Circle the correct options.

A well-organized complaint letter presents the [**situation / solution**] in paragraph 1. It then moves on to a [**problem / suggestion**] in paragraph 2. In paragraph 3, it sometimes presents [**an opinion / only facts**]. Finally, in the last paragraph, the letter often [**makes a request / only gives a summary**].

C Read *Write it right!* Then write the more formal highlighted expressions 1–5 in the chart.

Write it right!

In a formal email or letter:

1 Begin your email with *Dear* + full name or *Dear Sir / Madam*. Sign off with *Sincerely (yours)*.

2 Put a colon (:) after the full name when you begin, but a comma (,) when you sign off.

3 Avoid contractions: ~~*I'm*~~ ***I am*** *writing to complain about ...*

4 Avoid informal language: *There were* ~~*lots of*~~ ***a number of*** (more formal) *inaccuracies in the article.*

"Well, actually ..."	1 ______
"about ..."	2 ______
"I think ..."	3 ______
"I want to point out ..."	4 ______
"Another problem is ..."	5 ______

D Complete 1–5, from different letters and emails, using formal expressions from C.

1 I am writing ______ the programming on your channel.

2 While you claim to have excellent customer service, ______, I had to call five times before someone could help me.

3 ______ the fact that there were a number of factual errors in your recent documentary.

4 ______ that there should be fewer stories on urban violence, especially in that time slot.

5 Your online store is not only hard to navigate. ______, it often lacks sufficient product information.

E **Your turn!** Write a 180-word letter or email complaining about a problem from 11A.

Before
Check the guidelines in B, and decide the main points you will make in each paragraph.

While
Re-read *Write it right!* Use at least four expressions from C, and check the level of formality.

After
Proofread your work carefully. Show it to another student before sending it to your teacher.

12 How optimistic are you?

1 Listening

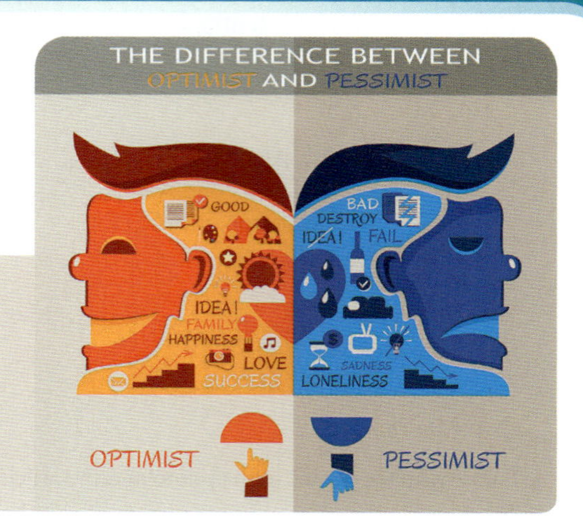

A 12.1 Complete the quotes from a radio show with *an optimist* or *a pessimist*. Listen to check. Which is your favorite?

1 "I used to be __________, but now I know nothing is going to turn out as I expect." Sandra Bullock
2 "__________ sees the difficulty in every opportunity; __________ sees the opportunity in every difficulty." Winston Churchill
3 "The man who is __________ before 48 knows too much; if he is __________ after it, he knows too little." Mark Twain

Common mistakes

Overall, I'd say I'm ~~optimist~~ *an optimist*, but I'm a bit ~~pessimist~~ *pessimistic* about the interview.
Optimist and *pessimist* are nouns. *Optimistic* and *pessimistic* are adjectives.

B 12.2 Listen to the radio show survey and circle the correct answers. Do you feel the same way?

C 12.3 Complete the highlighted expressions in 1–4, using your intuition. Listen to check. Do you have similar ones in your language?

feet	fingers	proportion	store	tunnel	world

1 I keep telling myself that it's **not the end of the __________** (= not a tragedy) if I fail an exam or two, but deep down, I know I'll be really upset. Anyway, I'm **keeping my __________ crossed** (= hoping for the best).
2 They're going through a rough time right now, so who knows **what the future has in __________** (= what will happen) for me.
3 I know we've lost all the games so far this season, but now with this new coach, there might be **a light at the end of the __________** (= some hope).
4 The media tends to **blow things out of __________** (= exaggerate), but, on the whole, I think we're doing OK. Anyway, I try to **keep my __________ on the ground** (= be practical and sensible).

D In groups, take turns miming and guessing the expressions in **C**. Then remember all you can of each conversation. Check in AS 12.2 on p.164. Anything you missed?

E Make it personal In pairs, answer 1–4. Any surprises?

1 Take the survey in **B**. Use expressions from **C** in your answers.
2 Create two other questions to ask each other. Who's more optimistic?
3 Who's the most / least optimistic person in your family? How well do you get along?
4 Does the weather affect your general feelings of optimism / pessimism?

I love cold, rainy days, you know. The grayer the better! I feel really good.

Really? Rainy days always get me down.

2 Listening

A 12.4 Listen to three conversations. O (optimistic) or P (pessimistic)? Have you ever had a similar experience?

Conversation 1	Conversation 2	Conversation 3
1 Ed ______	3 Peter ______	5 Tom ______
2 Sonia ______	4 Kate ______	6 Linda ______

B 12.4 Listen again and check (✔) what you can infer about each person.

1 Ed wasn't surprised he got fired.
2 Sonia thinks Ed's age might have been a problem in the past.
3 Kate likes expensive cars.
4 Kate probably had a big car before.
5 Linda doesn't mind packing.
6 Linda has probably been to Paris before.

C Make it personal Take turns role playing an optimist / pessimist.

1 12.5 **How to say it** Complete the chart. Listen, check, and repeat, copying the intonation.

	Optimism and pessimism	
	What they said	What they meant
1	Let's hope for the ______ .	Let's hope things will turn out well.
2	No ______ is good news.	
3	Look on the ______ side.	Try to find something good about this situation.
4	Better safe than ______ .	It's better to be cautious so you don't regret it later.
5	Yeah, ______ on! (informal)	What you want probably won't happen.
6	That's wishful ______ .	What you want is not realistic.

2 Choose two situations and role play them with a partner. Use *How to say it* expressions.

A ☹ You've just failed an important test. You think you might have to take the course again.
B ☺ Convince **A** that taking the course again will be a good idea.

A ☺ You've just inherited $1 million. You want to quit your job, invest the money, and live off the interest.
B ☹ You think quitting a steady job is too risky.

A ☺ You love to live dangerously. You want to go mountain climbing next weekend.
B ☹ You're scared of extreme sports. Remind **A** of all the risks involved.

3 Language in use

A 12.6 Listen to part 1 of an online program and match conversations 1–4 to pictures a–d. Label the items.

DYING TECHNOLOGIES: WHAT WE SAY ABOUT WHAT THE EXPERTS SAY

a ☐ ______

"Wireless chargers for smartphones are already on the market, and the possibility of Power WiFi is not that far off."
Yes, definitely. Soon you won't have to shout "Watch out! You're going to trip over that thing!" anymore. But we're talking [1] ______ years from now, at least.

b ☐ ______

"Very soon, people are going to be driving into a gas station for a recharge. Or maybe to fill up the tank with a clean [2] ______ , like ethanol."
Gas is bound to be replaced **by** ☐ greener fuels, but the combustion engine won't be going anywhere until electric cars become less [3] ______ .

c ☐ ______

"In the past few years, subscriptions have dropped **by** ☐ more than 50%. By the end of the decade, we'll be using [4] ______ only."
Yes, this trend is likely to continue, except in more remote areas, where there are relatively few cell phone [5] ______ .

d ☐ ______

"**By** ☐ 2020, printed newspapers and magazines will have disappeared without a trace. Online subscriptions are much cheaper."
Newsstands are still going to be around for a while. They'll attract new customers **by** ☐ selling [6] ______ and lottery tickets, for example.

B 12.7 Read the infographic in A and predict the missing information. Listen to part 2 to check. Did you guess correctly? Any you disagreed with?

> I'm not so sure about the first one. I think it will take ... years.

C Read *Uses of by*. Then write 1–4 next to the bold words in A.

Uses of *by*

By is the 30th most common word in English. Here are four important uses:

1 Expresses "not later than":
*I'll get back to you **by** Monday.*

2 Answers the question *how*:
*We're going **by** car.*

3 Indicates the amount:
*Prices have increased **by** 20%.*

4 Identifies the "doer" in passive sentences:
*The telephone was invented **by** Bell.*

D **Make it personal** In pairs, answer 1–4. Similar opinions?

1 Order the technologies in A in the order you think they will disappear.
2 Will you miss them? Why (not)?
3 Which other everyday items / jobs / activities would you like to disappear?
4 What do you think they should be replaced by?

doing dishes   ironing   plastic bags   postal workers   watches

> I think watches are totally useless. I know what time it is by looking at my phone.

4 Grammar: Talking about the future (1)

A Read the grammar box and write the correct numbers (1–3) next to the examples. Then find four more examples of 1 and 2 in the infographic.

Predictions with *going to*, *will*, future perfect, and future continuous

☐ TV sets **will / are going to become** increasingly rare.
☐ People **will / are going to be riding** driverless cars.
☐ Bookstores **will have disappeared** by 2030.

1 Actions completed before some point in the future.
2 Actions in progress at some point in the future.
3 Future predictions in general.

Will and *going to* are often interchangeable, but *going to* is more common when you are sure of your prediction because there is evidence:
*Watch out! You'**re going to spill** coffee on your phone.*

Common mistake

By the end of this lesson, you ~~will read~~ *will have read* 129 pages of *Identities 1*.

B More predictions! Correct four mistakes in the predictions below. There may be more than one answer.

ALSO ON THEIR WAY OUT

Prescription glasses
With laser eye surgery and contact lenses, it's possible that in the not-too-distant future we'll have lived in a world free of glasses. Sunglasses will still around for a while, though, for sure.

Writing by hand
By the end of the decade, possibly before that, handwriting as an educational requirement will be dropping from the national curriculum. By the time you read this, you won't write a letter by hand for ages.

C Read *Other ways to make predictions*. Rephrase three sentences in **B** using *be likely to* and *be bound to*.

Other ways to make predictions

You can use *be (un)likely to* and *be bound to* when making predictions. *Be bound to* is more definite:
Next year **is likely to be** better than this year. (I'm pretty sure it will be better.)
Climate change **is bound to get** worse. (I'm almost certain it will get worse.)

D Make it personal In groups, guess what life will be like in 2050. Who predicts the brightest future?

English food household chores marriage post offices school tests shopping

I think ... are going to ...

... are bound to ...

By ... I think ... will have ...

... will be ... *-ing*

What do you think the future has in store for us as far as household chores?

I'm sure people won't be spending their free time vacuuming or ironing.

5 Reading

A In groups, make a list of things you know about Mars in one minute. Which group has the longest list?

Scientists have found water on Mars, right? But I'm not sure whether it's drinkable.

Common mistake

I don't believe there's intelligent life ~~in~~ *on* other planets.

B In pairs, explore the photo: *where*, *what*, *who*, *when*, and *why*? Read paragraph 1 to check. Does the writer feel optimistic or pessimistic about the project?

C Read only the first sentence of paragraph 2 and guess why the writer feels this way. Then read to check. Do the same for paragraphs 3–5. Were you surprised?

Not the kind of place to raise your kids. Or is it?

After the blockbuster movie *The Martian* in 2015, it seems we've been witnessing a new wave of enthusiasm for the idea that in the near future, some of us are going to be living on Mars. A Dutch nonprofit organization called Mars One, for example, is hoping to send four people on a one-way trip to Mars by 2026, as the beginning of a permanent human colony, which could in the long run ease overcrowding on Earth. To be honest, I still **have my doubts** [1] about whether this is a viable mission.

To begin with, getting there will be a nightmare. A trip to Mars will take up to nine months, which is a long time, especially when four people will be floating around in a tiny capsule, subjected to low gravity and insanely high levels of radiation. Then there are the inevitable equipment failures, which could **pose** [2] **a threat** to the whole mission. But that's just the beginning.

People seem to **overlook** [3] **the fact that** Mars is horribly inhospitable. The average temperature is minus 63 degrees Celsius, far too cold for it to rain, and people would need to **figure out** [4] **a way** to endure the year-long cold. Then there's breathing. The atmosphere is 96% carbon dioxide, so oxygen must be artificially synthesized, which will be **hard to pull off** [5]. And extremely dangerous, since peaks of oxygen may be potentially lethal, too.

Another key question is how the crew's health will be affected. Their bones and muscles evolved under Earth's gravity and on Mars they will weigh 30% of what they weigh on Earth. This means they're bound to lose a lot of muscle mass – and that includes the heart. Speaking of heart, their feelings of isolation and loneliness will probably be devastating, especially as time goes on. We don't **have a clue** [6] how this will affect their mental health.

And finally, the costs are going to be quite literally astronomical. At an estimated cost of $6 billion (!) for the first flight, the whole project begs the question: Is colonizing Mars worth the investment – and the risk? Wouldn't it be wiser to use this money to fix our own planet first?

D Read *How to know if a writer is certain*. Then re-read the article and write + (more certain) or – (less certain) for 1–5, according to the text. Underline the evidence.

1 There will be technical problems in the spacecraft.
2 Too much oxygen will kill them.
3 Their hearts will get weaker.
4 They will go crazy eventually.
5 The mission will cost $6 billion.

How to know if a writer is certain

	more certain	less certain
adverbs	The whole thing will **inevitably** fail.	It will cost $10 million, **possibly** $20 million.
adjectives	It's **bound** to go wrong.	There are a lot of **potential** problems.
expressions	It's off to a bad start, **without a doubt**.	**Who knows** what's in store for us.
modals	It'**ll** be a disaster.	It **might** backfire eventually.

E ▶ 12.8 Read and listen. Notice the schwa /ə/ in the words ending in *-al* and *-able*.

F **Make it personal** In pairs, answer 1–3. Anything in common?

1 Why would anyone volunteer for a mission like that? Would you?
2 How would you answer the last question in paragraph 5? Give three reasons.
3 Imagine you're one of the astronauts. You can take three personal objects with you. What would you take and why? (Remember: No phones!)

I think I'd take a photo of my family.

You mean, so you could feel close to them, even if you couldn't see them?

6 Vocabulary: Expressions for discussing innovation

A Match the bold words 1–6 in the article in 5C with their meanings a–f. Then in pairs, test each other. Say the highlighted expression from memory and give an example sentence.

a ☐ achieve c 1 feelings of uncertainty e ☐ find
b ☐ ignore d ☐ relevant information f ☐ represent

Doubts ...

Have my doubts. I have my doubts about life on Mars.

B Complete the forum entries with the highlighted expressions 1–6 in 5C. Who do you agree with?

Cars that drive themselves: a blessing or a curse?

Aron4: The problem with the scientists behind this new driverless car is that they tend to [1] __________ a lot of people actually enjoy driving – at least I know I do. So I [2] __________ whether self-driving cars will ever become popular.

Paula87: As far as the technology itself is concerned, I imagine a self-driving car wouldn't be [3] __________ . In fact, lots of prototypes already exist and have been tested on roads, with very few accidents, which means they probably won't [4] __________ to pedestrians and other drivers.

JJWilcox: Everyone's hyped up about driverless cars, but the truth is, we don't [5] __________ what our roads will be like with thousands of these. How safe and reliable are these cars, really?

Freerider©: Another car? Really? What the government should do is [6] __________ to persuade people to use their bikes or public transportation.

C **Make it personal** Rate each innovation below from 1 (unnecessary) to 4 (very necessary). In groups, share your ideas. Which innovation is most (least) popular?

Stuff we might see by 2025:

the end of physical classrooms DNA mapping at birth to manage disease risk pills to replace sleep
4D TVs cosmetic face transplants the end of baldness music written by machines

I gave "music written by machines" a 2.

Me too. Machines are bound to be less creative than people!

7 Language in use

A In groups, make a list of excuses people usually make in situations 1–3. Which cartoon do you like best?

1 Leaving work early

2 Traffic violations

3 Being late

When people want to leave work early, they often say, "I'm not feeling well."

B 12.9 Listen to Don's excuses and take notes. Who do you think believed him?

	2:00 p.m.	3:00 p.m.	4:00 p.m.
1 Who's he talking to?			
2 What's the excuse?			
3 Why did he make it?			

C 12.10 Complete the text with the words from the mind map. Listen to Don's conversation the next day to check.

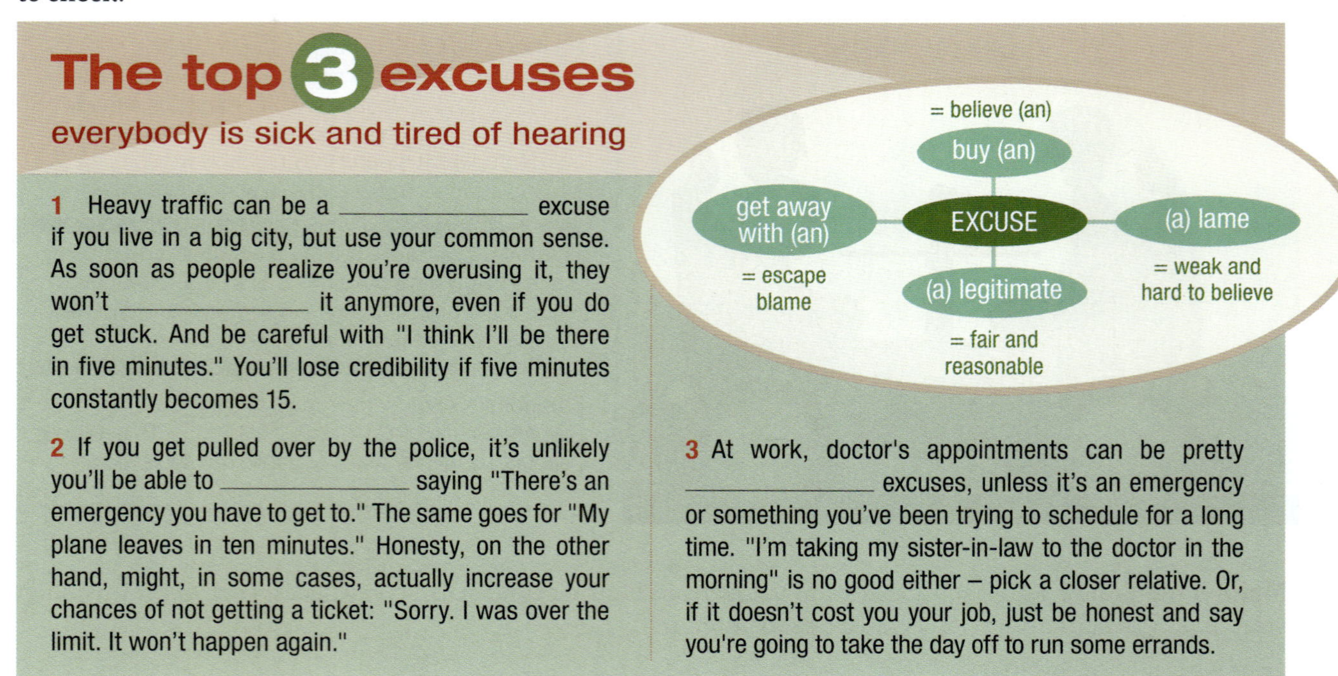

The top 3 excuses
everybody is sick and tired of hearing

EXCUSE: buy (an) = believe (an); get away with (an) = escape blame; (a) lame = weak and hard to believe; (a) legitimate = fair and reasonable

1 Heavy traffic can be a ______________ excuse if you live in a big city, but use your common sense. As soon as people realize you're overusing it, they won't ______________ it anymore, even if you do get stuck. And be careful with "I think I'll be there in five minutes." You'll lose credibility if five minutes constantly becomes 15.

2 If you get pulled over by the police, it's unlikely you'll be able to ______________ saying "There's an emergency you have to get to." The same goes for "My plane leaves in ten minutes." Honesty, on the other hand, might, in some cases, actually increase your chances of not getting a ticket: "Sorry. I was over the limit. It won't happen again."

3 At work, doctor's appointments can be pretty ______________ excuses, unless it's an emergency or something you've been trying to schedule for a long time. "I'm taking my sister-in-law to the doctor in the morning" is no good either – pick a closer relative. Or, if it doesn't cost you your job, just be honest and say you're going to take the day off to run some errands.

D **Make it personal** In pairs, talk about the last lame excuse you or someone else made. Did you / the other person buy it?

Last week my oldest friend forgot to call me on my birthday and said her phone was stolen. Of course I didn't buy it. I mean, she could have Skyped me.

Pretty lame, huh? Or at least sent an e-card or message!

8 Grammar: Talking about the future (2)

A Study the examples and complete rules a–d with 1–4. Then write the correct rule (a–d) next to the quotes in 7C.

Expressing plans and intentions, decisions, and scheduled events

Listen, I have to go. The bus **leaves** at seven.
I'm going to join a gym. I**'m signing up** today!

My battery is almost dead. I**'ll give** you a call later!
I'm not sure, but maybe I**'ll take** a course this summer.

Use the ... 1 simple present 2 present continuous as future 3 future with *going to* 4 future with *will*

a ___ for a decision or promise you make at the moment you're speaking.
b ___ for events on a schedule or timetable, with verbs like *open*, *close*, *arrive*, and *start*.
c ___ for plans and intentions you're not sure of with expressions like *I guess*, *I think*, and *probably*.
d ___ or ___ for a fixed decision or plan you've already made.

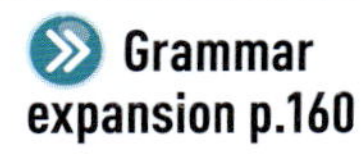
Grammar expansion p.160

B 12.11 Don's boss, Miranda, is having a difficult day at the office. Circle the best answers 1–6. Listen to check.

1 I [**'ll fire** / **'m going to fire**] Sue Ann. She's been late every day for two weeks!
2 Please talk to her first. Or I [**'ll talk** / **'m talking**] to her for you.
3 OK, I [**give** / **'ll give**] her one more chance. But this is the last one!
4 Excuse me, Miranda, I [**'ll probably be** / **'m probably being**] late tomorrow.
5 I [**'m taking** / **'ll take**] my grandmother to the doctor.
6 Unacceptable! Our meeting [**starts** / **will start**] at 9:00 a.m.! One more excuse and you're fired!

C Read *Time clauses*. Then complete 1–4 with a suitable verb.

Time clauses

Always use the simple present in time clauses with words like *when*, *after*, *as soon as*, *before*, and *until*:

I'm going to buy a car **as soon as** I turn 18. (= immediately after)
I'm finishing the report **before** I leave.
I won't leave **until** the rain stops. (= up to the point that)

Common mistake

I think she'll get promoted as soon as she ~~will graduate~~ *graduates*.

1 Going abroad: "I'm not going abroad until my English ________ better."
2 Saving money: "I'm going to start saving money when my boss ________ me a raise."
3 Finishing an assignment: "I'll get started after I ________ the dishes and check my newsfeed."
4 Eating healthier food: "I'll change my diet when my doctor ________ I'm in trouble."

D Rewrite 1–4 in C using the words below. Which sentence is true for you?

1 as soon as 2 until 3 before 4 until

I'm going abroad as soon as my English is better.

E **Make it personal** In pairs, share stories about 1–3. Make one untrue. Can your partner guess which one?

1 Something you're not going to do even though you should. What's your excuse?
2 Someone you're meeting in the next few days even though you'd rather not. If you make an excuse, will he/she buy it?
3 Something old / useless you think you'll throw away soon. What's wrong with it?

I think I'll throw away all of my CDs this week. They take up a lot of space.

Me too. I'm getting rid of mine as soon as I can upload all of them.

9 Listening

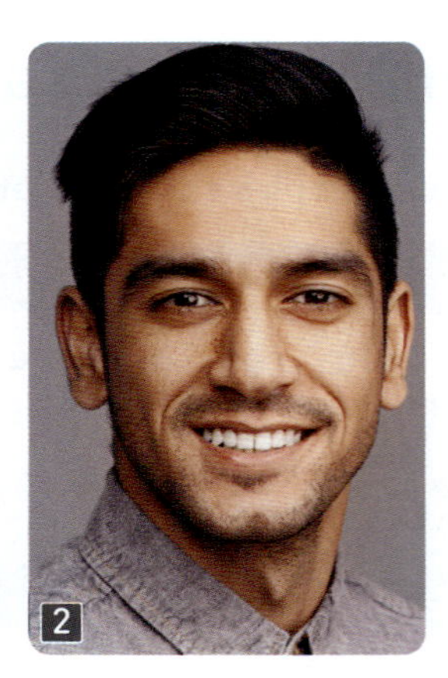

A 12.12 Listen to Fred talking about a contest he entered. Answer 1–3.

1 What does Fred have to do?
2 What was the example he gave Tina?
3 How much older is Fred in photo 2?

B 12.13 Listen to Fred 10 years later and complete sentences 1–4. One choice is used twice. Is Fred pleased with his decisions?

a expected to	b didn't expect to	c wondered if he'd

When Fred was younger, he ...

1 ______ look this old.
2 ______ become a teacher.
3 ______ have a girlfriend.
4 ______ to live at home after graduation.

C 12.12 & 12.13 Complete 1–7 with the correct prepositions. Listen again to check. Did you understand all the highlighted expressions?

1 I'm taking part ______ a writing contest.
2 I could do ______ a little extra cash.
3 What ______ earth is that?
4 You could start with something ______ the lines of "Dear Tina ..."
5 Well, it's now a number of years ______ the road.
6 It may not satisfy me totally ______ a personal level.
7 That should be the least ______ your problems.

10 Keep talking

A Think ahead 10 years. What would you say now to your future self? Make notes on at least three topics.

career family life fitness and health friends looks love life money studies travel

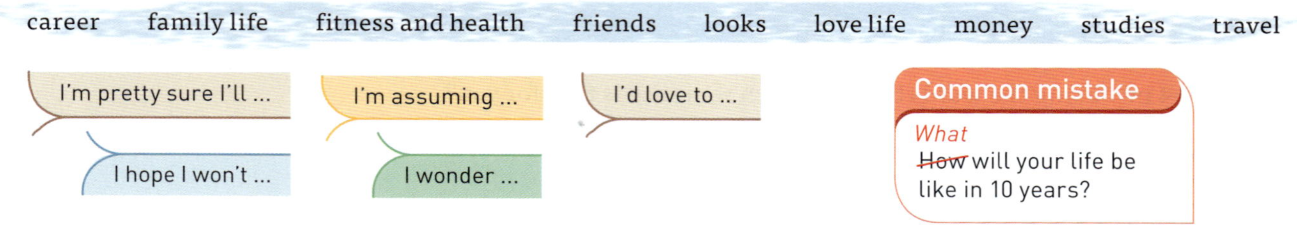

Common mistake

What
~~How~~ will your life be like in 10 years?

B In groups, compare ideas about your future selves. Any coincidences?

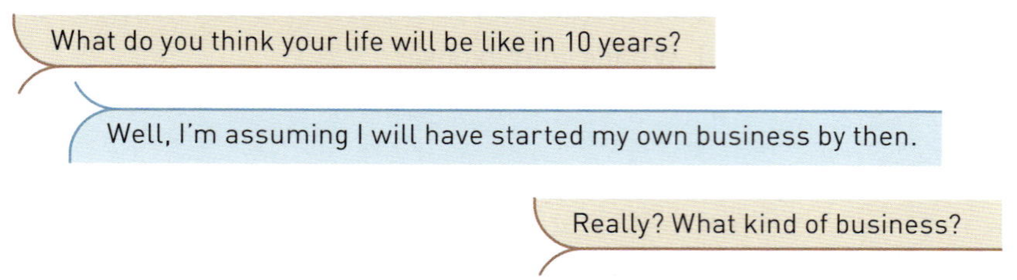

11 Writing: An email to your future self

A Read Nina's email to her future self. Are any of your ideas from 10A mentioned?

From: Present Nina
Subject: Future Me
To: Future Nina

Dear Future Me,

I've just come across a website that allows someone to send an email to his or her "future self" 10 years from now. I thought, "What a cool idea!" And so, here it is: my first email to you, "Future Me." Today is August 30, 2016, so, when you read this, [1]you'll be celebrating your 27th birthday. I know you're not too crazy about birthday parties, so I hope you make it through this one! Well, at least you'll be surrounded by all the people you love, that's for sure.

Next year you're going off to college. Or maybe you'll end up taking a year off to travel around the world and do some volunteer work. Who knows? By 2022, [2]you'll have graduated and found a nice job in your field. Aren't you lucky that, unlike some of your classmates, you'll be able to build a career from your passion – looking after animals? Call me an optimist, but I'm sure [3]you'll become one of the best vets in the city!

As to marriage ... Well, I could be wrong, of course, but I have my doubts you'll want to settle down and have kids before you're in your thirties. You've always valued your freedom more than anything else and something tells me you'll want to enjoy your single life for as long as you can. Hmm ... What else? Oh, that trip to Cappadocia, Turkey, to go hot-air ballooning? When you read this email again, [4]you'll have done that – maybe more than once! Trust me!

Aren't you proud of yourself for writing this email in English? Wow! [5]You'll be an advanced student next year! Doesn't time fly? You may be a bit tired of studying English right now, but stick with it! I'm sure it will have been worthwhile in the end.

Future Nina, you'll have a bright future, wherever you are and whatever you may be doing. I'll do my best to help, I promise.

Love,
Present Nina

B In pairs, explain the purpose of each paragraph.

I think the first one explains what the email is about.

Yes, and it tells us something about Nina. It's an introduction.

C Read *Write it right!* Then complete rules 1–2 with *after* or *before*.

Write it right!

Use adverbs for emphasis and to show how certain you are of something:

I hope that, by the end of the year, my boss will have **finally** promoted me to assistant manager. I'll **definitely** be making more money, I know, but my workload will **inevitably** increase, too.

In sentences with *will*, adverbs usually go ...

1 ________ *will* and ________ the main verb.
2 ________ the auxiliary *be*, but ________ the auxiliary *have*.

D Add these adverbs to the underlined phrases in A (1–5).

1 (probably) *you'll probably be celebrating*
2 (hopefully) ________
3 (eventually) ________
4 (certainly) ________
5 (officially) ________

E Your turn! Write an email of 200–250 words to your future self.

Before
Choose three or four topics from *Keep talking* in 10A.

While
Refer to B and make sure each paragraph has a clear purpose. Re-read *Write it right!* and use a variety of adverbs in your predictions.

After
Post your writing, and if possible, set a delivery date to receive your own email.

Review 6

Units 11–12

1 Listening

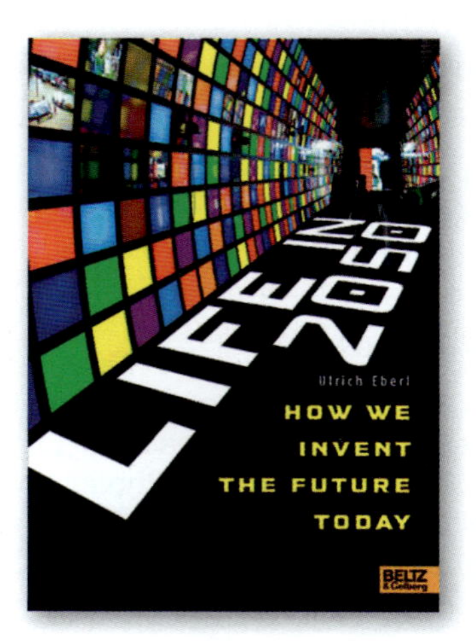

A R6.1 Listen to a conversation about Ulrich Eberl's book *Life in 2050*. Complete the sentences.

By 2050 ...

1 you'll be using a computer the size of a __________ .
2 a computer will be able to __________ a car.
3 there will be __________ farms in cities.
4 cars will be __________ to each other.
5 a "smart apartment" will recognize your __________ .
6 one in every six people will be over the age of __________ .

B **Make it personal** In groups, suggest as many innovations as you can for 2050 in two minutes. Which group has the most interesting ones?

I think food production will have doubled by 2050.

We'll be eating a lot more ...

2 Grammar

A Report the conversation using the words in parentheses.

GINA: I have something to tell you. (Gina told Len ...)

Gina told Len that she had something to tell him.

LEN: Really? Is it good news? (Len asked Gina ...)
GINA: Not really. (Gina admitted ...) I fell asleep during my interview last week. (She explained ...)
LEN: I don't believe it! (Len said ...)
GINA: It's true. (Gina assured Len ...) I don't think I got the job. (She added ...)
LEN: It's unlikely. (Len warned Gina ...) But some bosses have a kind heart! (But he reminded her ...)

B Report what happened next using the words in parentheses.

1 "Call your interviewer in the morning." (Len urged Gina ...)
2 "Please give me another chance." (Gina begged her interviewer ...)
3 "I'll go to bed early from now on." (She promised ...)
4 "I can't schedule another interview." (First, her interviewer refused ...)
5 "OK, I'll think it over and call you next week." (Then he agreed ...)

C Circle the correct future form for each of Gina's sentences.

1 [**I'm going to have** / **I'll have**] another interview tomorrow after all.
2 [**I'm getting** / **I get**] there early. That's for sure.
3 Maybe [**I'll go** / **I'm going**] to sleep at 9:00 p.m., too.
4 As soon as [**I'll get** / **I get**] home, I'll start preparing.

D **Make it personal** In pairs, role play one of these situations.

1 Report an embarrassing incident that happened to you or someone you know.
2 Apologize for something you've done and say what you've decided to do differently.

3 Reading

A Read the blog about the future. The main purpose of the blog is to ...

- [ ] frighten people.
- [ ] encourage people to read about environmental problems.
- [ ] encourage people to join the organization and take action.

FIFTY YEARS FROM NOW ... by David Montalbán

When most people think about the future, they only think of positive developments: advances in medicine and technology, better living conditions, higher salaries. Concernedcitizens.id. is more realistic. The future is in our hands only if we are aware and responsible. Some of these facts may shock you!

- In a recent year, 22 million people, many of them poor, were displaced by natural disasters. People living in coastal areas will continue to suffer in the years ahead. Yet, despite enormous evidence to the contrary, some scientists still argue that computer models are "not sophisticated enough" to predict climate change. Is it that they don't want to spend money to control carbon monoxide emissions that raise the earth's temperature? What can you do to prevent global warming?
- By 2050, the Earth's population will have increased from 7 billion to 9.6 billion people. There will not be enough resources for so many people, especially if flooding and drought increase due to climate change. We will need more recycling and more solar energy. Farmers will need incentives to grow food in an environmentally sound way. But do you know how to prevent overuse of fertilizers or how to increase sustainable farming on dry land? And do you recycle all you can?

If these and other facts concern you, become involved! Contact us at concernedcitizens.id to see how you can get help. The future is now!

B In pairs, search on "global warming" or "preserving our resources." Then answer one of the writer's questions in a way you think he'd agree with.

4 Self-test

Correct the two mistakes in each sentence. Check your answers in Units 11 and 12. What's your score, 1–20?

1 I try to keep up the news, even though it's often bias.
2 My girlfriend said me she was sorry and admitted me she was wrong.
3 I promised her to keep the secret, and I agreed her not to tell anyone.
4 I explained my teacher I'm not sure of the answer.
5 My mother persuaded me apologize and she made me to call right away.
6 I'm definitely optimist, so I'm keeping my fingers cross about the future.
7 We're going there on bus, and as soon as we'll arrive, I'll be in touch.
8 By the time you read this, you will almost finish *Identities*, and you will likely to know a lot of English!
9 I'm giving you a call later. Maybe I'm taking a nap first.
10 I visit Larry this weekend, so I won't see you until I'll get back.

5 Point of view

Choose a topic. Then support your opinion in 100–150 words, and record your answer. Ask a partner for feedback. How can you be more convincing?

a You think gossip is part of human nature and no big deal. OR
You think gossip can be very dangerous and should be avoided at all cost.

b You think the economic situation is bad, and there's a lot to be pessimistic about. OR
You think there will always be jobs for people who are well qualified, and it's important to be optimistic.

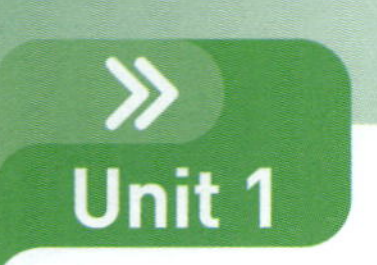

1 *stop*, *remember*, *forget*, and *try* do after 1.2

I **stopped to buy** some meat for dinner. (= I stopped at the store in order to buy meat.) I **stopped buying** meat when I became a vegetarian. (= I no longer buy meat.)
I **remembered to call** Dad on his birthday. (= I didn't forget to call Dad.) I'm sure I talked to Dad last week, but I don't even **remember calling** him. (= I don't have a memory of the fact that I called Dad.)
I sometimes **forget to call** my parents to say I'll be late. (= I don't always remember to call my parents.) I'll **never forget calling** my parents to say I was getting married. They were so thrilled! (= I remember clearly calling my parents.)
I'm **trying to concentrate**. Please be quiet. (= I'm attempting to concentrate.) I **tried writing** down new words, but I still couldn't remember them. (= I experimented with writing down new words.)

More on *try* and *forget*

Only use *try* + *-ing* when the meaning is "to experiment with something." When the meaning is "to attempt," use an infinitive:
I've been **trying to be** nicer to my little sister.

Only use *forget* + *-ing* to remember the past. Otherwise, use the infinitive.
I sometimes **forget to set** the alarm, and then I'm late for school.

2 Using the infinitive with adjectives: More on negative sentences do after 1.4

Pay close attention to the position of the negative. Whether it goes with the verb or the adjective often depends on what's being emphasized.
It's important for you **not** to go. (= You shouldn't go.) It's **not** important for you to go. (= You don't have to go.)
It's critical for my daughter **not** to fail her exam. (= She must pass.) It's **not** critical for my daughter to pass her exam. (= It's OK if she fails.)

Sometimes if you move the negative, the sentence no longer makes sense. When in doubt, say the sentence aloud.
It's essential **not** to feel intimidated during an interview. (= Relax and don't feel intimidated.)
~~It's **not** essential to feel intimidated during an interview~~. (= Meaning is unclear.)

Sometimes both choices are possible and have a very similar meaning.	
It's **not** helpful to ... It's helpful **not** to ...	pressure your children. (= You shouldn't pressure them.)

1A Complete 1–8 with the infinitive or *-ing* form of the verbs.

1 I remember _________ (meet) Tim at a party last year. He was thinner then.
2 We stopped _________ (look) at the flowers. They were really beautiful.
3 I'm trying _________ (finish) as fast as I can! Be patient.
4 She stopped _________ (go) to dance class. She said it was really boring.
5 At the last minute, we remembered _________ (take) an umbrella. It's a good thing because it started pouring!
6 He forgot _________ (check) that the door was locked, and a robber walked in.
7 I tried _________ (take) French classes, but in the end, I realized I liked English better.
8 I just can't forget _________ (see) Tom again after all these years. I think I'm still in love!

1B **Make it personal** Write and share three facts about yourself. Use *remember*, *stop*, *try*, or *forget*.

2A Match the sentence beginnings with the most logical ending.

1 It's important not to — a ☐ agree with everything your teenager says.
2 It's not important to — b ☐ contradict your children in front of their friends. It could embarrass them.

3 It's not essential for you to — a ☐ understand your children at all times.
4 It's essential for you not to — b ☐ have rigid opinions.

5 It's not critical for older parents to — a ☐ be stuck in the past.
6 It's critical for older parents not to — b ☐ be up-to-date with technology.

2B Choose two sentences you agree with from A. Then give a reason for your opinion.

2C Circle the most logical options. When both seem possible, circle both.

[1][**It's important not to / It's not important to**] think all teenagers are alike. People mature at different rates, and [2][**it's useful not to / it's not useful to**] make comparisons. If you want to have a good relationship with your teen, [3][**it's essential not to / it's not essential to**] make unrealistic demands. In addition, things were very different when you were young, and it's [4][**critical not to / not critical to**] be close-minded. Teens listen to their friends more than their parents, and it's [5][**helpful not to / not helpful to**] begin sentences with "When I was your age ... "

Bonus! Language in song

♪ It's been a hard day's night, and I've been working like a dog.

- What do you think the expression "a hard day's night" means?
- Give the singer from 1.3 on page 11 some advice beginning with "It's important (not) to ..."

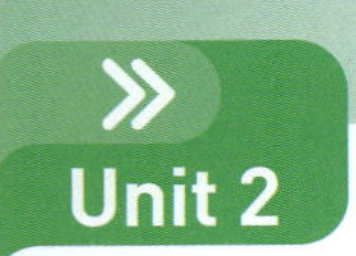

1 Sentences with complements and conjunctions do after 2.2

Sentences with complements can be followed by a conjunction and another sentence.

Less formal	The most difficult thing about having children is it's expensive,	**and**	it's hard work, too.
	The advantage of working is I make money,	**so**	I'm looking for a job.
	The great thing about exercise is losing weight,	**but**	it's time-consuming.
More formal	The problem with teenagers is they don't think.	**Furthermore,**	they don't listen.
	The problem with English is pronunciation.	**Therefore,**	I need more practice.
	The great thing about technology is being connected all the time.	**However,**	it's expensive.

Common mistake

The problem with coffee is it keeps me ~~up so~~ *up, so* I never drink it at night.

The great thing about coffee is the ~~taste, however~~ *taste. However,* it keeps me up.

2 More on modals do after 2.4

Using modals in negative sentences

	Present	Past
Maybe it's true.	There might / may **not** be aliens.	It might / may **not** have visited us.
I'm pretty sure it's true.	It must **not** be a ghost.	You must **not** have seen him.
I really doubt it's true.	You can'**t** / couldn'**t** be serious!	It can'**t** / couldn'**t** have been an alien.

Common mistake

He ~~mustn't~~ *must not* have been home. He would have opened the door. I'm pretty sure.

Mustn't expresses prohibition in British English (American English = *can't*), but it cannot express probability.

Using modals in continuous sentences

	Present	Past
Maybe it's true.	They **might** / **may (not) be watching** TV.	He **might** / **may (not) have been** robbing the house.
I'm pretty sure it's true.	It **must (not) be raining**.	You **must (not) have been paying attention**.
I really doubt it's true.	You **can't** / **couldn't be thinking** clearly!	We **can't / couldn't have been driving** that fast.

Common mistake

He ~~must have been~~ *was probably* being influenced by others.

Modal verbs are not used in the passive in continuous tenses.

1A Combine two advantages of fast food, or an advantage and a disadvantage, to give five opinions with conjunctions. Watch your punctuation!

Advantages	Disadvantages
it's ready made	it's not fresh
it tastes good	it usually has too much salt
it doesn't go bad	you don't know how old it is
it's not expensive	it's bad for you
you always enjoy your meal	children need healthy food
children love it	
they sell it everywhere	

The good thing about fast food is that it's ready made. However, you don't know how old it is.

1B Share in pairs. How many different combinations did you make in A?

2A Rewrite the underlined parts of the sentences with an affirmative or negative modal verb.

1 I really doubt there's life on other planets. We would have had some visitors by now.
2 I'm worried about Tim. He didn't answer his phone, but maybe he was sleeping.
3 I'm pretty sure Sheila didn't take her keys, and that's why she had to sleep in a hotel.
4 I'm pretty sure Amy wasn't paying attention. That's why she had an accident.
5 I really doubt a monkey was climbing in the window! You must have seen a shadow.
6 Roger didn't show up for his appointment because I'm pretty sure he didn't remember it.

2B Complete the story with past modal verbs in the continuous form, using the verbs in parentheses.

Ape costume or the real thing?

No one would believe this, but a gorilla [1]*might have been living* (maybe / live) in my neighborhood last year. It was filmed on video at about 1:00 a.m. one Saturday night. At that moment, a car [2]_________ (probably / approach) because the headlights revealed a gorilla's face on a video the neighbors had installed to monitor coyotes. Then, suddenly, it disappeared.

It [3]_________ (maybe / hide) behind some parked cars because no one could find it. I think the gorilla was frightened. It [4]_________ (probably / not / expect) to see anyone.

When I told the story to my brother, though, he said the neighborhood [5]_________ (probably / imagine) things. A gorilla [6]_________ (very much doubt / walk) in the neighborhood. A person [7]_________ (probably / wear) an ape costume. He or she [8]_________ (maybe / come) home from a party.

2C Make it personal Using modals, share something surprising about your own neighborhood that you can't explain.

I think someone might be living on our roof. I found a shoe in the elevator!

Bonus! Language in song

♫ All day long I think of things, but nothing seems to satisfy. Think I'll lose my mind if I don't find something to pacify.

Rewrite this song lyric from 2.1, beginning with "The most difficult thing about my day is ... " Then combine the two sentences in the song with a conjunction.

1 Uses of the past perfect do after 3.2

The past perfect is used to avoid misunderstanding.	
When my boyfriend **got** home,	he **texted** me. (= the actions occurred almost simultaneously)
	he **had already texted** me. (= he texted before he got home)
By the time my boyfriend got home,	he **had (already) texted** me. (= identical in meaning to above)

1 Always use the past perfect with *by the time*. Add *already* to avoid ambiguity.
2 We often avoid the past perfect when a misunderstanding is unlikely, even if one action clearly takes place before another.
- I **didn't get up** in time to have breakfast before I left for school.
- When the singer **walked** on stage, everyone **applauded.**

Common mistake

Oh hi, I ~~hadn't seen~~ *didn't see* you earlier. Sorry I didn't say "hello."

The past perfect is common with these expressions:
I was already working **by the time** I'd started college.
I didn't start studying English **until after** I'd finished high school.
I had studied English **before** / **previously**, but I didn't remember much.
I had **already** bought a house when I got married.
I hadn't bought a house **yet** when I had children.
I **still** hadn't saved much money when I turned 30.
Up until last year, I'd never met anyone from the U.S.

2 Past narration do after 3.4

Use *used to* and *would* to set the scene. Then use past tenses to show the order of events and whether they were continuous.

We **used to live** in an old house, and every so often we **would hear** noises. One day, I **was brushing** my teeth when I **heard** a strange, high-pitched sound. Before I could figure out where it **was coming** from, I **saw** glass on the floor. Someone or something **had broken** the window.

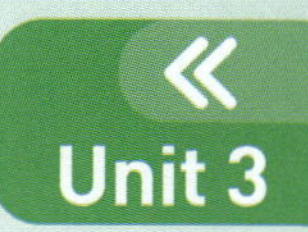

1A Complete the conversations with the correct form of the verbs in parentheses.

1 A: When I was a child, I really ________ (enjoy) playing alone.
B: Really? I never did.

2 A: When I arrived at the party, everyone ________ (leave).
B: You mean no one was there at all?

3 A: When Susanna arrived at the airport, her brother ________ (greet) her warmly.
B: I bet she was really happy to see him.

4 A: Hello, when I ________ (call) this morning for an appointment, no one ________ (answer) the phone.
B: Oh, we're so sorry. When would you like to come?

5 A: When Amy met George, she ________ (already / date) several other guys.
B: Yes, but he was "the one" for her from the second she saw him!

6 A: I was so worried about Tim when he disappeared on our hike.
B: Yes, when Sue and I finally saw him, we ________ (run) up and ________ (hug) him.

1B Make it personal Complete 1–6 so they are true for you. Use each verb only once. Share with a partner. Did you learn anything new?

be decide do go learn start

1 Up until last year, I ______________________________ .
2 I __________ yet when I ______________________________ .
3 Before I __________ , I __________ never ______________ .
4 Until after __________ , I ______________________________ .
5 By the time I __________ , I __________ already ______________ .
6 I still __________ when I ______________________________ .

2A Circle the correct forms to complete the story.

I [1][**used to love** / **would love**] going to the beach, and I would go there whenever we could. One day I [2][**was** / **had been**] in the car with some friends when all of a sudden, I [3][**realized** / **had realized**] I had left my bathing suit at home. By the time I [4][**discovered** / **had discovered**] I didn't have it, we [5][**drove** / **had driven**] for over three hours. I still [6][**didn't go** / **hadn't gone**] swimming that summer, so I decided to make a bathing suit. First, I [7][**took** / **had taken**] my blouse, and I cut off the sleeves. Then I [8][**rolled** / **had rolled**] up the bottom and tied it to look like a bikini. I [9][**saw** / **had seen**] a friend do that previously, and it looked like a real bathing suit. Then I [10][**did** / **had done**] the same with my jeans. And here's the selfie I [11][**took** / **had taken**]! Only after I [12][**went** / **had gone**] swimming and everyone had complimented me on my new bathing suit, did I realize that I [13][**had** / **'d had**] no clothes to wear home!

2B Make it personal When was the last time you left something important at home? Complete the paragraph. Who has the best story?

One day I ________ when I realized I'd forgotten my ________ . By the time I remembered, I ________ . When I arrived at ________ , I had to ________ . To this day, I still ______________________ .

Bonus! Language in song

♪ I **used to rule** the world, Seas **would rise** when I **gave** the word, Now in the morning I sleep alone, Sweep the streets I **used to own**.

Which verbs in **bold** can be replaced by a different past form?

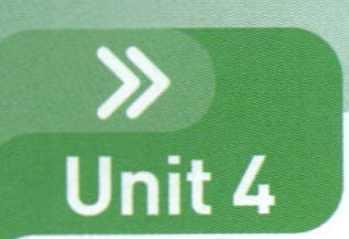

1 Using conjunctions do after 4.2

Common conjunctions fall into several categories of meaning.

Adding	Comparing / Contrasting	Conceding
besides	unlike	although
moreover	while	even though
what's more	whereas	though
	but	despite
	however	in spite of

Some can be followed by more parts of speech than others. Notice the position of *not* in negative statements.

Although **Even though** **While**	my phone's **not** expensive, (sentence)	it works great.
Despite **In spite of**	the fact that it's **not** expensive, (clause) **not** being expensive, (*-ing* form)	it has tons of features.
	the expense, (noun)	I buy a new phone every year.

2 More on reflexive pronouns do after 4.4

Some verbs are commonly used with reflexive pronouns.

Be careful! You'll **cut yourself**.
Melanie dived into the pool and **hurt herself**.
I really **enjoyed myself** last night at the party.
I met Sam at the concert when he came up and **introduced himself**.
Can you believe John and Louise **taught themselves** to speak Arabic?

Other verbs: *prepare, dry, help, imagine, express*

Other verbs, however, only use a reflexive pronoun for emphasis.

I forgot to **shave** today. I hope it's not obvious!
I forgot to **shave myself**. I was in a really big hurry this morning.

Other verbs: *feel, shower, get dressed, get up*

And some verbs, such as *concentrate* or *focus*, don't use reflexive pronouns.

I couldn't **concentrate** in class today. I was so tired!

1A Combine 1–7 in two different ways, using the conjunctions in parentheses.

1 I did a lot of research. I was taken in by the phone company's offer. (*despite + -ing; although*)
Despite doing a lot of research, I was taken in by the phone company's offer.
Although I did a lot of research, I was taken in by the phone company's offer.
2 I still failed my English test. I studied all night. (*in spite of* + clause; *even though*)
3 I'm able to work at my own pace. I'm not a fan of the flipped classroom. (*in spite of + -ing; although*)
4 My friends don't make much money. They still have nicer clothes than I do. (*despite* + clause; *while*)
5 Mountain climbing can be dangerous. I really enjoy it. (*despite* + noun; *while*)
6 I read lots of hotel reviews before I went to Berlin. I still paid too much. (*in spite of* + clause; *though*)
7 My brother is a genius. He's a nice person. (*besides + -ing; what's more*)

1B Make it personal Changing only the second part of the sentence in A, share four facts about yourself. Any surprises?

Although I did a lot of research, I still bought the wrong computer.

1C Find and correct Amanda's four mistakes. Then role play the conversation ending with "No, none at all!"

JIM: Your English has really improved in the last year.
AMANDA: You really think so? Despite study every day, grammar is still difficult.
JIM: But you have a really good accent.
AMANDA: Well, in spite of I might have a good accent, I still have a long way to go.
JIM: Maybe you could practice grammar by having a language exchange: you know, find someone who wants to learn Portuguese.
AMANDA: That's a good idea. I really try. However that my English will never be perfect. Conjunctions are so difficult!
JIM: Well, you just have to feel comfortable.
AMANDA: Yes, you're right. In spite of it's challenging, I should keep at it.
JIM: Yes, that's it.
AMANDA: How's my grammar today? Did I make any mistakes?
JIM: Well, just a few small ones!

2A Circle the correct options to complete the paragraph about Sayeed's visit to New York.

Every night I dreamed about my vacation. In my dream, I was staying [1]**[myself / ø]** in an expensive hotel, right off Fifth Avenue with my cousin Laura. Every morning we got up [2]**[ourselves / ø]** early to sightsee. Wherever we went, we dressed [3]**[ourselves / ø]** fashionably. In fancy restaurants, I would often introduce [4]**[myself / ø]** to famous actors. We taught [5]**[ourselves / ø]** to think like celebrities, and in general, we felt great [6]**[ourselves / ø]**! But, of course, it was all a dream, and at 7:00 every morning, I had to wake up [7]**[myself / ø]**, shower [8]**[myself / ø]**, and go to work.

2B Correct the mistakes.

1 I'm having trouble focusing myself in class. I'm always tired.
2 The students looked at them in the mirror and were pleasantly surprised by their appearance.
3 I went to a concert last night, and I really enjoyed.
4 When my daughter concentrates herself, she can succeed at anything.
5 My grandparents were immigrants, but they taught himself to speak perfect English.

Bonus! Language in song

♫ It took myself by surprise I must say. When I found out yesterday. Don't you know that I heard itself through the grapevine?

Are the reflexive pronouns correct? Correct the mistakes.

1 Imaginary situations: *hope, wish, if only,* and *supposing* do after 5.2

Future	I **hope you'll be** quiet during the performance. (= I don't know if you'll be quiet.)
Present	I **wish you'd be** quiet when I'm talking. (= You're not quiet, and it's annoying me.)
Past	I **hope** I **didn't fail** my test. (= I don't know if I failed.)
Past	I **wish** I **hadn't failed** my test. (= I failed, and I'm sorry I did.)
Future	**If only** I **could see** Sarah again. (= I don't think I'll ever see her again and I miss her so much.)
Past	**If only** I **could have seen** Sarah again. (= I didn't see her and I'm sure we would have gotten back together.)
Future	**Supposing** Sarah **wanted** to go out with you again, would you say yes? (= It's unlikely Sarah will want to go out with you again.)
Past	**Supposing** Sarah **had wanted** to go out with you again, would you have said yes? (= She didn't want to go out with you again.)

Common mistake

I ~~wish~~ *hope* I'll be able to go out tonight.

2 Shortening conditional sentences do after 5.4

Zero, first, second, third, and mixed conditionals can all be shortened when the information referred to is understood. The auxiliary cannot be contracted.		
Zero	My brother never **helps** me. If / When he **does** (help me),	I feel better.
First	I don't think my sister **is coming.** If she **is** (coming),	I'll be really happy.
Second	I **don't have** my parents' help. If I **did** (have my parents' help),	I'd go to college.
Third	I **didn't have** my parents' help. If I **had** (had my parents' help),	I would have gone to college.
Mixed	We **didn't make** any money. If we **had** (made money),	we wouldn't be living here any longer.

All conditionals can be contracted in a shorter way also.	
First	**With** my parents' help, I'll be able to go to college.
Third	**Without** my parents' help, I wouldn't have gone to college.

1A Complete the sentences with the correct form of *hope* or *wish* and the verb.

1 A: I ________ Ann ________ (call) me tomorrow. I really need to talk to her!
B: Oh, I'm sure she will.

2 A: I ________ my mother ________ (spend) more time with me when I was young.
B: I feel the same way. Mine was always working.

3 A: I really ________ I ________ (not fail) my final exams.
B: I'm sure you'll do well if you study!

4 A: I ________ I ________ (know) how to drive. It's such a useful skill.
B: Why don't you take lessons?

5 A: John ________ he ________ (not quit) school.
B: Yes, that wasn't too smart. You need a college education these days.

6 A: I ________ I ________ (not upset) my little brother when I yelled at him.
B: I don't think he's upset. Look, he's smiling!

1B Which is the full form? Write *had* or *would*.

1 Sue wishes she'**d** apologized sooner. *had*
2 Jim wishes I'**d** asked him to the party.
3 I wish they'**d** hurry up and finish.
4 We all wish they'**d** come to visit last year.
5 I wish they'**d** decide about this year.
6 I wish you'**d** sent the package yesterday.

1C **Make it personal** Share three hopes and three wishes that are true for you.

I really hope I ... , and I really wish I ...

2A Rewrite these short sentences using the word *if*.

1 With hard work, you can learn anything.
If you work hard, you can learn anything.
2 Without good grades, I never would have gotten into college.
3 With really good luck, maybe I'll win the lottery.
4 Without studying really hard, I wouldn't have passed the exam.
5 Without a lot of practice, you'll never learn to speak English.
6 Without the help of my parents, I wouldn't be living in this house today.

2B Shorten the underlined parts of each sentences, beginning with the word in parentheses.

When I was young, I didn't have many role models. [1]<u>If I'd had good role models</u> (with), I wouldn't have ended up in so much trouble. [2]<u>If I hadn't had the support of my neighbor Melanie</u> (without), I'd still be on the streets. She convinced me that I should go back to school. [3]<u>If I didn't go back to school</u> (if), she said, I'd be tempted to live a life of crime. [4]<u>But if I had a good education</u> (with), I'd have a satisfying career. I really listened to her. [5]<u>If I hadn't listened to her</u> (if), I might still be running around with those guys. I'll always be grateful to Melanie. [6]<u>If I didn't have her</u> (without), who knows where I'd be today.

2C **Make it personal** Write three sentences about your own role model. Be sure to use short conditional sentences. Choose from these topics or one of your own.

Someone who helped you ...
make friends stay out of trouble choose a career
understand your parents learn a new skill
meet your boyfriend / girlfriend

I'll always remember the boy who sat next to me at my new school. Without him ...

Bonus! Language in song

♫ I can be your hero, baby, I can kiss away the pain.

Rewrite this song line beginning with *I hope*, *I wish*, or *If only*.

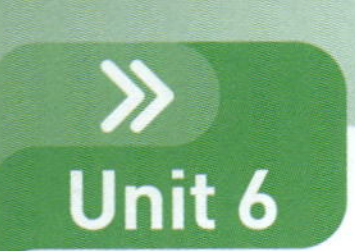

1 Questions in the passive do after 6.2

		Subject	*be*	Verb (+ *by*)
Simple present	Are	you	–	(ever) watched by your parents?
Present continuous	Are	you	being	bullied online?
Simple past	Were	you	–	(ever) spied on as a child?
Present perfect	Has	your profile	(ever) been	broken into?
Future	Will	teachers	be	replaced by computers?

The pattern is the same with question words.

How often	has	your profile	been	accessed?

Causative sentences are always passive in meaning. The causative with *get* is a little more informal.

	Auxiliary	Subject	*have* or *get*	Object	Verb (+ *by*)
Present continuous	Are	you	having getting	your hair	cut by Ralph?
Simple past	Did	Amy	have get	her sentence	reduced?

Using the passive

The passive is very common in English and makes impersonal questions sound polite.
Can the phone **be exchanged** after 30 days?
Could I **have** my hard drive **checked**, please?

Common mistake

How many people ~~were~~ *was* your profile seen by?

Be careful with subject-verb agreement!

2 Uses of *whatever* do after 6.2

In spoken English, ***whatever*** often expresses strong advice or a warning:
- **Whatever** you do, don't talk about politics on Facebook®.

Whatever is also used to end conversations and avoid arguments:
- "You spend far too long online!" "Yeah, yeah, **whatever** (you say)."

Fixed expressions like ***whatever that means*** and ***whatever it's called*** can be used when you don't know, remember, or understand something:
- Mom says she's going to keep tabs on me "selectively," **whatever** that means.

1A Put the words in order to make questions. (Each has one extra word.)

1 to / by / ever / will / replaced / paper books / be / e-books / ?
2 does / why / still / is / considered / the iPad / a revolution in teaching / ?
3 being / students' / should / from the classroom / banned / be / native languages / ?
4 removed / be / from / always / photos / have / Facebook® / you / when friends ask you to / ?
5 privacy / can / your / be / how / you / violated by credit card companies / ?

1B Make it personal Ask and answer the questions. How many similar opinions?

1C Make conversations 1–4 more natural and polite. Replace the underlined sentences with sentences in the passive.

1 A: <u>I 'd like you to check my computer, please</u>.
B: OK, right this way.
2 A: <u>Should you replace my battery</u>?
B: Yes, that would be a good idea.
3 A: Will you repair this water damage by <u>tomorrow</u>?
B: We'll certainly try our best.
4 A: <u>Have you fixed my phone yet</u>?
B: We're very busy today, ma'am. I promise we'll get to it.

1D Trivia time! Complete 1–5 with questions in the passive. Then search on "fun trivia" and create two more questions.

1 Where ____________________ ?
The Soccer World Cup? I think it was held in Brazil in 2014, wasn't it?

2 How many ____________________ ?
The song *Imagine*? I'm sure it's been recorded well over 100 times. And translated, too!

3 Who ____________________ ?
Everyone knows that! The Sistine Chapel was painted by Michelangelo.

4 Where ____________________ ?
Ceviche? That's that dish with raw fish and citrus juices, isn't it? I think it's eaten throughout Latin America.

5 Where in the world ____________________ ?
It's obvious you haven't been to Paris. The Mona Lisa can be seen at the Louvre!

2A Replace the underlined phrases with these expressions. There is one extra.

whatever you do | whatever the cost | whatever time | whatever | whatever that means

1 A: Oh no, why isn't the site loading?
B: It says here "bad gateway," <u>but I'm not sure what that is</u>. Let's try Bruno's iPad.
2 A: So you're moving on Sunday?
B: Yeah, and <u>even if it's really expensive</u>, I've decided to use a moving company.
3 A: But you said you wanted to go to the concert!
B: <u>It doesn't matter</u>. I've changed my mind.
4 A: I'm taking my first trip abroad next month.
B: Great, but don't let your credit cards out of your sight, <u>under any circumstances</u>.

2B Make it personal Start a conversation about home, school or leisure. How many ideas can you think of?

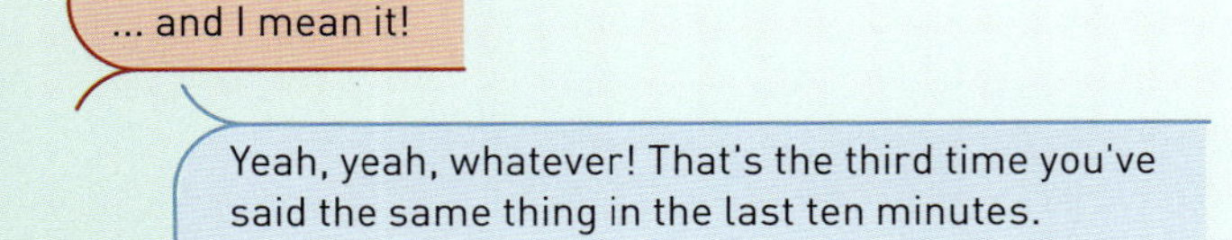

Bonus! Language in song

♫ I always feel like somebody's watching me. And I have no privacy.

Make the first sentence in this song line passive.

Grammar expansion

1 More on *so* — do after 7.2

So vs. *such* as intensifiers		
I'm	**so**	excited about the concert.
It's going to be		great!
I'm	**such**	a fan of Bruno Mars.
He's		a great singer.
There are	**so many**	people out there.
I've never heard	**so much**	noise.
Use *so* + adjective, but use *such* + (adjective +) noun. Use *so many* + count nouns, but *so much* + non-count nouns.		

Expressing purpose with *so as (not) to*		
I left an hour early	**so as to**	be on time for the interview.
I gave up my seat	**so as not to**	seem selfish.
So as (not) to means "in order (not) to," but is more formal. The negative *so as not to* is more common in conversation than the affirmative *so as to*.		

2 *because*, *because of*, and *for* — do after 7.2

I couldn't go to the concert	**because of**	the expense. rain.
	because	it was expensive. I didn't have an umbrella.
John was fired	**for**	arguing with his boss.

More on *for*	
To express a reason	*For* meaning "because" or "as a result of" can replace *because of* in very few situations. Memorize phrases with *for* when you hear them. ▸ I canceled my trip **for (because of)** health reasons. ▸ John married Sue **for (because of)** her money.
	When in doubt, use *because of*. *For* to express a reason is often ungrammatical. ▸ I didn't buy a ticket ~~**for**~~ **because of** the expense. ▸ I felt sick on the plane ~~**for**~~ **because of** turbulence.
	Only use *for* to express a reason when an *-ing* form follows. ▸ She was arrested **for** arguing with a police officer. ▸ I yelled at my brother **for not** turning off the lights.
To express a purpose	*For* is often used, however, to express purpose. ▸ I went to the store **for** some bread. ▸ I sent in the paperwork **for** my application.

3 Other ways of specifying — do after 7.4

Either ... or, both ... and, and *not only ... but also*
You choose the music. **Either** Adele **or** Shakira is fine. I really like **both** Taylor Swift **and** Katy Perry. I listen **not only** to rock **but also** to jazz.

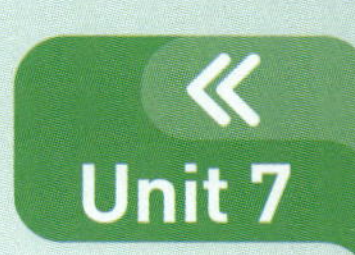

1A Make sentences with *so, such, so much*, or *so many*. Then suggest a solution for each problem.

1 ... noise outside that I can't sleep.
2 .... people with cars that it's impossible to park.
3 ... good desserts, but I can't eat any because I'm on a diet.
4 ... exciting to travel to new places, but I don't have any money.
5 .... homework that I'll never finish it all before Monday.
6 ... nice person, but when we didn't agree, he refused to speak to me.

There's so much noise outside that I can't sleep!

Why don't you just shut the window?

1B Make five sentences using one item in each column.

A	B	C
1 I walk to school	so as not to in order not to	burn out.
2 I call my parents every day		forget any vocabulary.
3 I take at least one vacation a year		have to wait for the bus.
4 I hardly ever go to museums		pay the entrance fee.
5 I read three books in English a year		worry them.

1C Make it personal Change three sentences in B so they are true. Share them. Any surprises?

I walk to school in order not to take the bus with my brother.

2A Correct the errors (1–6) in the story.

I was so excited that I was going to see Shakira in concert, but when we got to the stadium, the concert had been canceled (1) for rain. (2) Because of it had just started, the organizers were totally unprepared. No one wanted to go home, and one woman was arrested (3) because jumping over a fence. (4) For the chaos, I was really scared someone might get hurt. (5) Because of there had been no warning, everyone was so upset. I just went home and went right to sleep (6) for my disappointment.

2B Complete the sentences using *for* and the correct form of these reasons.

not come home on time	leave the refrigerator open	speak English	talk back to my boss	write the best essay

1 I was fired ____________ . She said I was totally rude.
2 My mother yelled at me ____________ . All of the food spoiled.
3 I got an award ____________ . I really worked hard at it.
4 I felt proud of myself ____________ . I was a little self-conscious of my accent, though.
6 I was punished ____________ . My parents were so worried.

3A Make sentences using *either ... or, both ... and*, or *not only ... but also*.

1 English / Chinese
2 Brazilian music / Latino music
3 the guitar / the piano
4 modern art / impressionism
5 novels / mysteries

3B Make it personal Guess whether your partner's sentences are true. If you think they're false, correct them.

I speak both English and Chinese.

That's false. You speak both English and Spanish, though!

Bonus! Language in song

♫ Music makes the people come together. Music mix the bourgeoisie and the rebel.

- Correct a grammatical mistake in this song line.
- Combine the two sentences starting with since or because.

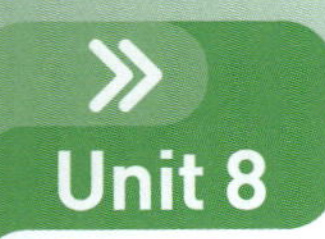

1 More on expressing ability do after 8.2

Present	I	**can / 'm able to**	speak five languages.	1
		can	give him a call now.	2
Past	I	**could / was able to**	see the ocean in the distance.	3
		was able to	get in touch with my brother.	4
Future	I	**'ll be able to**	speak French a year from now.	5
Present perfect	I	**can / 'll be able to**	see you tomorrow.	6
		've been able to	swim since I was three.	7
Verb + verb	I'd love to	**be able to**	come to your wedding.	8

Use *be able to*, but not *can*:

- for specific past events. (sentence 4)
- for something you will learn little by little. (sentence 5)
- with perfect tenses. (sentence 7)
- after another verb. (sentence 8)

Use *can*, but not *be able to*, when you offer to do something. (sentence 2)

2 Uses of *be supposed to* do after 8.2

We	**were supposed to**	arrive in the morning, but there was a delay.
I	**had to**	wait hours because I missed my connection.
We	**weren't supposed to**	have any of these headaches. I expected an easy trip!
I	**didn't have to**	be understanding, but I decided to be nice about it.

Be supposed to is often used to express something that turned out differently than expected. *Have to* is often used to express something that was inevitable.

Common mistake

The bus ~~had to~~ *was supposed to* be here at 2:30. Where is it?

3 Obligation and advice in the past do after 8.4

Obligation	I **had to** get a visa to enter Russia.	I **didn't have** to get a visa to go to Bermuda. My passport was good enough.
Strong advice	You'**d better** have packed some warm clothes before you left! It's freezing here.	I know you packed quickly, but you'**d better not have** forgotten your coat!
Advice	You **should have** / **ought to have** visited Times Square. Too bad you didn't.	You **shouldn't have** missed it. Well, too late now!

Remember! *Must have* in the past expresses probability, not obligation.
I **must have left** my passport at home. (= I'm pretty sure I left it at home.)

1A Circle the most logical options.

1 Don't worry. I [**can** / **'m able to**] speak to your brother today and ask for help.
2 I was terrified when the rollercoaster started its descent, but I [**could** / **was able to**] hold on tight.
3 Even though I can't cook very well now, I'm taking lessons, and I'm sure I [**can** / **'ll be able to**] cook next year.
4 Don't worry. I [**can** / **'m able to**] call the travel agency and ask if there's another flight.
5 I [**'ve been able to** / **can**] save money to buy a house, and I'm moving next week.
6 I'd like to [**can** / **be able to**] fly, but my heart starts to race at the thought of getting on a plane.

1B In pairs, which rules from 1 helped you choose the correct answer?

The first one sounds like an offer, so you have to use *can*.

2A Complete the sentences with the correct form of *have to* or *be supposed to* and the verbs.

1 Our plane ________ (arrive) by 10 p.m., but it didn't come in until midnight, so we ________ (spend) the night in a hotel.
2 I know Barry is difficult! He ________ (be) away today, but he came to work unexpectedly, so I ________ (invite) him to the picnic with everyone else.
3 My Mom ________ (be) here! If she hadn't come home early, she wouldn't have caught us looking at her computer.
4 My boyfriend ________ (meet) me at the airport, but he always thinks of others. He didn't want me to take the bus.
5 There was no parking at all! I ________ (drive) around the neighborhood for at least a half hour.
6 We ________ (get) our test results last Friday, but we didn't, so I ________ (live) with my anxiety all last weekend. I'm glad I passed in the end!

2B Make it personal Thinking on your feet! Share three things that you didn't expect to happen, but did. What did you do?

Well, I wasn't supposed to fail math because I did my homework every day, but when I did, I had to find a tutor.

3A Are these conversations logical? Correct the mistakes in the underlined words.

1 A: Oh, no! I can't find our passports. But maybe they're in this bag.
B: You <u>should have brought</u> them, or they won't let us on the plane. I reminded you three times!
2 A: I loved the U.S. It's a shame I didn't have time to go to the Grand Canyon.
B: You<u>'d better have found</u> time to go there. Who knows when you'll be back in Arizona.
3 A: Look at that rain! You <u>didn't have to leave</u> the windows open. Our carpet will be ruined!
B: Don't worry so much! I'm pretty sure I closed them.
4 A: I found out my license had expired, and I <u>should have taken</u> another driving test.
B: That sounds awful! I'm sure it's not what you were expecting.

3B Make it personal Share three fears and regrets using *(didn't) have to*, *had better (not) have*, and *was(n't) supposed to have*. Your partner will cheer you up.

I'd better not have left my car unlocked! It might be gone!

Bonus! Language in song

♫ How am I supposed to live without you? How am I supposed to carry on? When all that I've been livin' for is gone.

Grammatically, *can* and *be able to* can both replace *be supposed to* in this song line. Sing the line to yourself. Which one do you think sounds better?

1 Common prepositions ending relative clauses do after 9.2

I gave the plants **to** a neighbor.	→	That's the neighbor (who / that) I gave the plants **to**.
We used to live **in** this house.		It's near the house (that) we used to live **in**.
I arrived **at** this airport.		Your flight leaves from the airport (that) you arrived **at**.
John talked **about** the movie.		It was the movie (that) John talked **about**.
The thief was jailed **for** the robbery.		The thief regrets the robbery (that) he was jailed **for**.
He was convicted **of** a crime.		It's a crime (that) he was convicted **of**.
I went on a trip **with** Amy.		Amy is the friend (who / that) I went on a trip **with**.

Common mistake

He's the guy ~~with who~~ (who) I went to the party ^ with.

She's the woman I was talking ^ to.

In conversation, the preposition goes at the end. In very formal English, you may use *whom:* "I'm afraid it's a company **with whom** we no longer have relations."

2 Using relative clauses: summary do after 9.4

Restrictive
I finished the book (**that**) I was reading. My uncle is someone (**who** / **that**) I've always looked up **to**. Our school makes rules (**that** / **which**) I don't agree with.
Marcia is a good friend **who** comes over often. School is something **that** stresses me out.
Millenials are people **whose** values I really admire. I bought a car **whose** brakes don't work.
That's the house **where** I was born. It was a time **when** I was really happy.

Common mistake

He was late, ~~what~~ which upset me.
My dad, who is usually a sound sleeper, woke up when I came in.

You only have one dad. Remember to add the commas!

Restrictive, reduced
All those **standing** in the back, please exit through the rear door.
People **jogging** regularly may be prone to injuries.
Anyone **caught** entering will be arrested.

Non-restrictive
My grandfather, **who** is 70, bought his house in 1984.
People talk too loudly on their phones, **which** really annoys me.
We went to the theater last night, **where** we were surprised to see Martha.

More on relative pronouns

You can only delete a relative pronoun when the clause:

1 refers to the object of the sentence.
I finished the book. I was reading it. → I finished the book (that) I was reading.

2 refers to the subject of the sentence, *be* is also deleted, or the verb changes to an *-ing* form.
A person is speaking. The person is my son. → The person (who is) speaking is my son.

1A Circle the correct alternatives. Then complete the sentences.

1 Something I often worry [**about** / **for**] is ...
2 An issue I'm really interested [**about** / **in**] is ...
3 A time I got yelled [**at** / **to**] was when I ...
4 An event I'm really looking forward [**of** / **to**] is ...
5 Something really worth fighting [**to** / **for**] is ...
6 The hardest two things I've had to choose [**of** / **between**] are ...
7 The kind of person I'd like to get married [**to** / **with**] is ...
8 Something I've often wondered [**of** / **about**] is ...
9 A place I'd like to spend some time [**in** / **on**] is ...
10 A job I'm thinking of applying [**for** / **to**] is ...
11 Something I'm really hoping [**of** / **for**] next week is ...
12 Something I'm never really sure [**to** / **of**] is ...

1B **Make it personal** Share three sentences with a partner. Any surprises?

Something I often worry about is the future of our planet.

2A Add commas where necessary.

1 My only brother who's three years older than me wants to join the army.
2 Sally stepped on my foot three times which really made me mad!
3 We never think about the problems that we should worry about most.
4 My mother who's writing a novel always wanted to be a novelist.
5 Anyone who's caught cheating on this test will have to repeat the course. I mean it!
6 The man who I once almost married just got arrested.

2B Combine the two sentences with *who*, *that*, *which*, *whose*, *where* or *when*, and true information.

1 I'm fascinated by a country. The country is ...
A country which I'm fascinated by is Japan.
2 I most enjoy spending time with a friend. The friend is ...
3 I take vacations somewhere. The place is ...
4 I really like the sense of humor of someone in this class. The classmate is ...
5 I love a musician's albums. The musician is ...
6 People never ... It really annoys me.

2C ~~Cross out~~ all optional relative pronouns (and any other optional words). Then complete the sentences.

1 The best place that I've ever been to is ...
2 The politicians who are running this country ...
3 A writer whose books I love is ...
4 The type of weather that makes me depressed is ...
5 ... is an activity which I'd really like to be good at.
6 The person in my family who I confide in most is ...
7 These days many people think ... , which is exactly the opposite of what I think.
8 People who are caught stealing sometimes ...

2D In groups, share four opinions from B and C. Who do you have most in common with?

A country that really fascinates me is Japan.

Really? Tell me why. It's a place I know very little about.

Bonus! Language in song

♪ I'm all lost in the supermarket. I can no longer shop happily. I came in here for that special offer. A guaranteed personality.

Combine two of the sentences in this song line with *which*. Do you need a comma before *which*?

1 Responding to indirect questions, negative questions, and tag questions do after 10.2

Answers to all three types of questions may not include the words "yes" or "no," but the meaning is clearly implied.		
Indirect question	**Do you know if** you're coming over?	Sure. I said I would, remember? (= Yes.) Not yet. I'll call you later. (= I don't know.)
Negative question	**Aren't you going** to school today?	I'm leaving right now. (= Yes.) Actually, I'm not feeling well, so I think I'll stay home. (= No.)
Tag question	You have a doctor's appointment today, **don't you?**	It's tomorrow. (= No.) I'll give them a call now. (= I'm not sure.)

Other types of indirect questions may not even sound like questions. They are statements and end with a period, not a question mark.	
Excuse me, **I'm wondering** which way the train station is.	Just turn right at the corner.
I can't understand why checkout is at 11 a.m.	We have other guests arriving and need to clean the rooms.
I'm curious to know whether this bag is leather.	Yes, of course. It's 100% natural leather.
My hesitation is if there's a better discount elsewhere, to be honest.	I can guarantee that our prices are the lowest around.

2 Questions with *be used to*, *get used to*, and *used to* do after 10.4

Questions follow the same patterns as other question forms in the appropriate tenses.	
Present continuous	I wonder if they**'re** slowly **getting used to** the spicy food in Seoul.
Past of *be*	You **weren't used to** the cold weather, **were** you?
Simple past	**Didn't** you **use to live** around here?
Present perfect	You**'ve gotten used to speaking** English by now, **haven't** you?
Modal verbs	**Shouldn't** you **be used to** your husband's snoring by now? You've been married 25 years!
Future with *will*	**Will** I ever **get used to living** abroad?

1A Complete the questions with the words in parentheses in the correct order and form. Then write N (negative question), I (indirect question), or T (tag question).

1 *Why isn't there* a room available today? I had a reservation. (be – neg / there / why) *N*
2 I'm curious to know ________________ the game last night. (win – past / we / whether)
3 Both you and Tom are going to the party tomorrow, ________________? (be – neg / you)
4 ________________ any smaller sizes? These are too big. (have – neg / you)
5 Do you have any idea ________________ to London? I'm totally confused. (go / train / this / if)
6 ________________ at this hotel before? He looks familiar. (stay – past, neg / that / guy)

1B Choose the most likely meaning for each response: *Yes*, *No*, or *I'm not sure*.

1 A: Isn't there a 20 percent discount on these pants?
B: Let me check with the manager.
2 A: Excuse me, could you tell me if there's a good restaurant on this street?
B: Actually, it's all residential down there.
3 A: We were in the same English class together last semester, weren't we?
B: You sure were a great student!
4 A: I can't understand why my car can't be fixed by tomorrow.
B: I'll take another look at our schedule.
5 A: I'd like to know whether these earrings are sterling silver.
B: For this price? But they're very attractive. I'm sure you'll enjoy them.
6 A: Hello, is this reception? I'm wondering if you can give me the WiFi password.
B: You're in Room 252? I'll call you in just a minute.

1C Choose three items and write three new sentences where B is a possible response.

2A Complete the sentences with a form of *be used to*, *get used to*, or *used to*.

1 A: I wonder if I ________ living here. It's so different from where I come from.
B: Give it time. I'm sure you will.
2 A: ________ work at Coffee Xpress, too? I'm positive I've seen you before.
B: No, but I was your next-door neighbor!
3 A: You ________ speaking English by now, haven't you? You've been in the U.S. for five years!
B: Not totally. I still wish I could speak French.
4 A: Your first winter in New York! ________ slowly ________ the cold weather and all the snow?
B: Little by little. But I'd still like to spend January on a beach in the Caribbean!
5 A: ________ travel more when you were younger?
B: No, I never traveled very much. I really didn't have the money.

2B Write three questions with *be used to*, *get used to*, or *used to* that you'd like to ask a classmate. Find the answers in your next class.

Bonus! Language in song

♫ Do you know where you're going to? Do you like the things that life is showing you? Where are you going to? Do you know?

Which song line is an indirect question? Which two lines can be rewritten as an indirect question?

1 More on reported speech do after 11.2

In some situations, the tense does not usually move back.
1 The statement is very recent. "I **want** to go to the movies tonight." → John said he **wants** to go to the movies tonight.
2 The statement is a universal truth. "The sun **rises** in the east and **sets** in the west." → My mother told me that the sun **rises** in the east and **sets** in the west.
3 The statement includes the modal verbs *might* and *should.* "I **might** go to Europe next summer." → Amy said she **might** go to Europe next summer. "We **should** call Mom more often." → They admitted they **should** call their mother more often.

Pronouns in reported sentences change to reflect the perspective of the speaker.

Direct sentence	Speaker	Reported sentence
"Why are **you** leaving?" Sarah's boss asked.	Sarah	My boss asked **me** why **I** was leaving.
	Sarah's friend	Sarah's boss asked **her** why **she** was leaving.

2 Reporting what people say do after 11.4

Notice the patterns possible for these verbs.

Verb	Correct	Incorrect	
I **said***	that I would call	~~her to call~~ ~~her that I would call~~	her parents.
I **told***	her that I would complain	~~to complain~~ ~~that I would complain~~	to her parents.
They **promised**	to keep that they would keep us that they would keep	~~us to keep~~	things secret.
They **agreed**	not to tell that they wouldn't tell	~~us not to tell~~ ~~wouldn't tell~~	anyone.
We **urged**	him to tell	~~to tell~~ ~~that he would tell~~ ~~him that he would tell~~	the truth.
He **threatened**	to call that he would call	~~her to call~~ ~~her that he would call~~	the police.
I **persuaded** We **begged**	them to tell	~~to tell~~ ~~that we would tell~~ ~~them that we would tell~~	their parents.

*Be careful! These sentences have different meanings. The second is a command.
"I'll call your parents." → I **said I would call** her parents.
"Call your parents." → I **said to call** her parents.
"I'll complain to your parents." → I **told her that I would complain** to her parents.
"Complain to your parents." → I **told her to complain** to her parents.

1A Change the sentences to reported speech. Pay careful attention to whether the tense moves back.

1 "You're going to get into trouble."
Sam warned Miles he ______________________ .
2 "I'll be at the coffee shop in five minutes." (very recent statement)
Ellen said she ______________________ .
3 "Stars only come out at night."
My teacher told us stars ______________________ .
4 "I might be a little late tonight."
Phil reminded me he ______________________ .
5 "I didn't tell anyone you and Ted broke up."
Melissa reassured me she ______________________ .
6 "I didn't break the window!"
Eric denied he ______________________ .

1B Report each sentence (a and b) using the correct pronouns.

1 "You can't take the day off, Sally."
a My boss told me ______________________ .
b Sally told her parents ______________________ .
2 "We're going to be moving, but we'll visit you often."
a My parents told me ______________________ .
b My parents told their friends ______________________ .
3 "What do you want?"
a The store owner asked us ______________________ .
b The boys explained to the store owner
______________________ .
4 "I don't have the rent money, so I can't pay you."
a My tenant Sue admitted to me ______________________ .
b I told my landlady ______________________ .

2A Correct the sentences so they are grammatical, paying attention to the underlined verbs. There may be more than one answer.

1 The guests noticed there had been a robbery, but they <u>agreed</u> me that they would stay calm.
The guests noticed there had been a robbery, but they agreed that they would stay (agreed to stay) calm.
2 Tim wasn't happy about lending me money, but I <u>promised</u> him to pay it back next week.
3 Lisa was very upset about failing her final exams, but I <u>persuaded</u> her that she wouldn't give up.
4 Bob had his credit cards stolen, but I <u>urged</u> him that he would keep his cool and call the bank to cancel them immediately.
5 Beth forgot all her lines during the play, and our director really lost it, but I <u>begged</u> him that he would give her a second chance.
6 Steve fell asleep in an important meeting, and his boss <u>threatened</u> him to fire him the next time it happened.
7 Our local TV station mispronounced my name, and I <u>said</u> them I wasn't happy at all about that.
8 Nancy's boyfriend is always asking her for money, and I <u>told</u> her stop seeing him.

2B Complete each sentence with the correct form of these verbs.

agree	beg	persuade	promise	threaten	urge

1 The way Larry __________ to call the police over a little loud music left me speechless. He shook his fist at us and started screaming!
2 Laura was caught looking through her boss's papers. I __________ her to apologize to him, but she just burst out laughing. (two answers)
3 George found a wallet on a bench. I urged him to try to find the owner, and eventually I __________ him to call the number inside.
4 Liz told me some juicy gossip, but I __________ not to tell a soul! So I really can't tell you, either. My lips are sealed. (two answers)

Bonus! Language in song

♫ You tell me that you're sorry. Didn't think I'd turn around and say that it's too late to apologize. It's too late.

Change the first sentence of this song line to reported speech beginning, "You told me that ... " and the second sentence (after "and") to reported speech beginning, "I said that ... "

1 More on predicting
do after 12.2

Both facts and predictions use *going to* or *will*.	
Fact	My sister **is going to be** / **will be** 21 in August.
Prediction	Checks **are going to** / **will disappear** within five years.

When you use the future continuous, you emphasize the ongoing nature of a prediction, but you may also use the future with *will*.	
Future with *will*	People **will live** on the moon by 2030.
Future continuous with *will*	People **will be living** there in small huts.

When you use the future perfect, you emphasize the completion of a prediction by a certain time. This tense is often used with *by the time*.	
Future perfect	By the time you get here, we **will have finished** dinner. Before the end of the year, I **will have spent** all my savings.

If you use *going to*, you sound more certain. Predictions based on present evidence often use *going to*.	
Future with *going to*	Global warming **is going to get** worse.
Future continuous with *going to*	We're **going to be paying** much higher rents a year from now. That's for sure!

When you are less sure of your prediction, you can use *may* or *might*.	
Future continuous with *might*	We **might all be living** on the moon a few years from now.
Future perfect with *may*	By 2050, they **may have sent** people to other planets, too!

Common mistake

Do not use the simple present or present continuous for predictions:

're going to spend / going to be spending
We ~~spend / 're spending~~ more by the end of the year.

2 More on the present continuous as future, *going to*, and *will*
do after 12.4

Use the present continuous as future or *going to* when your plan or decision is already made.
I'**m meeting** Pedro after class.
We'**re going to see** a movie.

However, if your plan is far in the future, use *going to:*
I'**m going to become** an engineer like my father.

Use the future with *will* when you're unsure about your plans:
I guess **we'll go** to the Rivoli for lunch.

Also use *will*, but not *going to* ...
1 when you make an offer or decide something as you're speaking:
- The phone's ringing. I'**ll get** it.

2 in stores and restaurants to express your intention:
- I'**ll take** the larger size.
- We'**ll** both **have** the fish.

3 to invite someone:
- **Will you join** us after class for coffee?

4 to make a promise:
- Officer, I promise **I won't speed** in the future!

1A Circle the best options.

1 A: Prices are through the roof! We [**'re going to be paying** / **'re paying**] even more by the end of the year.
B: That's for sure! We [**'ll be** / **'ll have been**] bankrupt soon.
2 A: Look how late we are! By the time we get to Bill and Marcy's, they [**will have left** / **will leave**] without us.
B: Stop worrying so much. I think they [**wait** / **'ll wait**] for us.
3 A: There [**are going to be** / **will be**] layoffs at our company. My boss told me!
B: Oh, no! We [**might be looking** / **might look**] for new jobs very soon!
4 A: By this time next year, we all [**will have graduated** / **will graduate**].
B: How can you be so sure? Maybe some of us [**will fail** / **will be failing**].

1B In pairs, answer these questions for each speaker in A. What other answers are possible?

- Is the event ongoing?
- Is it complete?
- Is the speaker sure?

In the first one, I think you can also say "We'll be paying ..." or even "We might be paying ... ." There's some evidence, but we can't be sure of the future.

2A Complete the conversations with a future form of the verbs in parentheses. There may be more than one answer.

1 A: ________ (you / come) to our party Saturday? We'd love to see you.
B: Oh, I wish I could, but I have some other plans.
2 A:I ________ (not do) it again! I promise.
B: That's what you said the last time! You ________ (not leave) home this weekend!
3 A: When I grow up, I ________ (study) architecture.
B: How can you be so sure? There are a lot of years between now and then.
4 A: What ________ (you / do) this weekend?
B: I ________ (go) camping. Helene invited me to go with her family.
5 A:Can I get you anything else?
B: No, I've decided. I ________ (take) the blue ones. Sorry to keep you waiting.
6 A: You failed your English exam? What happened?
B: I don't really know. I guess I ________ (talk) to my teacher on Monday and find out.

2B In pairs, try to explain the reasons for your choices in A before checking with your teacher.

In the first one, I chose will because it was an invitation: "Will you come to our party on Saturday?"

Oh, I decided the friend already knew about the party, so I chose "Are you coming to our party on Saturday?"

2C Make it personal Write three questions to ask a classmate about the future. How long can you continue the conversation?

What are you planning to do over the summer?

Bonus! Language in song

♫ I missed the last bus. I'll take the next train. I try but you see, it's hard to explain.

Rewrite the line "I'll take the next train" in two ways: (1) You've made a plan and have already bought your train ticket, and (2) You're not very sure what you'll do.

Selected audio scripts

R1.1 *page 26 exercise 1*

A = Amy, J = Joe

A: Did you grow up around here?
J: Well, no, we moved here when I was 16 so I could start over.
A: What do you mean?
J: You know how teenagers do some stupid things. They say our minds aren't fully developed until we're 25. I had some problems – peer pressure, that sort of thing.
A: And you had to leave town?
J: Well, that's one way to look at it. My friends weren't the best influence. The biggest problem was that they convinced me to take risks. Need I say more?
A: Oh! I guess not ...
J: And so my grandparents decided it was time to leave.
A: Your grandparents? Did they live with you?
J: Yes, I was raised by them. They were great. My grandfather was a movie actor, and my grandmother a novelist.
A: Wow! That must have been cool!
J: And how about you? What was your childhood like?
A: Well, I ...

3.3 *page 29 exercises 2B and C*

M = Marco, L = Lucas, A = Ana

M: But that wasn't the worst part.
L: It wasn't?
M: No. It had been a stressful day, lots of tests, lots of traffic, the treadmill ... and I wanted to relax before going back home, so I decided to catch a movie that night.
L: On your own?
M: Yeah. For a change, you know. I got there ten minutes before the movie started, got myself a soft drink, walked into the theater, sat down, and closed my eyes, as I waited for the lights to dim. I didn't even remember the name of the movie, you know ... I just wanted to relax for a while.
M: A bit. So, anyway, I sit down, and I glance across the room, and I see someone who looks familiar. I mean, really familiar.
L: Uh huh.
M: But the theater was really dark, so I couldn't get a good look at her. Well, the lights go out, the movie starts, and the next thing I know the woman moves three rows back and sits right in front of me.
A: OK, go on.
M: I couldn't take my eyes off her ... I kept staring at her and, bingo, it was my sister-in-law – or at least that's what I thought.
A: That's what you thought?
L: Oh no!
M: I wanted to say hi ... So, I whispered something in her ear and gave her hair a little pull, you know. I was sure she'd be happy to see me there.
L: Oh boy. Here it comes.
A: You pulled the woman's hair?
M: Very, very lightly, just to get her attention.
L: And then what?
M: You wouldn't believe what happens next.

3.4 *page 29 exercise 2D*

L: And then what?
M: You wouldn't believe what happens next. The woman's hair comes off.
L: What? She was wearing a wig?
M: Yeah. It was totally false.
A: Oh, boy!
M: So she turns around and screams and ...
L: Oh no!
M: Before I know it, everybody's staring at us, telling us to be quiet, and ...
A: So what happens next?
M: I don't know. I just apologized, got up, and ran to the exit.
L: Oh, man.
M: I've never been so embarrassed in my entire life.

3.11 *page 33 exercises 6C and D*

S = Sue, A = Ann

S: So, Ann ... How did you two meet?
A: Well, I was doing a college assignment. It was nearly midnight, and I was **sick and tired** of studying. So I took a break and took the dog for a walk.
S: That late?
A: Yeah! Every **now and then** I do that. Anyway, then I saw this guy walking his dog, and he looked really familiar. Turns out it was Vince, an old boyfriend from high school! I'd seen him on Facebook®, but I never thought we'd meet **face to face** again after all these years.
S: Wow! Did he recognize you?
A: Yeah. We met for coffee the very next day. Then time went by, and we started seeing each other nearly every day. Before we knew it, we were madly in love.
S: You seem very happy!
A: I am. Well, naturally, there have been problems along the way, and we've had our **ups and downs**. But we're crazy about each other, and I want him in my life for **better or worse**.
S: Wait a second! Are you talking marriage?
A: Sure. Maybe this year, maybe next year, maybe five years from now. But it's going to happen **sooner or later**. It's written in the stars.
S: Wow! To think how it all started ... Talk about serendipity!
A: Ser-en-dipity, yeah, love it! Definitely my favorite word in the English language.

5.9 *page 56 exercise 7A*

DJ = DJ, K = Keith, L = Lorna

DJ: Welcome back to *Oops, wrong again*, your weekly radio show about unusual careers. Keith, your story reminded me of the Beatles back in 1962.
K: You mean when they got rejected by Decca records?
DJ: Exactly. Apparently Decca's executives wrote to them saying that guitar groups were on the way out, or something like that. Can you believe it?
K: I bet they wouldn't have sent that letter if they'd had a crystal ball at the time. The best-selling band in history!
L: Oops! But at least they signed the Rolling Stones soon afterwards. And what about J.K. Rowling? She got rejected by twelve different publishers.
K: Twelve?
L: Yeah. They thought the book was far too long for kids.
DJ: So what happened in the end?
L: Well, she found a publisher whose president gave it to his eight-year-old daughter. Guess what? She loved it. So they agreed to publish Harry Potter.
K: I really look up to Rowling. What a fighter she is. If she didn't have that kind of willpower, she might have given up ...
DJ: That's so true, ... and she wouldn't be one of the wealthiest women in the world today.
K: Oops! Walt Disney had his ups and downs, too. He was fired from his job as a newspaper editor, wasn't he?
L: He sure was! In 1919. They said he lacked imagination and had no good ideas. Maybe if he hadn't had so much faith in himself, we wouldn't have Mickey Mouse today!
DJ: And that would be a real shame ... That sure is swell! See ya soon!

7.7 *page 74 exercise 3C*

J = Josh, L = Liz

J: But the show was rescheduled, right?
L: It was, eventually, but I couldn't miss work again. But in September, she was scheduled to play in Mexico City and ...
J: No! You ...
L: You know, since I was on vacation, I thought I'd give her a second chance. Plus, I have friends there, so finding a place to stay wouldn't be a problem. Besides, ...
J: Can't believe you went to Mexico! You lucky ...
L: I did! So, anyway, I borrowed money for the tickets and ...
J: I didn't know you were such a fan.
L: I am! Anyway, on the big day, I left home early so I'd have plenty of time to get to the airport.
J: Uh huh.
L: So I got on the plane and, guess what ...
J: Engine failure!
L: No! But something was wrong with the air-conditioning and, well, we nearly froze to death, so the plane was diverted back to ...
J: Kansas! No way!
L: Yep. I could have taken one the next day, but, you know, I was so fed up with the whole thing ... I just gave up. It wasn't meant to be, I guess.
J: But ...
L: In the end I downloaded the show just to have a taste of what I missed.

J: Sniff sniff. She'll go on another tour soon. Don't worry.
L: I hope so!

8.6 *page 84 exercises 3A and C*

D = Diego, L = Louise

D: So, in the end, did you go to Rita's party?
L: Yeah, Diego, but I wasn't able to get there until after 10, so I missed most of it.
D: How come?
L: Well, long story short there's a fence around our apartment complex, and, believe it or not, I couldn't get out.
D: What?
L: Yeah. I'd lost my key to the gate and couldn't find the spare one. So I couldn't get out onto the street!
D: That's so like you. But you were able to make it to the party ...
L: Well, I climbed the fence and ...
D: You what?
L: Yeah. My brother even took a photo. Look!
D: Why would he do that?
L: To embarrass me on Instagram®, obviously. You know him, Diego ...

8.7 *page 84 exercises 3B and C*

D: But ... I don't get it. Why didn't you simply call your parents?
L: I did! But there was no coverage where they were!
D: No way!
L: I know! I mean, what are the odds of that happening?
D: But, but ... I thought you were afraid of heights.
L: Oh, no, on the contrary. Actually, in school, everyone used to call me spider girl, because, well ... I could climb just about anything.
D: So you're telling me you were able to climb the fence? All dressed up like that?
L: Yeah.
D: Wow! I'm impressed. Did you at least enjoy the party?
L: Not exactly. I ran into Zack and his new girlfriend.
D: Oh, no! Of all people!
L: Yeah. I still have feelings for him, you know, and I think he could see it in my eyes ... So that kind of spoiled the fun ...
D: Hmm ... it's been what since you broke up, a month or two?
L: Yeah. I still kind of miss him.

10.6 *page 106 exercise 3B*

Conversation 1

R = Receptionist, M = Marty

R: 6 a.m. to 10 a.m. Enjoy your stay, Mr. Falcon.
M: Thanks. Erm ... one more thing, I was wondering if I could get a late checkout on Wednesday.
R: I'm sorry, but you need to check out by noon.
M: Listen, my flight doesn't leave until 5:00 ... what am I supposed to do until then?
R: I'm really sorry, sir.
M: Can I speak to the manager, please?
R: Erm, she's on her lunch break.
M: Can you tell me what time she'll be back?
R: At around 2:00, sir.
M: Thank you.
R: My pleasure. Have a nice day!
M: Oh, by the way, I need a wake-up call tomorrow morning.
R: Of course. Just dial 000, set the time, and the system will wake you up.
M: You mean I have to use the phone in the room?
R: Yes, sir.
M: OK, thanks.

Conversation 2

S = Salesperson, M = Marty

S: ... the green ones over there.
M: Would you happen to know whether these are machine-washable?
S: Yes, I think they are, sir.
M: You mean they won't shrink?
S: Let me take a look at the label just in case. Erm ... it doesn't say anything. I'll check with the manager.
M: No need to, thanks. They're $19.99, aren't they, you said?
S: Erm ... No, $90.99 plus tax.
M: How much?
S: $90.99.
M: Wow! Over a hundred dollars?! That's a rip-off! Aren't these things supposed to cost about 20 bucks?
S: Actually, $90.99 is less than the suggested retail price, sir. They're 100 percent cotton.
M: Really? Wow! If you say so ... Well, OK, I'll take them.
S: Great! How would you like to pay?
M: Do you accept international credit cards? I'm living in London now.
S: Sure. Sir, I'm afraid your card didn't go through.
M: Really? That's weird. I use this card all the time.
S: Yeah.
M: Erm ... Can you try again, please?
S: Oh, of course. No, sorry. Don't you have another card?
M: Yeah. Do you ...

Conversation 3

F = Fiona, M = Marty

F: Spencer and White Rent a Car. Fiona speaking. How may I help you?
M: Erm ... My car broke down and I don't know what to do. I'm lost in the middle of nowhere.
F: OK. The fastest way to report a car breakdown is via our app. Do you know whether you have it installed on your phone? That way, we'll know exactly where you are and send someone over.
M: Yeah, but I don't have a login or a password. Can't you help me over the phone?
F: Erm, just a minute. Please hold. ... Yes, sir, I can now help you! Could I have your name, please?
M: Marty Falcon.
F: And your reservation number?
M: 8983F.
F: It says "invalid reservation number."
M: What do you mean? It's the number on the document.
F: Hmm ... It seems there's been a mix up. Hmm ... Let me see if I can correct it and fix things up. Hold the line, please. ...Thanks for holding. Mr. Falcon, do you remember if any warning lights came on?
M: Warning lights? You mean something that lights up red or is it blue? – like on the dashboard?
F: Yes.
M: Well, yeah, the "check engine" light was on, but, er, I figured it was nothing serious, so I just ...
F: I see. Do you know what your exact location is?
M: No, I don't! I'm *completely* lost and in the middle of nowhere.
F: OK. Hold the line, please.

10.12 *page 111 exercise 9C*

Mariana from Caracas, Venezuela

I love Vermont ... and the campus ... But, well, I was born and raised in Caracas, so I kind of miss the hustle and bustle of life there – you know, the noise, the crowds, even the traffic! I'm sure I'll get used to the peace and quiet eventually... Well, at least I hope so. The upside, though, is that life here is generally healthier ... plus, I'm no longer the couch potato I used to be, which is a good thing, of course.

Ignacio from Montevideo, Uruguay

I grew up in a big house, so my sisters and I had our own bedrooms ... So, erm, I'm not used to sharing a room with anyone – let alone someone I barely know. Besides, my roommate isn't very talkative, which doesn't exactly help. He's so quiet it's weird sometimes. I mean, it's been two months and we, erm, we hardly know each other. Not that I've tried too hard, to be honest, so I guess it's my fault as much as his. Mom says we'll get used to living together. I hope she's right.

Ines from Lisbon, Portugal

It's, erm, it's been tough. I'm fresh out of high school, where there was, you know, far more hand-holding and guidance. So, erm, I guess in many ways I'm not used to being treated as an adult. Also, at school our final grade was based mostly on exams. Here we have regular assignments, quizzes, projects and exams, which can be a little overwhelming. I wonder if I'll ever get used to working this hard. Plus, you need a lot of self-discipline, which is definitely not my strong suit.

Diego from Bogota, Colombia

My father got transferred to Miami when I was little boy, and we lived there for, what, three years, so, erm, well, when I came here, I was used to life in the States ... I mean, there was less of a culture clash than I'd anticipated. But ... it took me a while to get used to the weather. It's freezing in Vermont in the winter! You have no idea, and it snows constantly. I was used to a mild climate. I even had to buy a whole new wardrobe!

Elena from Moscow, Russia

The first few weeks were kind of fun, but then I started to feel terribly homesick. I wasn't used to being away from my parents for more than couple of days. I'm an only child, and we're a very close-knit family and, well, even though we Skype at least once a week and What'sApp constantly, it's not really the same. They try to act strong, but deep down I know they wish they could catch the first plane and take me back home.

 **12.2** *page 127 exercise 1D*

A = Announcer, R= Rob, L = Lisa, M = Mike, T = Teresa

A: We're ready to survey our first guest over here on the right. And your name is ...

R: Rob.

A: OK, Rob, let's begin by talking about school tests. You said you're 19, so that means you're in college?

R: Uh huh, it's my second year.

A: How optimistic are you about your exams?

R: You mean my finals?

A: Yeah.

R: Hmm ... I haven't been putting a lot of effort into my work and it, it turns out I've had a couple of Fs ... I keep telling myself that it's not the end of the world if I fail an exam or two, but deep down, I know I'll be really upset.

A: So what are you going to do about it?

R: I guess I'd better start studying. Anyway, I'm keeping my fingers crossed.

A: So you're "unsure" about your exams?

R: You could say that again!

A: Let's try someone else. OK, in front. Your name?

L: Lisa.

A: Good. Let me ask you Lisa ... how optimistic are you about your career?

L: Well, I'm studying pharmacy, and right now I have a part-time job at ID drugs.

A: The drugstore chain?

L: Uh huh. It's great training. But they're going through a rough time right now, so who knows what the future has in store for me. If they have to let some people go, I'm pretty sure I'm at the top of the list. I mean, I've been there for less than a year, and I haven't even graduated from college yet.

A: Hmm ... So it doesn't look good?

L: Nope.

A: I'm sorry to hear that! What about your future in general?

L: All I can tell you is I'm feeling pretty down right now.

A: Let's try someone else. And you're ...

M: Mike.

A: OK, Mike. How optimistic are you about your team's chances of winning the championship?

M: You mean soccer?

A: Well, it could be any sport, soccer, football, baseb...

M: Hmm ... well, my soccer team hasn't been doing too well. We haven't won a single game.

A: You haven't?

M: No, but ... well, I know we've lost all the games so far this season, but now with this new coach, there might be a light at the end of the tunnel. I'm trying not to let it get me down.

A: Does that mean you're optimistic?

M: I just have no idea really, to be honest.

v Time for just one more. You, over here. And your name?

T: Teresa.

A: OK, Teresa, how optimistic are you about the country's economy?

T: Well, it sort of depends on who you ask, doesn't it? If you watch the eight o'clock news, you get the impression that we're on the brink of chaos. I mean, the ... the media tends to blow things out of proportion but, on the whole, I think we're doing OK. Anyway, I try to keep my feet on the ground and save a little every month, you know, just in case. But I think we're definitely headed in the right direction.

A: Thank you. You're a lot more confident than I am!

Phrasal verb list

Transitive phrasal verbs

Phrasal verb	Meaning
A	
ask someone **over**	invite someone
B	
block something **out**	prevent from passing through (light, noise)
blow something **out**	extinguish (a candle)
blow something **up**	explode; fill with air (a balloon); make larger (a photo)
bring something **about**	cause to happen
bring someone or something **back**	return
bring someone **down**	depress
bring something **out**	introduce a new product
bring someone **up**	raise (a child)
bring something **up**	bring to someone's attention
build something **up**	increase
burn something **down**	burn completely
C	
call someone **back**	return a phone call
call someone **in**	ask for someone's presence
call something **off**	cancel
call someone **up**	contact by phone
carry something **out**	conduct an experiment / plan
cash in on something	profit
catch up on something	get recent information; do something there wasn't time for earlier
charge something **up**	charge with electricity
check someone / something **out**	examine closely
check up on someone	make sure a person is OK
cheer someone **up**	make happier
clean someone / something **up**	clean completely
clear something **up**	clarify
close something **down**	force (a business / store) to close
come away with something	learn something useful
come down to something	be the most important point
come down with something	get an illness
come up against someone / something	be faced with a difficult person / situation
come up with something	invent
count on someone / something	depend on
cover something **up**	cover completely; conceal to avoid responsibility
cross something **out**	draw a line through
cut something **down**	bring down (a tree); reduce
cut someone **off**	interrupt someone
cut something **off**	remove; stop the supply of
cut something **out**	remove; stop doing an action
cut something **up**	cut into small pieces
D	
do something **over**	do again
do someone / something **up**	make more beautiful
draw something **together**	unite
dream something **up**	invent
drink something **up**	drink completely
drop someone / something **off**	take someplace
drop out of something	quit
E	
empty something **out**	empty completely
end up with something	have an unexpected result
F	
face up to something	accept something unpleasant
fall back on something	use an old idea
fall for someone	feel romantic love
fall for something	be tricked into believing
figure someone / something **out**	understand with thought
fill someone **in**	explain
fill something **in**	complete with information
fill something **out**	complete (a form)
fill something **up**	fill completely
find something **out**	learn information
fix something **up**	redecorate (a home); solve
follow something **through** / **follow through on** something	complete
G	
get something **across**	help someone understand
get around to something	finally do something
get away with something	avoid the consequences
get back at someone	retaliate, harm someone (for an offense or wrong act)
get off something	leave (a bus, train, plane)
get on something	board (a bus, train, plane)
get out of something	leave (a car); avoid doing something
get something **out of** something	benefit from
get through with something	finish
get to someone / something	reach; upset someone
get together with someone	meet
give something **away**	give something no longer needed or wanted
give something **back**	return
give something **out**	distribute
give something **up**	quit
give up on someone / something	stop hoping for change / trying to make something happen
go after someone / something	try to get / win
go along with something	agree
go over something	review
go through with something	finish / continue something difficult
grow out of something	stop doing (over time, as one becomes an adult)
H	
hand something **in**	submit
hand something **out**	distribute
hang something **up**	put on a hanger or hook
help someone **out**	assist
K	
keep someone or something **away**	cause to stay at a distance
keep something **on**	not remove (clothing / jewelry)
keep someone or something **out**	prevent from entering
keep up with someone	stay in touch
keep up with someone or something	go as fast as

Phrasal verb list

Phrasal verb	Meaning
L	
lay someone **off**	fire for economic reasons
lay something **out**	arrange
leave something **on**	not turn off (a light or appliance); not remove (clothing or jewelry)
leave something **out**	not include, omit
let someone **down**	disappoint
let someone or something **in**	allow to enter
let someone **off**	allow to leave (a bus, train); not punish
let someone or something **out**	allow to leave
light something **up**	illuminate
look after someone or something	take care of
look down on someone	think one is better, disparage
look into something	research
look out for someone	watch, protect
look somone or something **over**	examine
look someone or something **up**	try to find
look up to someone	admire, respect
M	
make something **up**	invent
make up for something	do something to apologize
miss out on something	lose the chance
move something **around**	change location
P	
pass something **out**	distribute
pass someone / something **up**	reject, not use
pay someone **back**	repay, return money
pay someone **off**	bribe
pay something **off**	pay a debt
pick someone / something **out**	identify, choose
pick someone **up**	give someone a ride
pick someone / something **up**	lift
pick something **up**	get / buy; learn something; answer the phone; get a disease
point someone / something **out**	indicate, show
put something **away**	return to its appropriate place
put something **back**	return to its original place
put someone / something **down**	stop holding; treat with disrespect
put something **off**	delay
put something **on**	get dressed / add jewelry (to the body)
put something **together**	assemble, build
put something **up**	build, erect
put up with someone / something	accept without complaining
R	
run into someone	meet
run out of something	not have enough
S	
see something **through**	complete
send something **back**	return
send something **out**	mail
set something **off**	cause to go off, explode
set something **up**	establish; prepare for use
settle on something	choose after consideration
show someone / something **off**	display the best qualities
shut something **off**	stop (a machine, light, supply)
sign someone **up**	register
stand up for someone / something	support
start something **over**	begin again
stick with / to someone / something	not quit, persevere
straighten something **up**	make neat
switch something **on**	start, turn on (a machine, light)
T	
take something **away**	remove
take something **back**	return; accept an item; retract a statement
take something **down**	remove (a hanging item)
take something **in**	notice, remember; make a clothing item smaller
take something **off**	remove clothing, jewelry
take someone **on**	hire
take something **on**	agree to a task
take someone **out**	invite and pay for someone
take something **out**	borrow from the library
take something **up**	start a new activity (as a habit)
talk someone **into**	persuade
talk something **over**	discuss
team up with someone	start to work with, do a task together
tear something **down**	destroy, demolish
tear something **up**	tear into small pieces
think back on something	remember
think something **over**	consider
think something **up**	invent, think of a new idea
throw something **away / out**	discard, put in the garbage / trash
touch something **up**	improve with small changes
try something **on**	put on to see if it fits, is desirable (clothing, shoes)
try something **out**	use an item / do an activity to see if it's desirable
turn something **around**	turn so the front faces the back; cause to get better
turn someone / something **down**	reject
turn something **down**	lower the volume / heat
turn someone **in**	identify to the police (after a crime)
turn something **in**	submit
turn someone / something **into**	change from one type / form to another
turn someone **off**	cause to lose interest, feel negatively
turn something **off**	stop (a machine / light)
turn something **on**	start (a machine / light)
turn something **out**	make, manufacture
turn something **over**	turn so the bottom is on the top
turn something **up**	raise (the volume / heat)
U	
use something **up**	use completely, consume
W	
wake someone **up**	cause to stop sleeping
walk out on someone	leave a spouse / child / romantic relationship
watch out for someone	protect
wipe something **out**	remove, destroy
work something **out**	calculate mathematically; solve a problem
write something **down**	create a written record (on paper)
write something **up**	write in a finished form

Intransitive phrasal verbs

Phrasal verb	Meaning
A	
act up	behave inappropriately
B	
blow up	explode; suddenly become angry
break down	stop functioning
break out	start suddenly (a war, fire, disease)
burn down	burn completely
C	
call back	return a phone call
carry on	continue doing something; behave in a silly / emotional way
catch on	become popular
check in	report arrival (at a hotel, airport)
check out	pay a bill and leave (a hotel)
cheer up	become happier
clear up	become better (a rash, infection; the weather)
close down	stop operating (a business)
come along	go with, accompany
come back	return
come down	become lower (a price)
come in	enter
come off	become unattached
come out	appear; be removed (a stain)
come up	arise (an issue)
D	
dress up	wear more formal clothes; a costume
drop in	visit unexpectedly
drop out	quit
E	
eat out	eat in a restaurant
empty out	empty completely
end up	do something unexpected; reach a final location / conclusion
F	
fall off	become unattached
fill out	become bigger
fill up	become completely full
find out	learn new information
follow through	finish, complete something
fool around	have fun (in a silly way)
G	
get ahead	make progress, succeed
get along	have a good relationship
get back	return
get by	survive
get off	leave (a bus, train)
get on	board (a bus, train)
get through	finish; survive
get together	meet
get up	get out of bed
give up	quit
go along	accompany; agree
go away	leave a place
go back	return
go down	decrease (a price, number)
go off	explode, detonate
go on	continue
go out	leave (a building / home); socialize
go over	succeed (an idea / speech)
go up	increase (a price, number); be built
grow up	become an adult

Phrasal verb	Meaning
H	
hang up	end a phone call
help out	do something helpful, useful
hold on	wait (often during a phone call)
K	
keep away	stay at a distance
keep on	continue
keep out	not enter
keep up	maintain speed / momentum
L	
lie down	recline (on a bed / floor / sofa)
light up	illuminate; look pleased, happy
look out	be careful
M	
make up	end an argument
miss out	lose the chance (for something good)
P	
pass out	become unconscious, faint
pay off	be worthwhile
pick up	improve
play around	have fun, not be serious
R	
run out	leave suddenly; not have enough (a supply)
S	
show up	appear
sign up	register
sit down	sit
slip up	make a mistake
stand up	rise (to one's feet)
start over	begin again
stay up	not go to bed
straighten up	make neat
T	
take off	leave, depart (a plane)
turn in	go to sleep
turn out	have a certain result
turn up	appear
W	
wake up	stop sleeping
watch out	be careful
work out	exercise; end successfully

Richmond

58 St Aldates
Oxford
OX1 1ST
United Kingdom

ISBN: 978-84-668-2083-7
DL: M-4705-2016
First Edition: February 2016
© Richmond / Santillana Educación S.L.

All rights reserved. No part of this book may be reproduced, stored in a retrieval system or transmitted in any form by any means, electronic, mechanical, photocopying, recording or otherwise, without the prior permission in writing of the Publisher.

Richmond publications may contain links to third party websites. We have no control over the content of these websites, which may change frequently, and we are not responsible for the content or the way it may be used with our materials. Teachers and students are advised to exercise discretion when assessing links.

Publishing Director: Deborah Tricker

Content Development: Debbie Goldblatt

Editors: Laura Miranda, Shona Rodger

Proofreaders: Emma Clarke, Tania Pattison, Sophie Sherlock

Project and Cover Design: Lorna Heaslip

Layout: Oliver Hutton (H D Design), Dave Kuzmicki

Picture Researcher: Magdalena Mayo

Illustrators: Iker Ayestaran, Ricardo Bessa, Paul Boston, Ben Challenor, Dermot Flynn, Matt Latchford, María Díaz Perera, Nick Radford

Digital Content: Luke Baxter

Audio Recording: Motivation Sound Studios

Photos:
Prats i Camps; S. Enríquez; 123RF; 500PX MARKETPLACE/ Olya Mruwka; A. G. E. FOTOSTOCK; ALAMY/STOCKFOLIO, David Noton Photography, jeremy sutton-hibbert, C12, Blend Images, Zuma Press Inc., ZUMA Press, Inc., Darren Robb, Lasse Kristensen, OJO Images Ltd, Aleksandr Bryliaev, Jan Hanus, B Christopher, Chuck Nacke, Vanessa Miles, Chris Rout, Eyecandy Images, Trinity Mirror / Mirrorpix, PhotoAlto sas, Stock Experiment, AF archive, Pictorial Press Ltd, Malcro, ZUMA Press, Inc, dpa picture alliance, Glasshouse Images, Fine Art, Pictorial Press Ltd., Wavebreak Media ltd, Eddie Gerald, Oleksandr Prykhodko, Mint Images Limited, ClassicStock, Dmitri Maruta, Keystone Pictures USA, Heritage Image Partnership Ltd, GL Archive, Golden Pixels LLC, Daniel Kaesler, epa european pressphoto agency b.v., Anatolii Babii; BROOKSIDE MUSEUM/ Saratoga County Historical Society; CARTOONSTOCK/ Marty Bucella, Mike Flanagan; CORDON PRESS/Kevin Dodge; FOTONONSTOP; FOURSQUARE; GETTY IMAGES SALES SPAIN/ Sean Gallup, Planet Flem, PeskyMonkey, Wonwoo Lee, Timur Emek, Stockbyte, Anna Pena, filo, Thinkstock, Kevin Winter, E+, Paul Popper/Popperfoto, Hill Street Studios, Ulrich Baumgarten, franckreporter, FineCollection, Ullstein Bild, Steve Granitz, Peter Dazeley, Jupiterimages, Jamie Farrant, Photos.com Plus, Bernhard Lang, Steve Hansen, Sergei Kozak, PhotoAlto/Sigrid Olsson, Michael Tran; HIGHRES PRESS STOCK/AbleStock.com; INSTAGRAM; ISTOCKPHOTO/Daniel Rodríguez Quintana, Getty Images Sales Spain, Alina Solovyova-Vincent, YekoPhotoStudio, Peeter Viisimaa, digitalskillet, andresrimaging, woranamphoto, Doug Bennett, Amanda Rohde, spinmysugar, shapecharge, caracterdesign, Yuri_Arcurs, damircudic, zlomari, andresr, Maridav, Nikada, rionm, DNY59; MAYANG MURNI ADNIN/www. mayang.com; PHOTODISC; REX SHUTTERSTOCK/Mars One/ Bryan Versteeg, Johnathan Hordle, Albanpix Ltd., Steve Meddle, Taipei Zoo, Sipa Press, Olycom SPA, MediaPunch, Startraks, Jim Smeal, Okauchi, ANL; VINE LABS, INC; Oliver Hutton; Doug Savage; Howdini.com/Touchstorm; Jennifer L. Price, PhD, Associate Professor of Psychology, Georgetown College; Mark Wolter www.woltersworld.com; Amanda Leroux; CREATIVE LABS; SERIDEC PHOTOIMAGENES CD; ARCHIVO SANTILLANA

The Publisher has made every effort to trace the owner of copyright material; however, the Publisher will correct any involuntary omission at the earliest opportunity.